# SOFTWARE PROJECTS

# WILEY SERIES IN
# SOFTWARE ENGINEERING PRACTICE

**Series Editors:**

**Patrick A.V. Hall,** *The Open University, UK*
**Martyn A. Ould,** *Praxis Systems plc, UK*

## Aims and scope

The focus of this series is the software creation and evolution processes and related organisational and automated systems necessary to support them. The aim is to produce books dealing with all aspects of software engineering, particularly exploitation of the best methods and tools for the development process.

The series covers the following topics:

- process models and software lifecycle

- project management, quality assurance, configuration management, process and product standards

- the external business environment and legal constraints

- computer aided software engineering (CASE) and integrated project support environments (IPSES)

- requirements analysis, specification and validation

- architectural design techniques, software components and re-use

- system design methods and verification

- system implementation, build and test

- maintenance and enhancement

- globalization

For a full list of titles in this series, see back pages.

# SOFTWARE PROJECTS

## EVOLUTIONARY VS.
## BIG-BANG DELIVERY

Felix Redmill

**JOHN WILEY & SONS**

Chichester • New York • Weinheim • Brisbane • Singapore • Toronto

Copyright © 1997 by John Wiley & Sons Ltd,
Baffins Lane, Chichester,
West Sussex PO19 1UD, England
*National*      01243 779777
*International* (+44) 1243 779777

e-mail (for orders and customer service enquiries): cs-books@wiley.co.uk

Visit our Home Page on http://www.wiley.co.uk
or
http://www.wiley.com

*Other Wiley Editorial Offices*

John Wiley & Sons, Inc., 605 Third Avenue,
New York, NY 10158-0012, USA

VCH Velagsgesellschaft mdlI, Pappelallee 3,
D-69469 Weinheim, Germany

Jacaranda Wiley Ltd, 33 Park Road, Milton,
Queensland 4064, Australia

John Wiley & Sons (Asia) Pte Ltd, 2 Clementi Loop #02-01,
Jin Xing Distripark, Singapore 129809

John Wiley & Sons (Canada) Ltd, 22 Worcester Road,
Rexdale, Ontario M9W 1L1, Canada

*British Library Cataloguing in Publication Data*

A catalogue record for this book is available from the British Library

ISBN   0 471 93343 0

Produced form camera-ready copy supplied by the author
Printed and bound in Great Britain by Bookcraft (Bath) Ltd, Midsomer Norton, Somerset
This book is printed on acid-free paper responsibly manufactured from sustainable forestation,
for which at least two trees are planted for each one used for paper production.

To all
who worked with me
in
NIS

# Contents

# Preface

*Big bang and evolutionary delivery*

In the title of this book, 'big bang' refers to the single delivery of a software-based system to its users at the end of a development project. Typically, such a project follows the 'waterfall model' of development. 'Evolutionary delivery' (ED) refers to the provision of a system in a number of planned deliveries throughout a project.

Implicit in the waterfall model (and big bang) are several problems, and ED is intended to overcome some of them. However, not only does it not resolve all of the traditional problems, but it also throws up problems of its own. These can be unexpected, can take a long time to understand, and, while they are being diagnosed, understood and resolved, can set back or even destroy a project.

*What's in the book*

This book is based on experience — of both waterfall-model and evolutionary-delivery projects. Part 1 considers the traditional problems of software development. It offers guidance on project management and software engineering principles and illustrates how projects fail due to a lack of them. It shows how failure using traditional methods led to the desire for a new basis for development, so it is *the path to evolutionary delivery*. It ends with an introduction to ED and its problems in Chapter 6.

Part 2 addresses the management of ED projects. It offers solutions to ED's problems and draws on personal experience of their application. It provides not only principles, but also guidance on good practice. Indeed, Chapters 10, 11, 12 and 14 present the details of procedures which were developed for, and have been used successfully in, ED projects. Part 2 is *the path through evolutionary delivery*.

Whereas the lessons of Part 2 are presented within the context of ED, the reader will, without difficulty, perceive that the principles are generally applicable, particularly those to do with management, strategic planning, communication, organisation and developer-customer relationships.

An understanding of the problems is a necessary prerequisite to solving them. An understanding of solutions which have already been successfully implemented is potentially even more valuable, for it obviates the need to reinvent them, it saves time and money, and it can save projects. The advice offered is both managerial and technical, and is intended not only for practitioners, such as project managers, software engineers, and development staff, but also for project customers such as senior management, strategic planners, and users of computer systems.

While the book offers guidance, in some cases in the form of step-by-step procedures, the reader should be aware that even these need to be tailored to the needs of particular circumstances if they are to be most effective.

*Routes through the book*

This book may be useful on at least two levels. First, it may be read or scanned for the principles which it offers, in which case the reader may expect to come away with a better understanding of the software development process and its problems, a feel for good practice, new ideas for improvement, and new insights into how it might be effected. Second, individual chapters may be studied for the lessons of what can go wrong, procedures of what to do, details of responsibilities for tasks, and advice on 'dos and don'ts'.

At the end of each chapter there is a brief review which includes a few extracts from the text. These by no means encapsulate the content of the chapter, but they offer indications to browsers of what they will find in it.

Those with time to read Chapter 1 will find that it offers a historical introduction to the problems of software development. It sets the scene for the book.

Project managers, software engineers, and all involved in development projects, who seek guidance on project issues in general, should find Chapters 2-5, 8, 13 and 15 particularly useful. For insight into ED, Chapter 6 offers an introduction and Chapters 8-14 provide detail. As already mentioned, the lessons of the ED chapters are in fact generally applicable. In addition, Chapter 7 offers an overview of an often neglected subject, but one which I consider of critical importance to projects — strategy. Project managers would do well to consider it.

Senior managers, including customers of systems being developed or to be developed, will find particular relevance in Chapters 3 and 4 which discuss project problems and include the roles of senior management in the discussions, Chapter 7 on strategy and its relationship to projects, Chapter 8 which includes the roles of project participants in the vital subject of creating a project infrastructure, and Chapter 15 which advises on culture and quality. In addition, they should find interest in Chapter 5 because it compares big bang and ED and Chapter 6 because it introduces ED. The other chapters, which give more details on development, are then at their disposal if interest goads them on to read them.

*Acknowledgements*

Appreciation is extended to Tom Gilb for many helpful conversations and arguments in my early days of employing evolutionary delivery, to George Sykens for offering a great deal of information and discussion when I was planning this book, to Peter Jesty, Stan Price and Les Hatton for reviewing the draft manuscript and making useful comments for its improvement, to Martyn Thomas for contributing the Foreword, and to Elizabeth Avery for help in creating the index.

Chapters 6 and 13 draw on papers by the author published by the Institution of Electrical Engineers and the Institution of Mechanical Engineers respectively. Acknowledgement is made to both institutions.

Throughout the book, the pronoun 'he' is used to imply 'he or she'. No inference should be drawn from this abbreviation and no offence is intended by it.

FR
November 1996.

# Foreword

## by Martyn Thomas

IT projects are inherently risky and, in the past thirty years, two generations of IT professionals have discovered a remarkable range of ways to make them even riskier. Years ago, someone coined the term *software crisis* to describe the intolerable level of project failures, cost and time overruns, and errors in delivered programs. Today the same phrase appears from time to time in the technical press but, with hindsight, we can see that there was no software *crisis*, for a crisis has a limited duration and the patient recovers or dies, whereas software development still suffers from the same chronic illness.

You do not have to look far for confirmation: the difficulties of large projects are often reported in the newspapers and, increasingly, the parties settle their dispute in court. The US Department of Defense said, a decade ago, that it 'had never had a successful software intensive project' and, quite recently, a senior official in the UK Ministry of Defence echoed the sentiment by saying that 'it is now possible to see that MoD has never yet awarded a software-intensive project to the right bidder'.

One reason why software suffers a chronic illness is that the tasks we routinely attempt get more complex every year. Complexity is the largest single cause of risk in IT projects and, on one scale, the size and complexity of many modern projects is dramatic evidence that, despite the failures, the software industry has been hugely successful. True, it is nearly thirty years since computers helped put men on the surface of the moon, but there is more computing power in most automobiles today than there was in the Lunar Excursion Module in 1969. Today we have aircraft that only fly because of the successful operation of millions of lines of software — commercial airliners like the Boeing 777™. We can install enterprise-wide software systems, such as SAP™ or PeopleSoft™, that support and automate the key business processes of multinational companies, operating in dozens of locations, accounting in many different currencies, integrating business areas from manufacturing and distribution to retail and cash collection.

The pace of change has been extraordinary. Since the world's first stored-program computer — the Manchester University 'baby', first run in June 1948 — the cost of processing, memory, data storage and data transmission has approximately halved every two years. The contrasts are dramatic: in the 1950s a three-minute telephone call between the USA and Europe cost about as much as a family car; in 1969 a large mainframe computer (an IBM 360/65, say) would typically have 512Kb of main memory, less than 100Mb of disk store, and a processor that was slower than the one in a modern cellular telephone. The IBM 360 needed air-conditioned, surgically clean accommodation and (I'm thinking now of the one in University College London) supported the computing needs of several thousand people, who punched their programs into 80-column cards.

Software and system design have changed dramatically too, from machine codes to Visual 4GLs, from fully custom to enterprise-wide packages and large-scale systems integration, from mainframe systems to client-server distributed processing architectures. New applications have created demands for extraordinary reliability and systems integrity. Twenty years ago it would have seemed heroic to build a computer system with the high integrity needed for railway signalling or the protection of a nuclear reactor. Today some companies can routinely build systems to these high standards — and demonstrate that they have done so, which is even more challenging.

With this high rate of change in both hardware and software, it is unsurprising that software developers believe that they need new approaches to building systems and that the experience of earlier decades must be irrelevant. It is unsurprising, self-evident, and wrong. IT projects still fail far too often, and they fail for the same reasons they always have: because the developers have lost control of the development, or lost sight of the real needs of the customer.

Developing IT systems is an engineering task. That should be obvious by now (the term 'software engineering' was coined in the 1960s) but software development remains a craft, rather than engineering, almost everywhere. Mature, stable processes lie at the heart of every engineering profession, and mature processes are, above all, the way in which experience is accumulated, refined, and made accessible. In a craft industry, without mature processes, experience is passed on haphazardly and unreliably, and the same mistakes occur over and over again.

Our 40+ year history has not been long enough to create these mature processes but there are hopeful signs. The Capability Maturity Model developed by the Software Engineering Institute at Carnegie Mellon University focuses on process maturity in software development organisations and is being adopted by many organisations to set improvement targets and demonstrate real progress. The widespread adoption of ISO9000-3 and TickIT in the UK is another positive sign. But where should the developing software engineer turn today to get the insight and experience, the knowledge of what has worked and what has failed, that is not yet taught in university courses?

Read this book. Felix Redmill has long experience in our industry, leading teams to build systems with challenging customer requirements, and monitoring projects run by other people. He has seen successes and failures, and learned from both. His accumulated experience is in this book and it will give you something worth a thousand times the cover price: insight and wisdom that will reduce the risks on your next project.

Experienced readers will not agree with every opinion in this book; but they will agree with enough that they will respect the experience and the intellect that have formed the opinions with which they disagree, and they will benefit from having their ideas challenged.

Whatever stage you have reached in your career, when you have read this you will be a better software engineer. That is important, because software development needs better engineers. Software is now too important to be left to amateurs, however gifted some of them may appear. The risks are too high, the consequences of failure too great.

Martyn Thomas
Praxis
October 1996

# One

## The path to evolutionary delivery

# 1

# Problems
# and Panaceas

'Evolutionary delivery' (ED) refers to the delivery of a computer system in stages over the course of a project, rather than in a single ('big bang') delivery at the end. Each delivery is not simply a new increment to be added to the existing system, but a new version of the system which may include changes to what had previously been delivered as well as new features.

Previous development methods were mostly based on the 'waterfall model' (explained in the next chapter) which leads to a 'big-bang' delivery at the end of the project. The problems inherent in 'big bang' pointed to a need for ED, but experience revealed not only that ED was not an automatic solution to most of them, but also that it threw up many problems of its own. Part 2 of this book presents these ED problems along with solutions which were devised for them.

Many project problems, however, are independent of the development model and the mode of delivery of the product, and are the result of the attitudes and interactions of the people involved. Part 1 examines these universal problems, as well as those inherent in the waterfall model and big-bang delivery. The Part begins, in this chapter, with a personal view of the history of software development, and ends with an introductory explanation of ED and its problems in Chapter 6.

## 1.1    A BRIEF HISTORY OF SOFTWARE DEVELOPMENT

There has always been reliable software. From the earliest days of computing, there have been success stories. The first stored program controlled telephone exchange was opened in the United States as long ago as 1965; the system was huge, and it was successful. The complex NASA space programmes have depended on software for control and communications. Now, the majority of the world's control functions are carried out by processors — in industry, commerce and the home. At the same time, there have also been numerous failed software development projects. Inestimable amounts of money have been wasted on projects which have been abandoned before completion, on software that has been developed but never used, and on systems which have contained disastrous flaws. It is from these failures that software development has derived its reputation.

In truth, the reputation of software as almost invariably being over budget, over time, and not to specification is not undeserved. Throughout the relatively short history of commercial software (a matter of only about fifty years), things have always been going wrong in its development; and, according to the developers, they have always been on the point of being put right.

In the 1960s, we heard that programming was about to be perfected; there were then to be no more bugs. In the 1970s, software engineering was about to change everything. In the 1980s, software engineering was still on its way in, and, what was more, computer-aided software engineering (CASE) tools were right behind it. Together, these would revolutionize software development projects. But the problems persisted. Also in the 1980s, however, there was the dawning of a recognition that engineering implies control and that control demands management, so project management as a discipline came into vogue — though project management skills were seldom evident. More recently, there has been the drive for quality. With each advance in thinking, in enlightenment as to the causes of problems, and in technology, there has been improvement, but still the problems persist.

As time has passed, the problems have been seen in different lights. In the 1960s, the emphasis was on programming. It was new, it was exciting, it was magic, it was known to only a few. The only drawback was the flaws in the programs — the 'bugs'. They would not go away. Perhaps their numbers would have been seen to diminish if change had been limited to improvements in programming technology. But change is never one-dimensional; as high-level languages replaced assembly code and debugging became easier, and as hardware memory became smaller and cheaper, so programs got longer and more complex, and the bug density remained about the same.

The expectation of perfect programming was, however, appealing. Such an idea matched the times, for practitioners of this new technology of software programming referred to it as an 'art'. They wanted to eat their cake today and still keep it for tomorrow's tea; they craved the status of 'scientists' or 'engineers', yet thrilled at being considered (and at thinking of themselves) as the custodians and exponents of a mysterious art. But which scientist would announce that perfection was around the next corner? The programmers gave themselves away by their naiveté, but it was to be some time before this was obvious to more than a few.

By the mid-1970s, perfection was still out of sight; and by now it was even deemed by some to be unreachable. The artists who had preached its imminence were losing their credibility: computers had spread their tentacles globally. Their influence extended not only into research, but also into industry, government and private life. It began to be recognized that a profession as widespread as software development required professionalism. It could not continue as an esoteric 'art'. Software had a bad image and this had to be cleaned up.

An engineering discipline was required. After all, software development was a technical occupation. As luck would have it, the term 'software engineering' was already gaining currency. It had been adopted at a NATO conference in Garmisch, Germany, in 1968, and since that date had been a reminder, at least to those at the leading edge of improvement, of the direction in which they needed to steer the change. But, as the use of the term radiated outwards from the serious software scientists to the semi-skilled programmers, it came to be interpreted as something quite different. Suddenly, to the programmers, programming was an engineering discipline and they were 'engineers'. Yet, the programmers themselves were the gullible dupes in this fraud. Being ignorant of the real meaning of engineering, they were unaware of their deficiencies as engineers. In spite of their self-defined elevation in status, software development continued to be problematic. The managers, perhaps naive, perhaps not altogether familiar with the meaning of engineering discipline either, believed software engineering to be on the way in, with significant improvement accompanying it. All that was required was a little time.

The trouble was that software engineering was seen as a technical improvement in programming rather than as a discipline for control. Some formality was introduced into programming, program specifications, and even system specifications; tools emerged to aid programmers and analysts. But while these tools were beneficial in that they aided the achievement of correctness, they did nothing to ensure effectiveness; moreover, they often locked their users into a set mode of operation which resulted in inflexibility. Programmers set about adjusting the problem to fit the standard solution provided by the tool, rather than considering how to use, or adapt, the tool to solve the problem. Nor did they frequently question whether they were using the right tool for the job.

By the mid-1980s, the accent was beginning to be on projects rather than merely on programming. The life cycle of a project was defined. Standards were realized by many to be important, but employed by few. Every programmer was a software engineer, but engineering discipline had penetrated a minority of software development organizations. CASE tools were the next panacea. These software-based tools, produced to automate the various tasks in the development process, had a mixed effect. Some, such as configuration management tools, were genuinely useful; others wasted their users' time. Tools made many tasks easier, but they often allowed, or even encouraged, a sloppy approach. But the most pernicious and extensive damage done by the 'tool culture' was the unquestioned reliance on tools which many programmers, analysts and designers developed, at the expense of an engineering attitude to understanding the problem in hand and then designing a solution appropriate to it.

Carrying out a task requires a method. If the task is repetitive, the method needs to be systematic; then a tool may be developed in support of it. If similar, rather than identical, versions of the task are to be repeated, the method may need to be varied in each case. To vary the method, the practitioner applying it needs to understand it and to understand how it applies to the task. With such understanding, the practitioner can adapt a tool (if the tool is adaptable) to support a varied method. However, when the practitioner carrying out a task believes (perhaps as the result of a tool supplier's advertising) that the tool is designed to support the task, rather than to support a given method of carrying out the task, trouble must ensue. Analysts, designers and programmers all sought tools to support tasks, without understanding the principles of the methods involved — either their own methods of tackling the tasks or the methods built into the design of the tools. They simply wanted to apply tools directly to tasks, and this is the antithesis of engineering — which emphasizes the understanding of fundamental principles. A small variation in the task from that for which the tool is designed renders the tool inapplicable, difficult to use, or subject to error. If the person applying the tool is lucky, the tool is inapplicable and is discovered to be so. The unlucky person manages to apply the tool but takes longer over carrying out the task and introduces error into the process. In the late 1980s, tool manufacturers acquired too great an influence over software developers. Their marketing, while not always accurate, was persuasive. It suggested to 'software engineers' that software could be thoughtlessly produced and tested. Had they been engineers the programmers and analysts would have recognized the flaw in this; as it was many brought their projects into difficulty by using tools which were sometimes inappropriate to the job in hand and often inappropriate to any job.

By the end of the 1980s, there was the realization that 'engineering' is not a synonym for 'techniques'; that it involves applying techniques in a controlled way so as to achieve the desired results within approved constraints; and that, therefore, a significant and essential element of engineering discipline is management — agreeing and understanding responsibilities, working to procedures which provide control mechanisms, and planning and coordinating teams and tasks so as to manage a project rather than merely the technical development of a system. So it came to be accepted, belatedly, that software engineering concerns not merely better programming but, importantly, the control of projects and the quality of products.

By the end of the 1980s, the quality drive, which had already become widespread (or, at least, widely spoken of) in industry, was beginning slowly to infiltrate the software development community. Gradually, software development companies and departments started to undergo quality improvement programmes, and by the 1990s some were beginning to seek certification to quality management standards. As they did so, it became clear that the quality software which had always been the goal would not be achieved merely by techniques, but might be approached by a combination of techniques, procedures and standards within the context of management and quality assurance.

Now, some years later, there is of a recognition by a few that standards and procedures can only take us a certain distance. Quality is not consistently achieved through the narrow constraints of rules, but rather by a genuine desire to achieve it. Quality management systems are necessary but not sufficient, and what is required is a 'quality culture' within which problems are not swept under the carpet and 'It meets objective measurable criteria' replaces 'it'll do' as the test of acceptance of a product. But a quality culture does not arise by chance. In the coming years it is going to be even more difficult for management to change the culture in their domains that it has been for them to introduce standards and quality management systems. Managers can point to the latter as 'being there' even if they are not being applied (which in most cases they still are not). But culture will not be changed by remote instructions or by documents. It responds only to leadership and example. Managers will need to develop an understanding of what culture is and what affects it, and to attend to their own behaviour as well as to what they say, so as to lead cultural improvement [Levene 97]. If they do not, quality will advance only as far as rules can take it.

Thus, by the 1990s, the astute could see that the successive philosopher's stones of the previous three decades, which they had recognized at the time as not being panaceas, had not been futile hopes or lost causes either. The 'perfect' programming of the 1960s could not materialize, but confidence in software could be greatly increased by a combination of disciplined programming, the use of tools, code inspections, configuration management, and testing. The concept of software engineering, misunderstood during the 1970s, would not lead to Utopia, but it had established a path towards a genuine engineering discipline. Many of the tools of the 1980s had been designed for enriching suppliers rather than supporting developers, but when the methods of software development, project management, and quality assurance were better understood, and the experience which had been gained in tool making was applied to creating tools to support them, real benefits accrued.

We should acknowledge success where we find it, and software has certainly been successful. In scarcely half a century since the first program was written, it has come to be the first choice for almost every control function, in the office, in the home, in industry, and in almost every product, from washing machines to aircraft. But success has followed a learning curve which has included a great deal of inefficiency and ineffectiveness. The proponents of the young discipline of software development have taken time to learn its lessons, and there are many lessons still to be learned. From a self-centred infant of the 1960s, it became a precocious child in the 1970s, then a self-opinionated adolescent in the 1980s. Now, in the mid-1990s, it has reached a state of young adulthood, beginning (but only beginning) to take the world seriously, beginning to listen to the criticism of its mistakes and to consider the lessons to be learned from them.

The result of this growing up, this learning curve, has been that more and more companies now take software development seriously, applying to it control procedures and quality assurance. But the speed of growth has meant that many (perhaps most) companies are still far behind, treating the development of software as a part-time task for one of the staff who claims to be adept at 'programming'. And even the advanced companies are not always respectful of the lessons of the past.

But it is generally recognized that the head-in-the-clouds notions of putting an industry right by this or that panacea were unrealistic and that fundamental improvement can only come from a better understanding and application of engineering principles in the development process and the assessment of the product against its objectives. For, what good is the bug-free program if it is the wrong program? The trend towards a more professional attitude continues and is typified by the gradual move away from the 'fire, aim, ready' approach of the 1970s, in which a sketchily designed solution to an unspecified problem was elaborately and cleverly coded. Now there is a recognition of the importance of adequate and accurate specification to achieving an effective solution, and this has led to more time being spent on defining the system to be developed, with proportionately less on building it. True engineering is based on striving for effectiveness as well as efficiency.

In the mid-1980s, when the story of this book began, many of what we now know to be the fundamental necessities of software engineering were not in place. For example, project management was often ignored or was not effectively or efficiently applied; there was little strategic planning of systems or projects, so project boundaries could not be defined; projects were often too large, and were allowed unconstrained growth. Since then we have gathered some wisdom. Yet, in our young adulthood, project management is still not very good — but it is better than before; strategic planning is recognized as a necessity — but it is hardly ever carried out; it is agreed that smaller projects stand a better chance of success than large ones — but projects continue to grow in size, complexity, and budget.

Despite the advance of technology and control techniques, we have not developed an immunity against software bugs. Projects continue to be late and over budget, systems continue not to meet their users' requirements, and the reports of project failures are as persistent as before.

## 1.3   SUMMARY AND EXTRACTS

This chapter has offered a brief and personal review of the history of software development. The following are extracts.

- When the practitioner carrying out a task believes (perhaps as the result of a tool supplier's advertising) that the tool is designed to support the task, rather than to support a method of carrying out the task, trouble must ensue ... If the person applying the tool is lucky, the tool is inapplicable and is discovered to be so. The unlucky person manages to apply the tool but takes longer over carrying out the task and introduces error into the process.

- 'Engineering' is not a synonym for 'techniques'; it involves applying techniques in a controlled way so as to achieve the desired results within approved constraints; and, therefore, a significant and essential element of engineering discipline is management—agreeing and understanding responsibilities, working to procedures which provide control mechanisms, and planning and coordinating teams and tasks so as to manage a project rather than merely the technical development of a system.

- Standards and procedures can only take us a certain distance. Quality is not consistently achieved through the narrow constraints of rules, but rather by a genuine desire to achieve it. Quality management systems are necessary but not sufficient, and what is required is a 'quality culture' within which problems are not swept under the carpet and 'It meets objective measurable criteria' replaces 'it'll do' as the test of acceptance of a product.

- A quality culture does not arise by chance ... Culture will not be changed by remote instructions or by documents. It responds only to leadership and example. Managers will need to develop an understanding of what culture is and what affects it, and to attend to their own behaviour as well as to what they say, so as to lead cultural improvement.

# 2

# A Natural Order of Events

In the mid-to-late 1980s, there was a surge in emphasis on the importance of good specification. This was in response to a recognition of the tendency of programmers to 'know what was needed' and to commence work before a design or even a specification had been prepared. The programmer would say to the customer, 'I know what you mean,' and immediately begin to 'cut code'. At the end of the project (prior to acceptance testing), the 'paperwork' would be completed by drawing up a design to conform to the system which had been produced. The intention often existed to prepare a specification document, for it was recognized that this would be useful when the system needed to be changed later, but time was hardly ever found to do this. The result of this process was that much of the software produced was the wrong software: at the end of two years or more of 'cutting code' the wrong system was produced. Sometimes it was well programmed, and occasionally it was well tested, but it did not meet the users' requirements. It was rare for a system to satisfy its users without modification, and many systems were abandoned altogether as so unusable as not to be worth modifying.

It was in this context that in the mid-1980s a colleague remarked to me that what we had was a culture of 'fire, aim, ready'. This really wasn't a very good joke, but I was impressed by it and have even repeated it several times since. It reflects just enough wit to appeal to those who haven't heard it before.

But what point was my colleague making? It was that it is not sensible to attempt to build a system before designing it, or to design it before it has been specified. And most of us would agree with that. Both experience and common sense have led us to conclude that a natural order of events in development is: specification, high-level design, further design at increasingly detailed levels, the programming of individual modules, the integration of modules to create sub-systems, the integration of sub-systems to create the system, validation of the system, and then delivery and acceptance testing. Validation is checking the system, by whatever means, to ensure that it conforms to its specification — that it is the right system for delivery to the customer.

## 2.1    THE WATERFALL MODEL

The model of development which reflects this 'natural order of events' is depicted in Figure 2.1 (this representation is concerned with the principle and shows only broad project stages). The horizontal spacing of the stages, along an imaginary time axis, suggests that one stage should not begin until the previous one has been completed. Thus, the output of one stage cascades down to be the specification for the next, leading to the title by which the model is known: the 'waterfall model'. It is this clear identification of the specification of any given stage which provides the basis for the verification of the work carried out. Verification is checking (by whatever means) to ensure that the product of any stage of the project is a faithful translation of its specification — the product of the previous stage. Thus, if the specification for a stage is clearly defined, there is also the definition of what the end product of the stage should be verified against. If an error occurs in translation and is not detected by verification, it becomes a feature of the next stage and will be propagated onwards into the system. Validation of the system against its original specification is intended to detect such occurrences — but by the time of

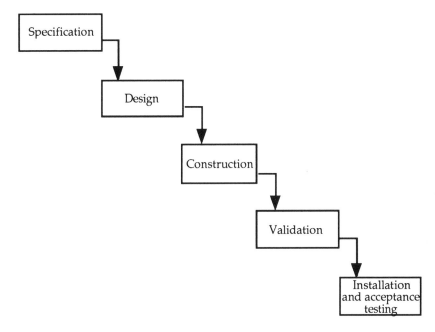

**Figure 2.1** A simple representation of the waterfall model

validation, correction may be an expensive process, if the error occurred at an early stage of the life cycle.

The stark representation of Figure 2.1 does not show the verification process. Not showing it undervalues the model, for the waterfall model does not preclude verification and feedback. Yet, many take the shadow for the substance and criticize the model, claiming that it does not allow for verification. This, it seems, reflects slavery to the model rather than the use of it as a tool. Nevertheless, a fairer representation would be that of Figure 2.2.

A great advantage of the waterfall model is that it represents basic engineering practice: that specification should precede design, design should precede construction, etc. This approach has, in theory, been the traditional basis of software development and, if it had been adhered to in all cases, a great deal less software would over the years have been abandoned as useless. But the fire-aim-ready culture of the magician programmers meant that the model was a representation of an ideal rather than of reality. It was often unfairly blamed for poor development practices — and we shall discuss these in the next chapter.

If the waterfall model is applied to an entire project, it produces a formal division of the project into a number of discrete stages each of which, by implication, must be completed before the commencement of the next. If this process is coupled with sound project management procedures, such as the formal signing off of each stage, it can provide a good basis for project control. However, if the project is large and the stages long, it can lead to the requirements specification being out of date before the system has been completed. But let us be clear about one thing: there is no suggestion in the model itself that it must be applied to an entire project. All the model provides is a statement of our agreed natural order of events. Thus, the waterfall model exhorts that we follow what we agree to be good practice; it can be applied to the development of a sub-system or a module as well as to a system. Further, as we shall see in Part 2, it is a sound basis for the development of each delivery of an evolutionary delivery project.

There are, however, two reservations to be mentioned concerning the waterfall model as a representation of the life cycle of a project. The first is a distinct disadvantage to those using it as a guide to development; the second is a limitation of the model.

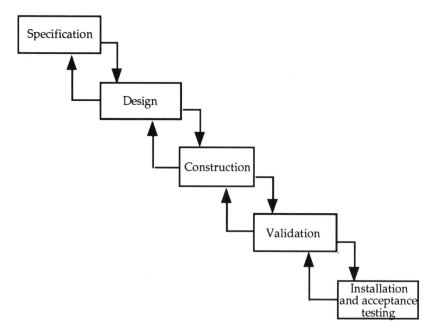

**Figure 2.2** A representation of the waterfall model showing feedback between stages

The first reservation, and the greatest disadvantage of the waterfall model, is that the product of the development process, 'the target system', is not available for testing or trial by its intended users until the end of the project. As we shall see in the next chapter, a frequent reason for software not meeting its users' requirements is that the requirements have changed between the time that they were specified and the time that the system is brought into service. The longer the time and the larger the project, the greater the risk of this occurring. There are ways of lessening the effect of the problem, such as good communication between the developers and the users, and providing the users with prototypes to demonstrate various aspects of the proposed system, but, in principle, the problem remains in the model.

The second reservation is that there is an implicit assumption in the model that all will go well throughout the project: the model suggests a unidirectional flow of activities through the project. It does not explicitly make provision for assessing risks and taking steps to manage them, which often means returning to an earlier stage of the project to make adjustments. As experience shows that projects seldom conform to their original plans, it is safe to assume that uncertainties existed from the beginning, even if they were not recognized or if no attempt was made to recognize them. A model which includes the assessment of risk is discussed in Section 2.3 below.

These two reservations suggest an assessment of the conditions under which the waterfall model is most effective: when the specification is complete, the risk of change is small, the solution has been clearly determined, and the project is expected to be short — less than a year of elapsed time. I do not say that it should not be used in other circumstances; only that, in my experience, its effectiveness diminishes as these circumstances cease to maintain.

The two problems just discussed refer to the waterfall model as the representation of a project. There is a third problem, and that is that the model starts at the project rather than at the strategy from which the project should have arisen. By not introducing the concept or the importance of strategy, a project model fails to warn the project manager of the likely difficulties ahead if the project does not have a firm foundation in business (rather than merely end user) needs. This topic is considered in the next chapter and is the subject of Chapter 7.

## 2.2    THE V MODEL

Something which the waterfall model does not show is the verification which
should occur at each stage of development. One means of illustrating verification
in the development process is by rearranging the waterfall model into the 'V'
model, as in Figure 2.3. In this, successive steps in the description of the system
(its specification and design) are expanded from those shown in the waterfall
model and depicted descending the left-hand side of the V. The detail
increases with each step, from a description of what is required to an overview
of the system which will meet the requirements, and then, by decomposition,
through a number of levels of increasing design detail, until the modules of
program code are defined. The number of levels of design is a matter for the
project manager and designers, and is (arbitrarily) shown as three in Figure
2.3.

At the base of the V, programming of the smallest individual units of
software is carried out. This process is the creation of the components from

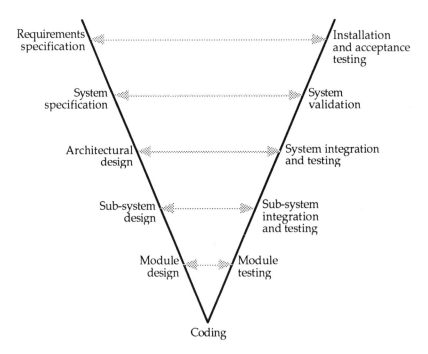

**Figure 2.3** The 'V' development model

which the system will be built. The successive steps in the building and confirmation of the system (its integration, verification, validation and acceptance testing) are then shown ascending the right-hand side.

Each step on the right-hand side of the V is equivalent to one on the left-hand side, such that the system description on the left forms the basis of testing its equivalent level of system integration on the right. Thus, it is against the module design that the formal module tests are carried out, against the sub-system design that an integrated sub-system is tested, and so on.

The V model is not different in principle from the waterfall model. It is a different view of the same staged process which reveals additional detail. Like the waterfall model, it is usually portrayed as a model of how a project is, or should be, structured. Also like the waterfall model, its application need not be restricted to the life cycle of an entire project; it can be applied to the development or change of a sub-system with equal effect.

## 2.3   THE SPIRAL MODEL

In any project, there is the need to pause from time to time, to review progress, question our direction and the intention which led to this direction, and perhaps to change course somewhat and take a fresh and more appropriate path. However far advanced we may be, there is likely to be a need to question earlier decisions and assess the risks which lie on the path ahead. The waterfall model does not illustrate this mode of operation. A development model which does is Boehm's spiral model [Boehm 88].

This is shown in Figure 2.4, with the project commencing at a point on the x axis to the left of the origin and proceeding clockwise around the origin. Progress is shown as an outward spiral, with every cycle going through the same sequence of activities, and the cycle's result being reviewed after the process has rotated through 360 degrees. A project would typically consist of a number of cycles, with the success of each being reviewed, and perhaps with a change of direction being initiated, before the next is commenced. Each quadrant in the figure depicts one or more activities.

The first quadrant identifies the definition stage of the cycle. In this, the objectives of the cycle, the constraints on it (such as limitations on time and resources), the preferred means of proceeding, and any alternative means of proceeding, are determined.

The second quadrant identifies the process of analysing the path ahead.

Here, the alternatives previously identified are evaluated and any risks involved in the way forward are identified, assessed and resolved. Risk analysis may involve administrative assessments, such as of competence and training, or technical assessments of the difficulties in development. If on evaluation an alternative means of proceeding is assessed to be preferable to the original choice, it may be taken. (See [Redmill 97] for an explanation of risk management and a qualitative process for carrying it out.)

The third quadrant depicts the carrying out of development. As with the other quadrants, what is developed depends on the stage of the project. It might be a specification or it might be a sub-system, or a new version of a system. Verification of what has been developed is also included in this quadrant.

The fourth quadrant indicates the planning of what is to be done in the next cycle of the process.

Thus, the spiral model proceeds in steps, with a pause and review at the end of each. It is directly concerned with risk and is, in fact, a risk-based model,

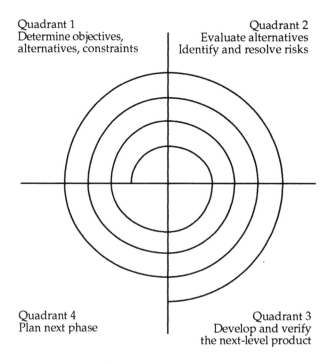

Figure 2.4 Boehm's Spiral Model of Development

rather than being product-based, as the waterfall model is. Once under way, a waterfall model project proceeds onwards towards completion of the development of the product along a predetermined path. But in a spiral model project, the risks are assessed at each step and the path which best overcomes the identified risks is taken. Thus the model inherently allows, and indeed implicitly provides for, the cancellation of the project if the risks suggest imminent failure.

The model may be used for the development of an entire system, a sub-system, or a component, or the enhancement of a system. But perhaps its most significant feature is its focus on the assessment of risk. It has reminded many project managers that the blind rush towards the distant goal of a product can be inefficient and ineffective if the path ahead is blocked. Indeed, one possible result of pausing, reviewing progress, and assessing future risks is the recognition that the present goal is not the ideal product. Then it may be appropriate to initiate a strategic review of the project.

## 2.4  THE MATRIX MODEL

The chances are that if a software developer has used a life cycle model it will have been one of the three described above. Yet, while each one offers certain advantages, they all share a major disadvantage: none of the three models reflects the true course of a project, for all define its stages as being sequential and do not allow for further work to be carried out on a stage after that stage has been 'completed'. In practice, there is a great deal of iteration between the stages of a project.

A further disadvantage of the three models is that none is truly a *system* life cycle model, for all are concerned only with the stages of a development project. For example, as we shall see in Chapter 14, when the waterfall model is extended to include a maintenance stage, this causes rather than resolves problems. To be fair, the models are intended as project tools and do not purport to represent life-cycle stages before the commencement of a project or after its end. Yet, it would be useful to represent life-cycle stages other than those during development. A model — the matrix model — which can overcome these two disadvantages is briefly described.

The diagrammatic form of the matrix model is (not surprisingly) a matrix, the rows of which represent the stages of the system life cycle which are of interest at the time of using the model. If only the development project is under consideration, the stages may be chosen, as in Figure 2.5, to be those of the waterfall model.

The columns of the matrix represent activities. When the activities are defined in 'course grain', they may take the titles of the stages themselves (as in Figure 2.5) because, typically, the title of a stage is indicative of the principal activity within the stage — or, at least, of the goal of the stage. For example, the main purpose of the specification stage is the production of a specification.

When more detail is required, the activities may be defined in 'finer grain'. Then the various activities which are necessary in a given stage may be listed. To pursue the specification stage example, the activities of requirements capture, requirements expression, requirements verification, and requirements analysis may be listed, as well as specification preparation and specification validation. Indeed, any activities of interest for a given purpose may be represented as columns of the model, as in Figure 2.6.

The cells of the matrix may be used for recording data concerning the activities (such as the time spent on them) when they are carried out, and, later, for making forecasts about the activities to be carried out on another occasion

| | Specification | Design | Construction | Validation | Installation and acceptance testing |
|---|---|---|---|---|---|
| Specification | | | | | |
| Design | | | | | |
| Construction | | | | | |
| Validation | | | | | |
| Installation and acceptance testing | | | | | |

Figure 2.5  The matrix model — a simple example

(for example, in another project).

During a project, the cells are used for storing the amount of effort invested in the activities defined in the column headings, during the stages defined in the row titles — but if a listed activity is not carried out in a particular stage, the appropriate cell of the matrix is unused. In the first place, the amount of effort may be recorded in absolute terms (for example, in man-hours or man-days), the model thus being used as a direct repository of relevant data. An advantage of this is that having such a repository (and a simple one) is an incentive to collect and employ the data for which it is to be used. Collecting the data implies monitoring the progress of the project and measuring the quantities (for example, manpower) which it takes to make the progress; employing the data implies, first, comparing it against the planned or forecast values of the quantities in question and, second, using it to make improved forecasts and plans for the remainder of the current project and for future projects.

At the end of a stage, or of the project, the figures which were earlier recorded in absolute terms may be converted into percentages. The effort expended on a particular activity carried out in a stage may be calculated as a proportion of the total effort expended during that stage, or of the total effort expended on that activity throughout the project. Similarly, the total effort spent on an activity may be calculated as a percentage of the total project effort. This is particularly useful in determining the proportion of project effort which is put into an activity like planning, which is (or should be) carried out at all stages. It is also useful when (say) a new technology has been used in the project and there is a need for a basis for estimation in the future.

The numbers in Figure 2.6 (only partially completed) offer an example of the use of the cells for storing percentages. They show that 58% of the requirements elicitation activity was carried out during the requirements elicitation and specification stage of the project, 21% during design, and so on.

If there is confidence that the figures in the cells are accurate representations of past projects, they offer an easy-to-use guide to estimation and planning for future projects. At the end of the first project in which the matrix model is used, the calculated percentages provide predictors of what may be expected in another similar project. But beware: they are only predictors, and their accuracy diminishes as the variables on which they depend change — variables such as the type of project, the type and composition of the team, and the team culture. Accuracy of prediction is also limited when it is based on a sample of one. But if the matrix is updated after each similar project, accuracy increases.

| | Requirements elicitation | Reqs. analysis and specification | Architectural design | Sub-system design | Module design | Coding | Code inspections | Dynamic module testing | Integration and testing | Validation | Installation | Acceptance testing | Maintenance | Risk management | Planning | Strategic involvement |
|---|---|---|---|---|---|---|---|---|---|---|---|---|---|---|---|---|
| Requirements elicitation and specification | 58 | | | | | 1 | | | | | | | | | | |
| Design | 21 | | | | | 18 | | | | | | | | | | |
| Coding | 4 | | | | | 58 | | | | | | | | | | |
| Integration | 2 | | | | | 8 | | | | | | | | | | |
| Validation | 3 | | | | | 2 | | | | | | | | | | |
| Installation and acceptance testing | 4 | | | | | 3 | | | | | | | | | | |
| Operation (first three months) | 8 | | | | | 10 | | | | | | | | | | |

**Figure 2.6** The matrix model — a more detailed example

It is most accurate if used in future projects by the same team which used it for the compilation of the figures in the past — but this is not a limitation on the matrix model, it is a fact of any estimation process.

In the same way as described above, the model can be used to provide the basis for recording the effort of any given activity during the project by allocating it a column of the matrix. This is particularly useful for activities such as risk management and planning which are not confined to one life-cycle stage. With planning being carried out by a number of people (project manager, development manager, team leaders, etc.) during all stages of a project, it would be interesting and useful to know how much effort was being invested in it — for example, with a view to improving the planning mechanism within the organization. The penultimate and anti-penultimate columns of the matrix of Figure 2.6 are labelled 'planning' and 'risk management' respectively.

A feature of the matrix model is that it is not confined to the project life cycle. It may be used for activities before the project commences (such as strategic planning) or after the project ends (such as maintenance and operation in a given mode). A separate matrix, with operations and maintenance activities, may be drawn up for the operations stage of a system's life cycle.

It is of immeasurable importance to have a sound strategic basis for a project and continued strategic involvement throughout (this is discussed in Chapter 7). While it is not often possible to identify the strategic planning which has gone into the project in advance of the 'first' project stage, it is certainly possible to measure the strategic input during the remainder of the life cycle. Thus, 'strategic involvement' is shown as the final activity (column) in the example of Figure 2.6.

Other distinct advantages of the matrix model, and a summary of some already mentioned are:

- The model's row titles offer guidance, like the waterfall model, on the stages of the life cycle. These may be defined broadly, as in Figure 2.5, or in greater detail so that they more closely reflect activities, as in Figure 2.6.
- The rows also offer guidance on the proper order in which an organisation expects the stages to be carried out.
- The activities represented by the column titles may also be defined in broad terms or in finer detail.
- It is not constrained to define only stages of a project, and also defines activities within stages — i.e., the matrix need not be square (see Figure

2.6). It then performs the added function of a checklist to remind the project manager of the need for the activities (such as strategic involvement) represented by the columns.

- It reminds us that change is always taking place in a system, and that nothing is wholly done 'in its place' only. Whether this is or is not recognised has an enormous impact on the way in which a project is managed, but the models in use contribute to its being ignored.

- The model provides a basis for recording what really goes on during (and after) a project. When empty, the model is a form for recording the time spent on the various activities, whenever they are carried out.

- It provides a predictor of what to expect in future projects. The cells, when containing percentage figures derived from one or more past projects, offer the basis for estimating the effort required for the various activities in future projects, not only in the particular stages in which they are traditionally supposed to be carried out, but in all stages.

The model offers some of the advantages of the waterfall model because its rows define the stages of the project. It also offers some of the advantages of the spiral model because it suggests the opportunity for change — and gives permission (makes it acceptable) to make change. However, it goes further and offers its own advantages. As will be seen in Chapter 9, it may be used to complement the other models.


## 2.5    THE THING ABOUT MODELS

The thing about models is that they are models. By definition, they are approximations, not the real thing.

But people tend to forget or ignore the approximations and limitations of the model they are using. Their implicit assumption is that they are dealing with the real thing. The price of this assumption is error.

If we know everything there is to know about something, we don't need a model of it: we have the thing itself, fully detailed. The problem of having something fully detailed is that there may be too much of it; we may have more detail, more complexity, than we can cope with. One reason, therefore, for creating a model is to limit the information we have to deal with to a manageable amount — while ensuring (or hoping) that it is sufficient for the purpose in hand. So a model is an approximation. Consequently, it is only likely to be reliable if it is used within the scope of application defined by the assumptions implicit within it. Thus, a valid criticism of a model may be that its accuracy within its defined scope of application is less than that claimed for it. It is not a valid criticism of a model to complain of its failure outside of its defined scope. A frequent problem is that models are used outside of their intended scope of application.

A city street map is a model. To make this perfect, we would have to make a map the size of the city, containing not only every street, but also every house, room, item of furniture and, indeed, every map in the city. Even if it were practical to create such a model, we would not need it, for it would be no different from the real thing which it would be as easy to study. But any model which is smaller and which contains less detail is a compromise of reality.

Usually our city map is adequate for finding streets and planning routes. But if it contained too much information, either it would be large, difficult to use and not portable, or the print would be too small to be legible. So it may not provide, for example, information on the numbering of houses along the streets, or on the gradients of streets. If the pedestrian with an aversion to hills or an inability to climb them assumes that because the map does not show hills there is none, he is attempting to use the map beyond its limitations and paying the price for doing this by making a false assumption.

On asking, 'What is to be the purpose of this model?' the model's creator attempts to minimize complexity by omitting all details not relevant to the stated purpose. But, if he omits a feature which is relevant, he has started with an incorrect assumption which would affect all calculations and decisions based on the model. If, for instance, a street map is being prepared for the purpose of planning walks for invalids, the lack of information on street gradients may indeed be a severe deficiency.

A street map is tangible, used in this discussion because it is a readily understood model. But there are also conceptual models, for example models of the structure, the education, or the health of society. The waterfall, V and spiral development models described above are conceptual. They are approximations to the development process, produced in order to illustrate certain points, and they include assumptions and limitations just as a street map does. Care should be observed when either employing or criticizing them. If both a model's deficiencies and its useful aspects are understood, it is possible to be guided by it while not being misled by its limitations. A developer should be prepared to introduce his own best practice to compensate for any limitations. In other words, a professional should possess professional discernment and judgement and be capable of applying them.

A model, then, is an approximation, created to be a vehicle for expressing or exploring certain defined phenomena. It is created to convey certain points, ignoring others which seem unimportant to the circumstances in hand. If these aspects were important, a different model would be necessary. The results or conclusions derived from a model must therefore also be approximate; but they would be valid within the context of the model's assumptions and limitations if the model is appropriate to its application. If the model is applied inappropriately, false conclusions are likely to be drawn. Because a model's users are usually not its creator, this often occurs: the fault for poor results frequently lies with the users for applying the model outside of its intended scope.

We saw above that the waterfall model reflects a natural order of events: that the stages of development should proceed in a given sequence. In order to emphasize this point, further detail is excluded from the model. Yet, if a developer is found not to carry out verification, or quality assurance, can we accept the excuse that these activities were not explicitly displayed on the waterfall model?

There is much which goes on within a development project which the model does not show. For example, within each stage, greater efficiency and higher quality can be achieved by the use of training for the staff, task procedures, standards, peer checks and formal verification of the work carried out, and quality assurance. These activities are presented in the model of Figure 2.7.

Because the waterfall model is not explicit on when and how verification should take place within a development project, it is useful to compliment it with the V model. The V model does not contradict the waterfall model; nor is it an alternative to it. It brings out different aspects of the same thing and is another view of the events defined and ordered in the waterfall model. The two models together provide a fuller description of the conduct of a project than either one on its own. Yet, I have heard people discussing whether to base their project on the waterfall or the V model. And I have known software engineering lecturers to give their students the choice of which to use in a project.

Different models are intended to illustrate different points. A model is only a guide, not a textbook. It is up to the user to understand the process which is represented in order to benefit, without being misled, from the guidance offered by the model. Developers need to understand the business of development, not follow a model blindly. Their natural reaction to a new model should be to seek to understand its benefits and limitations, in order to know when and where to employ it within its intended scope of use. The developer can then recognize those aspects on which the model does not offer guidance and, if guidance is required, seek it elsewhere, while deriving the advantages of the model where it is valid. But too often developers do not understand the process which a model represents and they seek not guidance but explicit direction from it. And here lies one of the big problems in software engineering. Too often 'software engineers' do not understand either software or engineering. Engineers should know what they are doing; and if a software engineer chooses to use the waterfall model as a tool, he should know why he is using it and in what context. He should also know what its limitations are. If he does not, he is wrong to choose it as a tool. It is unacceptable for an engineer to blame his tools for his own inadequacies.

Sensible use of a model requires discernment, but too often users are not discerning. A model is a symbol, but they want a sign to follow blindly. Models and tools should serve us; we should not be slaves to them.

I labour this point because it was fashionable in the mid-to-late 1980s to make the waterfall model the scapegoat for all the failures of software

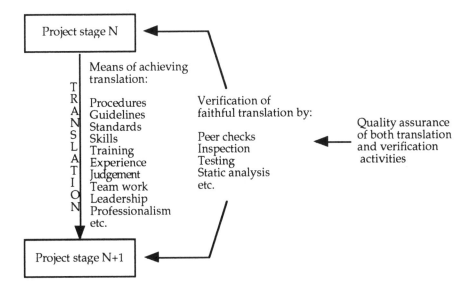

**Figure 2.7** Examples of activities carried out in a development stage

development projects. It was an easy target — because of its recognized shortcomings, the obvious failures of projects, and the lack of understanding of the real problems which existed in the projects (and still do). But the waterfall model, and models in general, have not let us down. We have let ourselves down in the application of the models. Let me raise a question here: do we 'follow' the waterfall model, or does the model represent what we do? The answer should be, 'A bit of both.' Before the creation of the model, there were development projects. Then came the model to represent what had been established as good practice and to guide the uninformed. It was the same with the spiral model. This was not a hypothesis of what might conceivably be useful, but Boehm's view of what goes on in practice. Thus, in development, we may begin by following a model. But then we must observe how well it serves us; and when we find that it does not serve us adequately, we must modify our way of working. If this is successful, we may modify the model — remembering that the modification may only be applicable in the circumstances of our type of project. In this way do both 'best practice' and useful models evolve. A problem comes when we publish the modified model without drawing attention to its limitations or to our special circumstances, thus giving the impression that it is suitable for universal application. Then, if its new users are not astute, they will follow it blindly and be led into trouble; their projects will fail.

## 2.6   SUMMARY AND EXTRACTS

This chapter has described the waterfall, V and spiral models, proposed a matrix model to compliment them, and made a commentary on the use of models in general. The following are extracts from the text.

*   There are two reservations concerning the waterfall model as a representation of the life cycle of a project. The first is that 'the target system' is not available for testing or trial by its intended users until the end of the project. The second is that there is an implicit assumption in the model that all will go well throughout the project: the model suggests a unidirectional flow of activities. It does not explicitly make provision for assessing risks and taking steps to manage them, which often means returning to an earlier stage of the project to make adjustments.

- The waterfall model is most effective when the specification is complete, the risk of change is small, the solution has been clearly determined, and the project is expected to be short — less than a year of elapsed time.

- The V model is not different in principle from the waterfall model. It is a different view of the same staged process which reveals additional detail.

- The spiral model proceeds in steps, with a pause and review at the end of each. It is directly concerned with risk and is, in fact, a risk-based model, rather than being product-based, as the waterfall model is ... It has reminded many project managers that the blind rush towards the distant goal of a product can be inefficient and ineffective if the path ahead is blocked.

- A feature of the matrix model is that it is not confined to the project life cycle. It may be used for activities before the project commences (such as strategic planning) or after the project ends (such as maintenance and operation in a given mode).

- The matrix model reminds us that change is always taking place in a system, and that nothing is wholly done 'in its place' only.

- People tend to forget or ignore the approximations and limitations of the model they are using. Their implicit assumption is that they are dealing with the real thing. The price of this assumption is error.

- The results or conclusions derived from a model must be approximate; but they would be valid within the context of the model's assumptions and limitations if the model is appropriate to its application. If the model is applied inappropriately, false conclusions are likely to be drawn.

- Too often developers do not understand the process which a model represents and they seek not guidance but explicit direction from it ... Engineers should know what they are doing; and if a software engineer chooses to use the waterfall model as a tool, he should know why he is using it and in what context. He should also know what its limitations are.

# 3

# Lessons in Software Development

It was mentioned in Chapter 1 that software development has traditionally suffered from a number of problems, and in Chapter 2 that the waterfall model has been blamed for many of them. In this chapter a number of the most frequent and consequential problems are discussed through the medium of personal experiences.

## 3.1   THE CUSTOMER'S PERSPECTIVE

Typically, a project manager has three goals with respect to a project: to deliver the product to specification, on time, and within budget (for a further discussion of this point, see the first part of Chapter 4). In fact, these are the three principal components of the agreement between the customer and the supplier (or developer) of the system, whether they are documented or implicit. So from the customer's point of view, these are the three things which can (and often do) go wrong.

This sounds simple, and it is. Yet, there is one qualification to be made. Whereas the agreement between the customer and the supplier demands that the system should meet its specification, the customer's and users' more frequent complaint is that it does not meet their requirements, which is almost certainly not the same thing. What they usually mean is that the system does not meet their requirements as they are at the time of delivery rather that at the time of specification. Nothing stands still; requirements change even as the system to fulfil them is being developed. If the developers do not keep up with the changes in the customer's organization as the project proceeds, there is a fair chance that the delivered system will not meet the real requirements at the time of delivery, even if it meets its specification.

Indeed, it is well known that not only do delivered systems frequently not meet their users' requirements, but also that they are late and over budget. So what are the causes? All things are in relationship with each other, and their relationships form not only chains of cause and effect, but also networks of interaction, multiple causes, and diverse consequences. What is seen as a cause from one point of view is seen as an effect from another. One person's problem is the cause of another person's problem. The three problems perceived by customers and users are seen by the developers merely as the effects of their own problems.

## 3.2   THE DEVELOPERS' PROBLEMS

Traditionally, developers have seen their problems as technical — and this has been their greatest problem. It is now recognized that the issues which have the most severe effects on projects are usually organizational, administrative, and social. If the developers would put themselves in their customers' shoes, they would recognize that in order to offer genuine quality, that is to say, to meet time, budget and specification requirements, they need to control their own problems. This control must come from project management. As we shall see in the next chapter and in Chapter 8, this does not merely imply technical competence but also, more importantly, a putting into place of the infrastructure necessary for the smooth running of the project.

The seeds of most of the serious problems are sown during the early stages of a project — at the contractual or authorization stage, in estimating and planning, in preparing the specification, and in failing to put an adequate project infrastructure in place. In the following subsections, I illustrate some of the issues by relating personal experiences.

### 3.2.1 Time and Budget Inadequate — An In-house Project

One of the most important lessons which I learned in the management of projects was to say NO.

Almost my first task when I became a development manager was to provide the project manager with estimates of cost and time for a certain proposed development project. As there was yet no specification, and the project manager had only an outline of what was required, I at first declined, suggesting that a specification should first be prepared.

'Come on,' said the project manager, 'we've got to play the game. We won't hold you to the figures that you give, but we've got to provide the Director with something so that he can authorize the project.'

I played the game, and proposed that the project, as understood, could be completed in (say) two years, with (say) five staff, for (say) one million pounds. This was in October of a given year. In the following January, a project proposal was submitted by the project manager to the Director for a project which would cost £1,000,000 and which would be completed in October of the following year. So, we had already lost three months! A month later, approval was given, for the project to be completed by the coming October at a cost of half a million pounds. Not only had the project manager 'played the game' very much to his own private rules, but the Director had halved both the time (as it was presented to him) and the cost. (I later discovered that doing this was a principle of that Director, on the basis that he did not trust his staff to provide him with honest estimates!) I protested to the project manager. He was adamant that the Director's position precluded challenge, that this was how things had always been, and that we just had to live with the decision and do what we could to meet his demand. I knew that it was impossible, but it was my first project as development manager and I was too inexperienced and timid to believe that I could buck the department's tradition.

Naturally the project was late and over budget, and naturally it was we the developers who got the blame. Only a couple of months into the project I became convinced that it would have been better to let the Director know the impossibility of his demand rather than accede to it and be seen to fail. When the next project came up, the same sequence of events occurred, except that, when he halved the cost and time, I did not carry on a futile discussion with the project manager but wrote to the Director to let him know that his terms could not be met. He called me to a meeting and insisted. I pointed out that as the experts employed by him, my staff and I had made a professional judgement and that we stood by it. If he wanted to override this judgement, we would naturally do our best to meet his demand, but he would need to accept responsibility for his directive. He seemed reluctant to accept the responsibility of contradicting the judgement of the 'experts', but he said that the project was so important that it required an earlier completion date. I replied that if he would authorize an increase in my staff complement, this might be possible. He said that the current freeze on recruitment did not permit this. I listed the projects for which I was responsible and invited him to choose the ones which he would permit to be late so that I could divert development staff from them. He declined, saying that all the projects were important. I pointed out that the project would therefore require the time and budget which we had estimated. He accepted this.

The Director saw his principal means of cutting timescales and costs as being to halve them at the time of project authorization. He had never been challenged on this, and to him this indicated that his theory of overestimation by his experts was valid. (He did not appear to have correlated the lateness and budget excesses at the ends of his projects with his own actions at their beginnings.) What is more, he had always managed to act without having to accept responsibility for the impossible project terms. Now, he did not want to take on a responsibility which he recognized as likely to be to his detriment later, and at the same time he seemed to appreciate having professionals who were prepared to support their judgement with confident argument. My saying NO showed the Director to be human.

It is important to distinguish between an estimate and a target. I was responsible for making an estimate, based on a professional understanding of the task ahead and how it would be tackled. The Director (or any other customer) may consider it necessary, for political or commercial reasons, to set a target, independent of the estimate. The project manager and developers may be forced to attempt to achieve the target, even though they perceive it to be unachievable, but this does not mean that the project manager should retract his professionally determined estimate and it should not prevent him from documenting it for future reference. Indeed, the more unachievable the target appears to be, the more important it is for the project manager to do so.

It is also crucial to distinguish between estimation and negotiation. The estimate was the best we could arrive at, given the available information, so I was not prepared to change it in response to the Director's challenge. However, the target was negotiable, as it was arbitrarily arrived at. A project manager should not fail to attempt to negotiate seemingly impossible targets, and the estimate is his main weapon in doing so. It is therefore worth investing resources in trying to obtain an accurate estimate. Sometimes, of course, when the commercial or political pressure on the customer is sufficiently strong, the target for achieving the product is not negotiable, and the development team must just get on with the job. Then, however, the project manager should negotiate to reduce the system's functionality, so that a usable system can be produced in the time available.

In the instance under discussion, the lessons did not end with the Director. Returning to the subject of my first project as development manager, I also discovered that the project manager had not acted on what he knew to be the case when he assured me that our estimates would only be used for making a business case and that there would be scope for adjusting them later. I discovered that when authorization for the project was given, it was subject to the 'usual' condition that the authorized cost and time could not be exceeded by more that 10%. I was left with twenty months to assemble a suitable team and develop the system — an impossible task, given that work had not yet even begun on the specification!

The lesson learned for future projects was to qualify all estimates and to be careful of how they were worded. For example, rather than say that a project could be completed in two years, I learned to say that, 'The estimate for the completion of the project, given the current information on the requirements, is two years from the date of receipt by the development team of the completed specification of requirements — given that authorization to proceed with the project has already been given.'

It was also obvious that having to make estimates before a specification had been prepared, and almost invariably in an extremely short time (typically one week), was hazardous. The first remedy was to document the limitations on the feasibility study, the most important of which were the shortage of information on the requirements and the limited time in which to investigate them. Then, in providing the estimates, we showed that the effect of these limitations was a diminution of confidence in the estimates themselves. This led to a recognition by senior management, as well as the customers and users, that a brief early study without adequate information was little more than a guess.

Our second remedy was to review our estimates when the specification had finally been agreed. Preparing the specification always revealed requirements which neither we nor even the users themselves had been aware of, and the review of estimates always led to greatly increased forecasts of cost, time and resources for the project. We therefore began to qualify our initial estimates with a 'subject to final estimates when the specification has been approved' clause. At first this was not appreciated by either senior management or the customers, but when they were shown that for previous projects the final costs and times to develop were always considerably in excess of the original estimates, they began to realize the wisdom of it. Gradually the culture changed.

So here is an important factor in the software engineering environment: culture. It is not difficult to recognize that successful development depends on the culture of the developers — for instance, whether they have a 'quality' culture. But success also depends on the culture of senior management — whether indeed they are quality-conscious, or even professional, in their attitude to development projects, and, as we shall see in Chapter 15, on what criteria they base their judgement of the success of a project.

Even in modern 'software engineering', early estimates are relied on too heavily. Re-estimating on the basis of the specification is carried out too seldom. Estimates can only be as good as the information on which they are based, and, prior to the approved specification, information is inadequate and unreliable. Estimation is difficult and likely to be inaccurate at the best of times, but two things currently increase its difficulty and accuracy. The first is that it is seldom carried out conscientiously, and the second is the fact that specifications change so frequently and so much.

The initial estimates should therefore be used only to judge whether or not the project is likely to be viable. It would be better if they were used only as a basis for giving approval for the preparation of the specification (see Section 9.3 of Chapter 9 for further discussion of this). When new estimates are made on the basis of the specification, negotiation should be carried out on whether the various requirements are cost-effective. In this way, senior management will possess more reliable information on which to base their decisions, fewer unnecessary requirements will be approved, and fewer projects will be judged to have failed when the real problem was inaccurate estimation in the first place rather than inefficient development later.

If developers are to have a reasonable chance of success, a serious and well-executed attempt at initial estimation is essential. Then the project manager must distinguish between estimates and targets and, while standing by his estimate, be prepared to negotiate the target. Later, the estimate should be reviewed. One of the greatest impediments to estimating is not systematically employing past experience. The greatest failure is the failure to learn from the past.

### 3.2.2  Time and Budget Inadequate — A Contracted-out Project

Contracting out suggests tendering. Tendering suggests competition for the award of the contract. Competition suggests that tenderers seek ways of minimizing their project price. How can tenderers minimize their price and still guarantee a profit? It is not unknown for them to rely for this on the near certainty of the purchaser providing a poor specification. Knowing that there will inevitably be a need for changes to an inferior specification, tenderers may confidently offer a low initial bid for the project — even one on which they would make a loss — with the intention of levying high charges on changes. For many years this has worked for them. What it means, however, is that the eventual time and cost of the project greatly exceed the initial 'estimates'. Given the circumstances, this leads to a false judgement of the overall success of the project.

A postscript to this, however, is a story which I heard recently. At the end of a certain project, the software house which had developed the system approached the customer and asked for an added £50,000 for extra time spent on the project. As this was unexpected and inappropriate in a fixed-price contract, the customer was thorough in investigating the reasons. It transpired that the developer had deliberately tendered a low price in order to win the contract and then, because the customer had sought no changes to the specification during development, had lost money on the project. It is not impossible to do a good job on a specification of requirements, and we need more customers who do so.

### 3.2.3  The Folly of Backward Estimation

It is 10.00 am, and I've got a date at Victoria Station at 8.00 pm. I don't want to be late, so I plan my journey. I will have to change trains, and a quick calculation suggests that the journey will take about one hour. That brings me back to 7.00 pm. Then there's the walk to the station and the wait to buy a ticket. Together they will take about fifteen minutes, so I'll need to leave home at about 6.45 pm. But suppose one of the trains is cancelled? I'd better leave a little extra time for that. Then, suppose there's a bomb scare in one of the stations? This would cause the underground network to be closed — and I wouldn't discover it until I arrived at the station to buy my ticket. Just in case this happens, I'd better leave enough time to take a bus. But then, I'd need to change buses, and the bus will be slower than the underground, so I'd better leave home at about 5.30 pm.

But isn't this too early? It's eating into all the other things I need to do today. But then, if I'm late she may not wait. It would be a chance missed if we didn't meet again, so I should do everything possible to make sure I'm on time.

Everything possible, or everything necessary? To do everything possible would mean considering every eventuality and making a contingency for it. If I did that, even now, at 10.00 am, it would already be too late to leave home. All right then — everything necessary. But what does that mean? If I leave any possibility unplanned, there remains a chance that I'll be late.

But what is the consequence of being late? I have already said she may not wait for me. But if we are as compatible as I seem to think, will she not have sensed that too and be just as keen for us to meet again? If so, will she not, if I am late, wait hoping that I will turn up? And if this is not so, then perhaps we were not so compatible after all. Perhaps the consequence of my being late would be no more than a disappointment — not great enough, in any case, to warrant elaborate contingency plans. So, I'll leave home at 6.45 pm as per the original plan, and hope that the underground trains are running normally.

At some time we must trust that 'things' will go 'according to plan'. But we do so having considered the possibilities, the risks, and the cost of putting contingencies in place. Estimating and planning go hand in hand. Preparing a sensible plan depends on estimation. Estimating, as seen in the case of my journey time, must be based on making a plan of what's to be done. They both require consideration of 'everything', as well as an assessment of the risks involved. In the end, estimation and planning require simultaneous risk assessment.

But in any given case the means of estimating must be realistic. Working backwards from the time of my assignation was a suitable way of both estimating and planning my rendezvous at Victoria Station. This was because the time available (the time between the present and the assignation) was greater than the time of my journey to get there. But in my first project as development manager, discussed in Section 3.2.1 above, I found myself with eight months in which to complete a project which had been estimated to require twenty-four. My staff calmly set about doing what they had done for some time — backward 'estimation'. This is of course not estimation at all; it involves dividing the time available into the stages of the project, not by allocating the various times actually estimated for each stage, but by proportionately allocating the available time among the intended stages. The result is a plan which shows the project ending at exactly the time appointed by the Director. I could see the folly of this, but I had already been talked into acquiescence by the project manager.

Naturally we did not complete the project according to the plan. Indeed, when the completion date found us still in the design stage of the project, with only an inferior specification to work from, we did not even have the wit to re-plan the project according to our own professional judgement. The project manager said that we could not risk telling the Director the whole truth, so our new plan extended the completion date by only six months. Thus, we re-planned a number of times, and each time it was we, the developers, who were seen to have failed.

It is better — no, it is vital — to report the truth as soon as it is known.

At the time of which I speak, it required a culture change — in the developers, the project manager, and senior management — for the truth to be acceptable. But, in the end, it was only the truth which set the tone for a new culture. If the truth had continued to be concealed, as it previously had been, there would never have been a change.

And the moral of this tale? Distinguish between targets and estimates. Backward estimation is not estimation at all, but usually a futile attempt to achieve an improbable target; use it for assignations but not for software development projects.

### 3.2.4 But Business Objectives May Demand Backward Estimation!

But what about the times when business objectives demand that a project is completed in a defined short time? If the time is too short, how can you avoid backward estimation?

Don't be silly. If sensible, forward, estimation reveals that the time available is inadequate, how can backward estimation change this and make the project viable? Recognizing the shortage of time is the first step to taking control of the situation. Then there are possibilities for action. The first is to be honest with the customer and affirm that production of a system to the full specification is impossible in the currently allocated time. You might then seek authority to reduce the functionality to that which is manageable in the time.

Or, if the specification has not yet been produced, a further option could be to use backward estimation wisely — not to plan the project but to determine its possible characteristics. For example, if experience of the type of project in prospect has led to a knowledge of the proportions of the total time which are typically spent on the various project stages, it is possible to estimate how large a project you could conduct in the time. For instance, if you know that it requires about 30% of the project duration to prepare a good specification, you might seek authority to use that proportion of the time available to capture and analyse the most important requirements. Then, the developed product would be sure to meet at least some of its strategic requirements, and there would be a fair chance of it being completed on time — not least because the project was kept small.

But whatever you do, do not be deceived into believing that packaging time into neat segments can provide more of it.

### 3.2.5  No Estimation — and the Desire for Estimating Tools

Frequently, 'estimates' of cost and time are guessed at or derived fraudulently rather than calculated by honest planning. Often they result from backward estimation based on a completion date decreed by senior management, as discussed above. Often, too, the greater part of estimating goes into guessing at what figures senior management would find acceptable and be prepared to authorize. Then there is the use of estimating tools.

In Chapter 1, I pointed to the danger of using tools without understanding them. I recall an instance when someone who was managing a project sought approval to purchase a certain estimation tool.

'How much does it cost?' he was asked. It turned out that it cost a lot of money.

'Why do we need it?'

'In order to improve our estimating,' he replied.

This was hardly a strong justification for the purchase, and he was asked for the documented estimates for the project to date.

The answer was that no such documents existed.

'Why not?'

'Because we're so overworked on the project that we have no time for estimating. That's why we need the tool.'

'Then how did you arrive at the targets to which you are now working?'

'They were what the Director wanted.'

We had come full circle. Because of stringent business requirements, demanding senior management, and inexperience in estimating and planning, the project manager had taken the option of backward estimation. Then, in the face of criticism, and recognizing that this was not estimating at all, his option was to find a tool which would, with neither effort nor knowledge on his part, provide him with estimates which would both silence his critics and help him (miraculously) to succeed in the project.

But it does not work like that.

'How does the tool work?'

He only knew that it worked on a statistical basis. The data for his project would be loaded into a database which already contained data from numerous other projects of many types, and statistical results would be produced.

'What gives you confidence that it will provide reliable estimates for this particular project?'

Well, the tool had been highly recommended, and that was a big influence.

But on examination of the facts, it turned out that, while accuracy on average was claimed, in any given project the guarantee was only for an accuracy to within about plus or minus 200% (beware of the word 'average'.)

So, he might have been lucky in his project, but he would not know if he was until the end of the project. Meanwhile, he had no basis for optimism, a principal reason for this being that he did not know the assumptions on which the tool was based. The tool was not purchased.

It is not sufficient to have statistical estimates, particularly when it is not known what data is contributing to the statistics. What is required in any given instance is an estimate for *this* project. If you are the project manager, the budget is *your* budget, and the timescale is *your* timescale. You are committed to develop the system within them, and you must have confidence in them. The only way to get that confidence is to carry out the estimates yourself, based on experience: the experience of *this* team carrying out *this* type of project using *this* technology. If you do not possess evidence on all those factors, you need to acquire what evidence exists. For example, the team may have changed somewhat since its last project and it has never had a project quite like this one: nevertheless, you can find out about the team in defined circumstances, you can find out about its leadership, and you can find out what technologies it has expertise in. If it has no expertise in any of the technologies to be used in the proposed project, you know that you must allow not only time for training but also a great deal more time for learning by practice.

A well balanced team always contains both experience and as yet undeveloped potential, so the project manager needs to consider the relative proportions in the current team before determining a rate of production. Then there is the question of what reliance can be placed on the specification: do we have experience of previous specifications from this customer?

If you estimate and get it wrong, you will have learned from the process — and you will be able to improve your forecasts as the project progresses. Would your senior management approve an estimate if you revealed that you had no idea what it was based on and that it was accurate to plus or minus 200%?

A frequent error in estimating is to be too optimistic. This is often rationalized, even with the experience of hindsight, with the comment, 'Well, if everything had gone according to plan, we could have met that target.' The fact is that things seldom go according to plan. There are numerous reasons why activities seldom take the time that they should take, and it is as well not only to take precautions against the problems by planning and risk management, but also to be practical rather than hopeful in estimating. A further relevant point is that plans seldom contain all the necessary activities. Time must be allowed for those which have not been thought of but which will reveal themselves later; there are always some of them.

A tool may be helpful. But if you are to place reliance on a tool, it should be one which you understand, not one which you hope can replace good judgement.

### 3.2.6 So Where's the Strategy ?

As development manager I had realized that one reason for a project's increasing time and cost was its increasing size (the increase in the volume of requirements as the project progressed). I had also recognized that many new requirements were the result of the appearance of new users, even late in the project. But it took me some time to appreciate the relationship between the appearance of new users throughout the project and the lack of strategic planning.

Although at least some of their requirements would have been inappropriate to the system under construction, I had no basis for rejecting or even challenging these new users: I had a specification of requirements for the system, but no strategic plan from which to define the project scope or a system boundary. The only project definition was the specification, and this was drawn up by the users rather than by senior management. There was no high-level plan to which the requirements should conform. I was unable to suggest that any new users' requirements should not be met by this system.

To define its boundary, one must understand a system in relation to other systems — including those not yet built, or even designed. For this to be so, there needs to be the conception of a number of systems at the same time, with their interrelationships defined — and this requires a strategic plan (see Chapter 7).

If there had been such a plan to define the terms of reference and business objectives not only of the system under construction but also of other related systems, I could have assessed each new set of requirements against the plan to determine which system should meet them. Then, even if that system was not due to be operational for a number of years, I could perhaps have kept the changes to my project manageable by explaining to the users how and when their requirements would be met.

In general, such a check can show that the proposed new requirements are not valid — if, for instance, the functions which they represented are being made redundant by the new system, or subsumed into other functions. As it was, there was no way for the developers to assess this, and I had to accept the new requirements. It would only be revealed later, when the system was operational, whether or not we had wasted resources in developing them.

When there is no strategic plan, a system is developed only to meet end users' requirements rather than business objectives. This is bottom-up management. Typically, this occurs when senior management is involved in the initiation of the project only to the extent of giving financial authorization.

On the other hand, when a project arises out of a strategic plan, a project manager has the basis for defining the project boundary and checking requirements to ensure that they do not fall outside of it. This can go a long way towards limiting the expansion of the project once development has commenced. It also goes a long way towards controlling the specification of requirements, and provides a basis for validating it.

Whereas strategic planning is not a project manager's responsibility, it is recommended that project managers enquire at the earliest possible opportunity about the origins of the project. If the project has no clear strategic foundation, the project manager will not be able to create one, and is unlikely to be able to reject the project, but he will have been warned. He should then anticipate not only change to the specification but also an increase in the size of the project, and he should allow for this in estimating.

Ideally, a business strategist and not the project manager should check new requirements against the strategic plan — as discussed in Chapter 7.

### 3.2.7  But What is it That You Want, Exactly ?

A specification is essential to successful development — the recognition of this was mentioned at the beginning of Chapter 2. But a specification which is incorrect, inconsistent, ambiguous, and full of gaps is as bad as no specification at all. Since the earliest times, software development projects have suffered from specification problems which range from the total lack of a specification, through specifications of such abominable quality that they are misleading, to specifications which are good but which change without proper control.

Coming to my new job of development manager, I found not only projects in their initial stages but also those which had been in progress for some time and those whose developed systems had been delivered for operation. I found myself immediately drawn into arguments over whether the delivered systems were fit for their purpose. The users maintained that they were not. My staff maintained that the systems were what the users had asked for. I proposed that reference to the specifications would settle the matter, but I found that there were no specifications.

The developers (my staff) were in a lose-lose situation. Traditionally, the users did not write specifications but called in the developers to act as systems analysts and investigate the requirements for any proposed system. Because they understood the users' domain, the developers believed that they also fully understood the system requirements, and, in an effort to save time for the users, pursued development without writing a specification. As we know, change is inexorable and, even if the specification had been perfect at the time of writing it, the true requirements would necessarily change even as development progressed. Inevitably, the developed system was not what the users wanted at the time of receiving it. Naturally the developers were blamed for the deficiencies, and they had no way of proving that the system was in fact what the users had asked for.

My solution was to let everyone know that we would not commence development on a system until a specification had been produced — and that it was the customer's responsibility to produce it. I thought that this support of my staff would be appreciated by them, but this was not the case. They argued that they were there to help the users and that I was jeopardizing their assistance by introducing a largely unnecessary step. The users too were against me because they had never produced a specification, they did not know how to prepare one, and they thought I was being dictatorial (which I was). I was unpopular with everyone.

I was feeling my way towards improving our development process. But I was also on a learning curve myself: I had to learn how to introduce change. I thought that because it was self-evident to me that new procedures were essential and that insistence on a specification would improve development quality, that it would also be self-evident to my staff. I had to learn, first, that lower-level staff with limited experience did not necessarily understand the principles of 'software engineering', and then that they had a much closer relationship with the users than I had imagined. I needed to introduce change by degrees, and to sell it rather than announce it in an authoritarian manner.

I also had to accept that it was not enough for me to remind the users that the specification was their responsibility and then to sit back and wait for it. It would not arrive. And if it did not arrive, there would be no development to be carried out and no work for my staff.

If specifications were to be developed, we had to assist the users to produce them. But there were more problems ahead. Requirements capture is a difficult business and the development staff were hardly more experienced in systems analysis than the users were. Preparing specifications requires attention to detail and good authorship, and at first the 'engineers' could see no good reason to write well. Gradually, however, things improved. We identified a suitable method of requirements capture and trained all the staff in its use. We kept emphasizing the importance of the specification stage of the project until everyone was convinced. Even the users were converted, and we induced them to join our teams and participate fully in requirements capture and analysis and the documentation of specifications. We found a specification standard and tailored it to our needs and from then onwards all specifications had to conform to it. We introduced Fagan's Inspection [Fagan 76, Redmill 88] as the means of quality control of specifications, and we arranged training in this not only for our own staff but also for the users. One of the criteria of inspection was that the specification should conform to the standard. When the authors discovered that inspection was being used to assist them in improving the quality of *their* documents and not to show them up as bad authors, they seemed to take greater pride in what they were doing, and their authorship improved enormously.

You will no doubt have noticed that I have been speaking of the users rather than the customer. The fact is that in those days the senior manager who should have been the customer was only involved to the extent of signing the authorization for the project budget. There were no formal business objectives, and the scope of the project was defined only by the users' requirements. There was bottom-up management and no strategy (see Section 3.2.6 above).

After our improvements in specification, one problem persisted, and this was that users' managers did not see it as their job, or their staff's, to provide information to the systems analysts. 'My staff's job is maintenance, they cannot spend their time talking to you,' they would say. 'Do you want a system to meet your needs?' I would ask. 'Then you must let us know your needs, and the best way to do that is to talk to us.' The users' managers said that their budgets did not permit a staffing level which provided for preparing specifications for the systems which they themselves needed. Senior managers assured me that they would provide sufficient staff to allow adequate participation in their projects, but these promises never seemed to show results. It took years before the users took a respectable part in their own projects, and it never reached the stage where they played an adequate part. It is perennially a difficult problem.

Our specification standard (which also served as a guideline) defined the form and content of specification documents, and in the main this was a success. However, one thing which was more a matter of culture than of procedure, and which therefore was more difficult to put in order, was that of defining acceptance criteria. It was rare for there to be no dispute between users and developers over whether a system met the users' requirements, even when a well-written specification existed. In many, if not most, cases, reference to the specification did not resolve the issue because acceptance criteria had not been thoroughly documented, or even considered at the specification stage.

It is one thing to specify that at least 90% of all responses by the system to a user's command should be within 1 second, but what about the other 10%? Even when there is no stated requirement, a single delayed response can be sufficient evidence to the users that the developers have done a bad job. Who is 'right' in the ensuing argument? It is as important to define maximum values and the variance of a distribution as it is to specify the mean.

Gradually we moved towards a culture of specifying acceptance criteria, but I can't say that we ever achieved an ideal state. Doing so requires clear and logical thinking, a questioning attitude, and users who are not only clear as to what they need but also who take time both to document their requirements and to interpret them into numerically defined criteria. None of these essentials is common. Even when the right people come together for a time, other forces such as promotion and a change of job tear them apart again.

Yet, over a period of time, we steadily improved our abilities, our approach, our relationships with our customers and users, and our quality procedures for requirements capture and specification, until we had in place:

- Trained systems analysts;
- A requirements capture and analysis method;
- Specification teams made up of both developers and users;
- A standard for specifications;
- A technique (Fagan's Inspection) for the quality control and assurance of documents;
- A change control procedure for specifications.

Even then, discovering what the users really wanted was not an easy task. The fact is that capturing and analysing requirements and preparing a specification are the most difficult aspects of the development process. Indeed, together they form a multi-dimensional issue. It is multi-dimensional because it depends not merely on the correct application of a technique but on a number of variables, including the following:

- Whether there is a business strategy in place;
- Whether there is an information systems strategy in place;
- Senior management competence, commitment and involvement;
- The structure of the customer's and users' organization;
- The competence of the systems analysts;
- Access to the real users;
- The commitment and calibre of middle and junior management;
- The writing ability of the author of the specification;
- Relationships between developers and users;
- Technical competence;
- The management of change.

Many of these topics are inter-personal and psychological. The issue is not merely technical, but also, importantly, whether we can get the information on requirements to cross the gap successfully between those who hold (or should hold) the knowledge and those who need it. But even that is not all. Those who should hold the information do not necessarily have it, so the holders of the information need to be found. Then, it is likely that they do not know that they hold it, or that they do not find it easy to express themselves, so ways must be found to extract the necessary information. Then, the information which crosses the gap is often misinterpreted by those who receive it, so when it is documented there are errors of translation.

I do not think that I should take this brief summary of specification problems further — the point is raised again in Chapter 5. It is sufficient now to caution project managers that this is the most difficult and error-prone of all the stages of a development project. There is no short cut: you need to have regard to the issues listed above, train your staff, manage them well, and pay attention to quality. If you want good quality, you must reject bad quality. Moreover, the time to reject bad quality is as early as possible. If you do not pay close attention to obtaining a good specification, and then be aware that it will change even as you strive to meet it, look out for trouble.

### 3.2.8  Who Wants the System, Anyway ?

If the senior manager responsible for the system—and therefore the developers' customer — and the potential users of the system do not participate in the development project, the changes which take place in their organization while the project is in progress are unlikely to be communicated to the developers.

As pointed out above, it was at first difficult to involve the customer and users in a project. Once we, the developers, showed ourselves to be helpful and open in our communication with them, the users were mostly interested and keen to be involved. But for a long time their managers did not, in the main, see their way clear to becoming involved or to facilitating the users' participation in projects.

Senior management's promises of greater user involvement were not kept. Although the senior managers could appreciate the importance of making the users accessible to the developers, the fact was that the users' in-line managers had to justify their staff on the basis of the 'real work'. Either they did not ask for staff to be justified on the basis of project representation, or the senior managers did not approve it, but the fact is that several frustrating years went by before there was adequate user representation on the projects.

Senior managers then, as now, perceived themselves as being too busy to participate in the management of the development of their systems. Eventually they compromised by appointing a middle manager to be a 'customer representative' on all projects. However, as we (the developers) became more professional, it became more difficult for the appropriate senior managers to avoid participation. As we identified problems, we documented them and made requests in writing for customer or user assistance. We were then able to attribute project delays to delays in receiving responses. We documented our validation test results against the acceptance criteria and could demonstrate that the system met its specification. Our change procedure ensured that all changes which had been communicated to us were documented and visible. Gradually the cooperation from the customers improved. By the time we began to employ evolutionary delivery, it was good.

Greater professionalism in the developers demands greater professionalism in the customer and users.

The customer's and users' roles in a project are not confined to producing a specification. If they are not involved throughout, the chance of failure is significantly increased.

### 3.2.9  Control Change or Fall Prey to It

The developers were all extremely helpful, and making changes to the requirements was easy: any of the users simply telephoned any one of three developers and explained the change. But at the end of the contract, the customer received a shock. The project cost twice the contract price. There was plenty of explanation for this: the numerous changes had been difficult to make; many had arrived after the design had been completed, so the system had had not only to be re-specified but also redesigned; further, many changes had arrived after the software had been written, so a great deal of work that had been done was abortive. When the customer asked for a statement of the changes, the developers presented a well documented list. When the customer asked the users to check the list, it turned out that they had not maintained a reliable record of their requests to the developers.

When a customer has such an experience, the need for a change control procedure is obvious — and Chapter 11 is devoted to this subject. Numerous project delays and budget over-runs have been due to uncontrolled change. This is not to suggest that change should not be allowed — its inevitability has already been remarked. But whether the project is contracted out or carried out in-house, there needs to be a change control procedure, and the procedure needs to be audited regularly to ensure that it is being observed.

## 3.3   SUMMARY AND EXTRACTS

In this chapter I have related a number of personal experiences of the problems which occur in software development. They include estimation — carrying it out badly or not at all and compromising it with impossible targets — the lack of strategic planning, and the absence of customers and users from the project.

The following are extracts which make some of the chapter's points.

- Whereas the agreement between customer and supplier demands that the system should meet its specification, the customer's and users' frequent complaint is that it does not meet their requirements, which is almost certainly not the same thing.

- What is seen as a cause from one point of view is seen as an effect from another. One person's problem is the cause of another person's problem.

- The seeds of most of the serious problems are sown during the early stages of a project — at the contractual or authorization stage, in estimating and planning, in preparing the specification, and in failing to put an adequate project infrastructure in place.

- It is important to distinguish between an estimate and a target.

- It is also crucial to distinguish between estimation and negotiation. A project manager should attempt to negotiate seemingly impossible targets, and the estimate is his main weapon in doing so.

- Successful development depends on the culture of the developers ... But success also depends on the culture of senior management — whether they are quality-conscious, or even professional, in their attitude to development projects, and on what criteria they base their judgement of the success of a project.

- Estimates can only be as good as the information on which they are based, and, prior to the approved specification, information is inadequate and unreliable.

- When new estimates are made on the basis of the specification, negotiation should be carried out on whether the various requirements are cost-effective. In this way, senior management will possess more reliable information on which to base their decisions, fewer unnecessary requirements will be approved, and fewer projects will be judged to have failed when the real problem was inaccurate estimation in the first place rather than inefficient development later.

- One of the greatest impediments to estimating is not systematically employing past experience.

- Backward estimation is not estimation at all, but usually a futile attempt to achieve an improbable target.

- A frequent error in estimating is to be too optimistic. This is often rationalized, even with the experience of hindsight, with the comment, 'Well, if everything had gone according to plan, we could have met that target.' The fact is that things seldom go according to plan ... it is as well to be practical rather than hopeful in estimating.

- If you are to place reliance on a tool, it should be one which you understand, not one which you hope can replace good judgement.

- To define its boundary, one must understand a system in relation to other systems ... and this requires a strategic plan

- When there is no strategic plan, a system is developed only to meet end users' requirements rather than business objectives. This is bottom-up management.

- If the project has no clear strategic foundation, the project manager will not be able to create one, and is unlikely to be able to reject the project, but he will have been warned.

- I had to learn how to introduce change ... I needed to introduce change by degrees, and to sell it rather than announce it in an authoritarian manner.

- Capturing and analysing requirements and preparing a specification are the most difficult aspects of the development process.

- If you want good quality, you must reject bad quality.

- If you do not pay close attention to obtaining a good specification, and then be aware that it will change even as you strive to meet it, look out for trouble.

# 4

# At the Mercy
# of the Project

When I first came into project management, an experienced project manager was kind enough to give me some advice. He drew a 'Y' on a white board and said that its three prongs symbolized the three goals of a project manager: time, budget, and quality. By 'quality' he meant conformity to the technical specification of requirements.

He then cautioned me that to think of achieving the criteria of all three goals was hopelessly ambitious. 'You've got to realize,' he said, 'that it's always a trade off. To achieve any one target means that you have to compromise the other two.' I was sceptical of this counsel, but I had to defer to a more senior, more experienced, and more confident project manager. Anyway, his Y diagram was novel and therefore persuasive.

Yet, how could 'quality' be independent of meeting our time and budget targets? If inadequate estimating, planning, coordination, or anything else has led to my missing these targets, does meeting the specification give me the right to claim to have done a 'quality' job? I put myself in the customer's shoes. If I order a car, do I consider that the garage has done a quality job if they provide the right make, model and colour, but deliver it late and charge a higher price than that agreed on? No. I decided that quality encompassed the complete service.

I reviewed my colleague's Y diagram. I changed his label of 'quality' to 'conformity to specification' and I put a 'Q' around the Y, as in Figure 4.1, symbolically to show that all three prongs are components of the quality of a project, and not just one of them.

It is true, of course, that during the course of a project there need to be trade-offs between the various prongs of the Y. For example, in order to test a design, we may need to purchase certain items of hardware earlier than planned, thus exceeding both time and budget in the design stage. But this should be an adjustment which is purely internal to the project. It is the project manager's responsibility not to allow such internal compromises to affect the total quality as seen by the customer at the end of the project. In discharging this responsibility, the project manager needs to understand the trade-offs being made and draw up plans to show why they are necessary, that they are temporary, and how the project criteria will be met in spite of them.

Although over a period of time I came to disagree with his basic premise

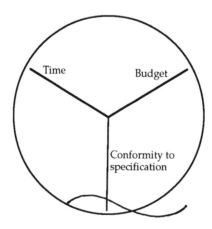

**Figure 4.1** The dimensions of project quality

of project management, I was thankful for my senior colleague's introduction to what in my opinion was a flawed definition of both project management and quality, because from the outset it set me thinking about what it takes to manage a successful project. If you commence a project with the notion that it will be impossible to meet more than one of the three agreed criteria, and that it is not even worth attempting to do so, something is seriously wrong. You stand a negligible chance of completing a successful project, for you have already accepted failure. And you have not been honest with the customer with whom you have made the agreements which you do not believe you can keep. In his ancient Chinese text on military strategy, *The Art of War*, Sun Tzu says that the victorious warrior wins first and then goes to war while the defeated warrior first goes to war and then seeks to win. Beware of starting off on the wrong foot.

The trouble is that project managers too often start off on the wrong foot. One reason why there is something seriously wrong with so many projects is that there is something seriously wrong with the attitudes of their project managers. There are many reasons for this.

## 4.1   THE WRONG PROJECT MANAGER

In recent years it has become more common to find 'dedicated' project managers — that is to say, people whose job it is to manage projects and who, having managed one project, take on the management of another. Such people gain experience in the job and may attend training courses, so the chances are that the standard of project management is, by and large, improving.

Previously, the responsibility for a project frequently lay entirely with an in-line manager. And frequently such a person was unfamiliar with development projects and glad to leave the whole business to subordinates. Thus, 'management' fell to the programmers, and the results have already been referred to in the previous chapters.

Later, when project management had come into vogue but was still seen almost entirely as a technical issue, it was common to appoint as project manager either an undistinguished junior manager who could be 'spared' from other duties, or a senior programmer on promotion or temporary promotion. In both cases the appointee usually had no experience and little or no training in management of any sort. Being almost wholly technically oriented, he was only competent to deal with purely technical problems —

though he often spent too much time resolving them himself rather than defining and then delegating the task to others.

However, when the more insidious symptoms of trouble within the project arose, such as lateness and over-spend, as they almost certainly do at some time in a project, the purely technical project manager was more at the mercy of the project than in control of it. In seeking the causes of problems, he concentrated on technical issues, and, as there are always technical improvements which can be made, he would always find something to 'fix'. But solving the small technical problems would not bring the project back on course. Being unaware of his own deficiencies in matters such as estimating, planning, coordinating, monitoring progress against plans, and the management of people, he was unable to recognize the ineffectiveness of his management of the project. He would work longer and longer hours, find more and more minor technical problems, resolve them with increasing frustration and anxiety, but still not be able to reverse the adverse trends in time and budget.

The first necessity of a software development project is a project manager who understands project management. Without this, the chances are stacked against success, whatever development model is being used.

## 4.2    PROJECT INFRASTRUCTURE

Perhaps the most important aspect of project management is the creation of the project infrastructure (see Chapter 8). The purpose of this is not to define what needs to be done during the project (this is the function of planning), or how to do it (this depends on the definition of project processes); it is to define clearly the wherewithal for doing what needs to be done. In this sense, the project infrastructure comprises the following three components.

- People. The project manager must determine who should be involved in the project, identify their roles and responsibilities, and ensure at the beginning of the project that each participant understands his role and has the authority, the competence, and the commitment to discharge it.
- Group communication. The project manager must define the teams and committees which need to work together on the project, from a high-level project board to the various working-level teams. He must define the responsibilities and authority of each group, determine the frequency

of the meetings of each group, identify the nature and details of each meeting, define the means of communication between people in each group and between groups in the project, and obtain the agreement of each person to attend all relevant meetings and discharge all their responsibilities.

* Documents. The project manager must identify the various types of documents to be produced on the project and devise a numbering and labelling system, filing system, and distribution system for each of them.

Creating the infrastructure for the project is akin to preparing the specification for the system to be developed. It is an essential prerequisite to development work. If the 'people' and communications infrastructures are not properly set up, there are doubts in people's minds as to what their responsibilities are, and some people are not even aware that they have responsibilities at all. Things which should be done 'fall between the cracks', with various persons believing that someone else is discharging the responsibility. When problems arise during the project, it takes a great deal longer than it should to determine who has responsibility for them (particularly when the customer and users are involved), to determine what action should be taken, and to implement the action plan. It is also more likely that inappropriate action will be taken and that further time will be lost in reviewing the situation, drawing up a revised action plan, and bringing the action to bear.

In the case of documents, it is not unusual to discover in the middle of a project that a scheme needs to be devised for distinguishing one type of document from another and one version of a document from another. Or, if a filing system has not been designed and put in place, it suddenly becomes apparent that there is no accepted set of master documents, no audit trail of document versions, and uncertainty as to the project documentation. By then, the task of creating the appropriate infrastructure is of increased difficulty, for all existing documents must be labelled retrospectively and a filing system for them designed. When such things occur, a project manager may accept it as an unexpected overhead which could not have been avoided, not appreciating that a considerable amount of time (which had not been planned for) could have been saved if the document infrastructure had been created at the initiation stage of the project.

There are often good reasons for planned activities to be carried out later or earlier than scheduled, and when they are, there may be a temporary loss or gain of time, with a reasonable expectation (at least if the project is adequately managed) that the project will eventually be back on course. But when unplanned activities become essential to the project, it is difficult to recover the time or the budget spent on them. And here lies the importance of the infrastructure: not only must it be in place, but, importantly, it must be put in place at the initiation stage.

Creating the project infrastructure is an important aspect of project planning, but it is seldom considered as such and seldom carried out effectively. Many project problems are due to the neglect, or late implementation, of the project infrastructure.

## 4.3    PLANNING

Project planning is seldom carried out well, even by the more competent project managers. One reason for this is that our culture — certainly our culture at work — requires us to be 'doing' rather than thinking, and planning is not considered to be 'doing'. I recall that in my early days as a project manager, even senior managers were impatient of planning. In fact, they were impatient of design too, and, indeed, of everything other than programming. 'Stop this messing around,' they would say, 'and get some real work done.' Programming was 'real work' because it was 'doing', and there was a visible end product — a mountain of paper.

I remember, too, going into a certain manager's office. He was of the same grade in the organization as I was. His door was closed but a little ajar, so, as I knocked I pushed the door and entered. The manager was leaning back in his chair, his hands were linked together behind his head, and he was gazing at the ceiling, apparently in thought. As he heard my knock, he simultaneously leaned forward, brought his arms to rest on the desk, and picked up his pen and held it in a writing position, so that he would be seen by the entrant (me) to be in a 'working' or 'doing' position. He did not want to be caught thinking!

As managers of software development projects, we need to recognize that the engineering content of our work lies in the planning, the design, the control. Programming is, in the main, equivalent to the technician's task in other engineering disciplines. Success depends on taking time to think. As a manager, we need to take time to plan, just as prior to programming we need to take time to design. And not only do project managers need to think, they also need to allow their staff time to think. If your staff are afraid to be caught thinking by you, something is wrong.

A second reason for planning not being well done is that it is often inadequately defined. It is frequently perceived only as the scheduling of events. Yet, before scheduling can be meaningful, there is the need to determine not only what needs to be done but also the value of doing it and the risk of not being successful. So planning demands not only estimation but also judgement.

Judgement needs also to extend to recognizing when a particular plan is no longer appropriate to the defined goal. As seen in Chapter 2, the spiral life cycle model emphasizes the need to review intended courses of action, assess their risks and, if necessary, change course. If a plan is too rigid and is seen as a mandate rather than a means of achieving a defined goal, it can lead to obstacles which might have been avoided by taking a different path. The plan is a sign which points the way to the goal, but if the indicated path becomes blocked, it is time to revise the plan. Beware of thinking that following it implicitly is in fact the goal. Do not grasp at the shadow and miss the substance.


## 4.4    PROJECT AND PRODUCT

When a task is to be carried out by a single individual, there are no overheads in coordination and communication between people. As the number of tasks increases and the size of a team grows, there is an increasing need to invest effort in coordinating the work of the individuals and ensuring communication between them. At a certain point, it is advantageous to have someone whose sole job it is to do this. Let us refer to him as the team leader.

A good team leader soon finds that effective communication depends not on calling the team together when it seems necessary, but on planning and employing a project infrastructure (see Section 4.2 above and Chapter 8), so a great deal of effort is put into this.

Then the team leader discovers that the infrastructure does not do the work but supports him in doing it, and that the infrastructure requires maintenance and change.

Gradually the team leader finds that his tasks are quite different from what they were when he was a 'worker'. Indeed, as his project and team become larger, it becomes clear that the activities necessary to facilitate team and project management are as numerous and demanding as those to carry on the development of the product. Perhaps he needs a support team in order to carry them out. The team leader has become a project manager and he had learned of the difference between product development and project management. A project manager who recognizes the distinction between project and product is fortunate, for it is seldom understood or even considered by project managers.

Failure to recognize this difference is one of the penalties for appointing a project manager of purely technical background (see Section 4.1 above). While the reason for the existence of the project is the need to develop the product (and so the development process is at the core of the project), the purpose of creating a project is to provide an infrastructure which facilitates the development of the product. The larger the project, the more essential it is to have such an infrastructure, and the greater the likely price, in over-runs of budget and time, if it does not exist.

When I preach the importance of an infrastructure, it is often argued that only large projects need such an overhead, and that it is unnecessarily cumbersome and expensive for small projects. But the principles which apply to large projects also apply to small ones. Without good project management, a small project is just as likely to fail as a large one. It is simply a matter of scale.

## 4.5   INTEGRITY

In my job, I need to rely on other people a great deal. We all do. Some time ago, I carried out a study of the reliability of people on whom I depended. During a period of one month, there were 24 deadlines to be met by people who had made promises to me. These included the delivery of documents, the provision of information, and the making of telephone calls at prearranged times or dates. Of the 24 promises, five were adhered to and two telephone calls were made to me in advance of deadlines to let me know that the deliveries would be late.

So, there was a reliability of 5 in 24, or 20.8%. If we consider the persons who telephoned me to have been reliable in that they did not allow me to wait in vain for something which would not arrive (although they were not so reliable that they kept their original promises), we get a figure of 7 in 24, or 29.2%.

Whereas this is the only such quantitative study that I have conducted, I am not surprised at the result: it seems consistent with experience. When I asked (some of) the defaulters why they had not let me know in advance, or at all, that they would not meet the promised deadline, it turned out that most had not even considered the idea. Reasons such as the pressing urgency of other tasks were considered sufficient to exonerate them from communicating their excuse to someone who depended on them (their customer). 'Good' reasons seemed, in the main, to negate the need for reliability, or even courtesy.

Most had good intentions: they thought that they would be able to meet the deadline but then ran out of time; they thought that they would be able to make the delivery soon after the promised time (and only be a little late). But once the date had passed and they had failed, they continued to give priority to other things: after all, the thing was late already; what did it matter if it was a little later? And, frequently, they were astonished or annoyed if I showed displeasure at their attitude. When told the excuse, the customer should accept it unquestioningly.

In the end, it seems that people give their word unthinkingly, make inadequate effort to keep it, and do not think it important to keep their customer informed of their progress and, in particular, of the prospect of their failure. It is enough that they can excuse themselves.

Are project managers any different from the majority of us in respect of integrity? Given the above results, we should be, and the best project managers are. But few are 'best', or even very good, and in the main we are not very different. We seem as susceptible as others to think that our own excuses are justifiable reasons for failure, and we accept feeble excuses from other project participants too readily. A lack of integrity is accepted as the norm.

Unless a project manager feels impelled to keep his word, and recognizes that not to keep his word is positively dishonest, he is unlikely to be successful, and the degree of difficulty of his task will be increased.

There are so many activities within a project, and there is such dependence between them, that failure to meet a deadline in a small activity can have an effect — often an unexpected effect — first on the task of which the activity is a component, then on the stage of the project, and finally on the project itself. It is not sufficient for a project manager to plan a schedule well. He must also identify the dependencies between activities and recognize the consequence of failure of any one of them. Then he must monitor progress *against the plans*. Finally, when he finds clues that things are not as they should be, he must take action to make things happen. And he must keep his word and expect the other members of the project team to keep theirs. This is a matter of culture.

## 4.6   MAKING THINGS HAPPEN

It was April, and the resource plans showed that the project would require expertise in the application of a certain proprietary database from the beginning of October. A person with the necessary expertise would have to be recruited. As it happened, someone in another part of the company was interested in being transferred to the development department, and the project manager arranged for him to commence work on 1st October. When he arrived, it was discovered by his team leader that he did not possess the required expertise (which was predictable, given his previous job). It then turned out that the project manager had known of the deficiency but had not given any thought to arranging an appropriate training course prior to the new recruit's joining the project. The database supplier was approached. Yes, they could provide the training we needed, but not until the middle of November.

There was a two-month delay before the chap was capable of useful work, and the project budget suffered to the extent of his salary and other inefficiencies. Re-scheduling reduced the project delay to two weeks. At the end of October, the project manager carefully explained in his monthly report to senior management that a delay of two weeks to the project was necessitated by the inability of the supplier to provide a training course when it was required.

On a number of occasions, I heard various senior managers remark on how good that project manager was at his job. 'He always writes a very clear report,' one said. 'He explains precisely why something has gone wrong.'

If senior management's judgement of excellence is based on the clarity of explanation of failure rather than on the record of success, then they are not performing their task of monitoring the project manager. The chances are that they will also have appointed the wrong person for the job in the first place.

It is said that there are three types of people: those who get up and make things happen, those who sit back and watch things happen, and those who sit back and wonder what the hell is happening. I should add, however, that we are not each fixed immutably into one of the three types; we all exhibit characteristics of each, depending on the circumstances, on our interest in the situation, on our confidence in ourselves and the people around us, and so on. But the fact is that successful project management demands a project manager who is of the first type when it comes to project management. There are so many things that can go wrong in a project, and it is so easy for a small problem with a simple solution to escalate into a disaster if it is not attended to quickly. A project manager needs to be permanently alert to small clues that things may not be as they should be. Having detected such a clue, the project manager needs to act, first to confirm the finding and then to correct the problem before it escalates.

Here's another story. A feudal lord in ancient China asked his physician, who came from a well-known family of physicians, which of his family was the most famous healer. The doctor said, 'My eldest brother is sensitive to the spirit of sickness. As he exorcises it before it materializes, his name is not known outside the house. My next brother detects and eradicates disease before the patient knows that he has it, so his name is unknown outside of the village. I can diagnose illness when my patients are in pain and have fever, I prescribe medicines, massage joints, and offer prayers, and when these are effective and my patients are relieved, they mention my name all over the place, even as far away as the city'.

It is the project managers who fix things which have gone dreadfully wrong who are usually the best known. But if you want to make things easy for yourself as a project manager, be sensitive to the spirit of problems before they materialize. This means not only formally monitoring the progress of the project, but also, and importantly, understanding people, knowing the other project participants and talking with them regularly, and being attuned to body language so as to detect early signals that something is not as it should be.

If a project manager is of the third type of person mentioned above (the one who wonders what is happening), you cannot blame him when the project goes wrong; it is senior management who are culpable for appointing him as project manager. If a project manager is of the second type, the question 'Why?' should be asked. Is it because he is disinterested and should be in another job? Is it because he is intimidated by the task, having not had experience or received training? Again senior management need to be monitoring the project manager's ability, attitude and achievement. Only if the project manager is of the first type, and at the same time is a leader who not only gets the best out of the other participants in the project team but does so harmoniously, are his projects likely to be successful.

## 4.7   THE CULTURE OF REPORTING PROBLEMS

I mentioned above that a project manager needs to be alert to clues within the project. Ideally, all problems should be reported immediately by whoever recognizes them, but this is not the way of our culture, as suggested by the following anecdote.

At the end of a certain month, a manager reported that one of his projects was going to be about two weeks late.

'Why didn't you report this before?'

'I didn't know until a couple of days ago,' he said.

So, what happened? It turned out that a team member in one of his project teams had required a document from a member of staff in another department. It had been promised for a certain day, and when it did not arrive the team member waited a week before asking for it. He didn't want to 'hassle' its provider because he thought he might be busy. By then, of course, the task which depended on the document was already late. The provider of the document said that he had not had time to write it but that he would do so the next week. It took six weeks to arrive.

'By the end of six weeks,' the manager said, 'the lateness of the task had caused the project stage to become so late that the whole project was affected.'

This reminded me of the cautionary tale of the horseshoe nail. Because of the nail, the shoe was lost; because of the shoe, the horse was lost; because of the horse, the rider was lost; because of the rider, the battle was lost; because of the battle, the kingdom was lost: and all because of a horseshoe nail.

The effects of small problems may be small at first, but they are almost certain to increase if neglected.

If the team member had insisted on getting the document when it was due, the problem might have been averted. If he had reported the problem early, a telephone call from the team leader or the manager could have resolved the situation. But the team member did not want to 'blow the whistle' on the person who had let him down because it might get him into trouble. But this is not so. Reporting the problem would not have got the person into trouble. No doubt he was busy. But why was he not busy doing what he had promised to do? (See Section 4.5 above on integrity.) A call to his manager need not have suggested that he was idling; rather it would have asked for his priorities to be rearranged because of the dependency of the project on his work.

What about detecting the clues? If the team leader or the manager had detected a clue that something was amiss, and acted on it, the situation might have been salvaged. But given that a project manager, or any other manager, cannot be everywhere at once, and that in any case he will inevitably miss some clues, we need confidence that staff will promptly report problems which they cannot themselves deal with.

But it is not in our culture to report problems. We find it easy to present glowing reports of trivial successes, but we sweep the problems under the carpet.

As project managers, we need to try to cultivate an attitude of not accepting problems. If the person spotting the problem does not possess the authority, the confidence, the resources, or the competence to solve it, then he should report it at the earliest indication. It should not be allowed to remain and fester. This is the basis of quality: detecting problems early, tracing them to their roots, eradicating them there, and so preventing recurrence. Too often in projects the same problem recurs because it has been ignored, or because it has been attended to with a 'quick fix' which did not get to its source.

If we are to generate a culture of problem reporting, we as managers must be prepared to support our staff and solve their problems. On one occasion, I was talking to a senior manager when one of his staff came up to us. He waited patiently until his manager attended to him, and then said, 'I have a problem.....'

The immediate response of his senior manager was, 'I don't want problems from you, I want solutions.'

Can you imagine that person seeking support from his manager again? What in future will happen to problems which he cannot solve? They will remain to develop into greater problems, and the person with the problem will become increasingly anguished because he has nowhere to turn for assistance. His work will suffer and he will be accused of not being 'up to it'. When the problem has got out of hand and is discovered, he will be blamed for it.

## 4.8  SUMMARY AND EXTRACTS

Project management is frequently perceived as the performance of a number of technical functions. Planning, monitoring and reporting are usually mentioned, and such activities as system integration and testing are given particularly detailed coverage by those who emphasize the development of the product to the almost complete exclusion of the management of the project.

This chapter has briefly reviewed a number of the areas of project management which frequently cause project problems. Management of the project has been distinguished development of the product, for if the attention of a project manager is directed entirely to the technical aspects of product development, the project is likely to fail.

Management is the business of identifying options and taking decisions, of identifying problems and planning and coordinating the implementation of their solutions. A project manager needs to be a thinker and coordinator rather than a technical expert — though it is important that he understands the domain in which he is working.

There are always technical problems. But the problems which have the greatest impact on projects are typically management and social issues. Above all, a project manager can only achieve success through other people. He must therefore have an understanding of social interaction. He must be a leader — and leadership involves creating and maintaining harmony as well as getting work done.

The following extracts make some of the chapter's points.

- It is the project manager's responsibility not to allow internal compromises to affect the total quality as seen by the customer at the end of the project ... The project manager needs to understand the trade-offs being made and draw up plans to show why they are necessary, that they are temporary, and how the project criteria will be met in spite of them.

- Perhaps the most important aspect of project management is the creation of the project infrastructure.

- As managers of software development projects, we need to recognize that the engineering content of our work lies in the planning, the design, the control.

- Not only do project managers need to think, they also need to allow their staff time to think. If your staff are afraid to be caught thinking by you, something is wrong.

- The plan is a sign which points the way to the goal, but if the indicated path becomes blocked, it is time to revise the plan. Beware of thinking that following it implicitly is in fact the goal.

- While the reason for the existence of the project is the need to develop the product, the purpose of creating a project is to provide an infrastructure which facilitates the development of the product.

- The principles which apply to large projects also apply to small ones. Without good project management, a small project is just as likely to fail as a large one. It is simply a matter of scale.

- We [project managers] seem as susceptible as others to think that our own excuses are justifiable reasons for failure, and we accept feeble excuses from other project participants too readily. A lack of integrity is accepted as the norm.

- It is the project managers who fix things which have gone dreadfully wrong who are usually the best known. But if you want to make things easy for yourself as a project manager, be sensitive to the spirit of problems before they materialize.

- It is not in our culture to report problems. We find it easy to present glowing reports of trivial successes, but we sweep the problems under the carpet.

- If we are to generate a culture of problem reporting, we as managers must be prepared to support our staff and solve their problems.

# 5

# The Waterfall Model is Dead, Long Live the Waterfall Model

## 5.1 THE WATERFALL MODEL IS DEAD

It was mentioned in Chapter 1 that during the 1980s there was increasing recognition that successful software development depended on the conduct of a project rather than merely on correct or efficient programming. Gradually the focus of attention shifted away from programs and towards projects. The shift from programmers to project managers was slower, however, and although there was a great deal of talk about project management, many projects lacked any defined decision-making process. Where 'project managers' existed, they often suffered from a lack of experience, training, or the right attitude, and, frequently, all of these.

In spite of the new focus on 'project management', this term was still applied mainly to technical affairs. Indeed, the technical view of project management was supported by books and courses which described the details and techniques of activities such as design and testing while omitting such management essentials as human interaction, team building and coordination. Risk management was seldom mentioned at all. Thinking software developers and academics concerned with the techniques of software development began more and more to question the traditional development process — represented by the waterfall model.

Linking the problems of software development — or, in many cases, their symptoms — to the waterfall model led a number of commentators, in the absence of any consideration of management, to the conclusion that the model was at fault. They believed that they had at last (again) found the cause of the problems; again it would only be necessary to make that certain little adjustment for all to be well — rather like the anticipated panaceas of perfect programming in the 1960s and software engineering in the 1970s. In this case, that certain little adjustment was to abandon the waterfall model and apply a new model to software development. Actually, as we shall see in the next chapter, the proposed adjustment was glibly stated, not previously tested and, in fact, extremely *un*certain.

By the mid-1980s, published papers were proclaiming that the waterfall model was the cause of the failure of software development projects, that its time was up, and that it was dead.

## 5.2   A SCAPEGOAT, NOT THE CAUSE

So an attempt was being made to discredit (and kill) the waterfall model. There was a noble motive to this — the abolition of software development failures — and which of us would not be happy to think that we had seen the last long project with an unwanted system at its end? Yet, every week I read of foundering projects, each with its single delivery not yet in sight, likely to be delayed still further, and at hugely increased cost. So the reports of the death of the waterfall model were greatly exaggerated. The model is still alive and many projects which follow it are still failing.

On the other hand, the waterfall model was falsely accused and wrongly indicted of being the cause of all of the problems. The authors of the accusations were mistaken for three main reasons. First, because they had not considered the role of management in a project; second, because they had considered the waterfall model as an absolute 'method' of development rather than within its limitations as a model (see Chapter 2 for a discussion of models); and third, because they had never tested any other means of software development and, in at least some cases, had apparently never developed software at all. They attributed development problems *en masse* to the waterfall model; but a great number of development failures resulted, and still result, from the deficiencies reported in the previous two chapters, and we can see from their descriptions that they are independent of the development model in use.

It is quite proper for theorists without practical experience to propose development models or to criticize those in use. It is not only the experience of practitioners which identifies 'best practice' and gives rise to improvements in operational models and procedures; it is also the research and analysis of academics. It is desirable and necessary for researchers to make their ideas known, and it is then incumbent on practitioners to test their theories.

But testing academic theories is not without problems, one being that time lags are typically great: the time between the proposal and its trial, the time for feedback from the trial to reach the proposer, the time for the proposer to correct the theory and adjust the proposal in the light of the feedback, and so on. An additional problem is that by the time the feedback from a trial reaches its academic proposer, the academic has often already moved on to a new topic and does not use the feedback to improve the theory.

In the 1980s, the theorists had not adequately analysed either what they were decrying or what they were proposing. In the first place, their accusations against the waterfall model were wild, over-generalized, and in many respects unfair. In the second place, their proposals for the model's replacement (with various forms of 'incremental' or 'evolutionary' development or delivery) were based not on experimental evidence but only on ideas — and untested ideas at that. One of the theorists came to give us a presentation of his methodology, and when I questioned him afterwards, he offered to provide us with a consulting service. I questioned him further and discovered that it would not be he who would do the consulting, for he was too busy, but one of his postgraduate students. I queried the wisdom of bringing a student to guide my staff, some of whom were very experienced in their field, but he brushed my doubt aside and assured me that the student knew the methodology well. I asked about the student's background, and it turned out that he had entered the postgraduate course immediately after gaining a first degree. He may have known the methodology well, but he had no experience (nor knowledge, I suspect) of the context of its application: software engineering. Beware of 'consultants' who wish to sell you, or train you in, a 'methodology' regardless of your problem. Such people abound, and they are likely to leave you with an unusable tool or inapplicable knowledge, less liquidity than you started with, and your problem still to be considered. If you seek help, make sure that any who purport to help you concern themselves with your problem first and their tool second. If they show an inclination to twist your problem into the shape of their tool rather than the other way round, leave them alone.

To return to the waterfall model, it is not entirely blameless. Its rigid staged approach to development has two significant disadvantages. It implies that a correct specification can be produced and that it will not need to be changed throughout the project; and it leads necessarily to the delivery of the entire system in a single 'big bang'. The problems inherent in these two issues are explained below.

## 5.3    THE TROUBLE WITH 'BIG BANG'

The waterfall model is a model for the development of 'something' — not necessarily an entire system. It may be used for the development of a sub-system, or, in the case of evolutionary delivery, of a delivery (this will be described at length in Part 2). But the product, whatever it is, only emerges at the end of the process. Thus, when an entire system is being developed, the customer and users do not have the opportunity to test or use it until it is complete.

This is perfectly normal for a product which is being bought off the shelf. Then an individual customer, although perhaps not contributing to the specification of the product, at least has the chance to inspect it before purchase and to test it before use. But for a computer system, for which the users may not have clear requirements, it is a different matter. It is not until they receive it that they can discover that it is not what they want. And the longer the project, the greater is the discrepancy likely to be between the users' actual requirements at the time of delivery and what they get. It is rather like a tailor measuring a boy of ten and then taking two years to make him a suit. The boy will have grown, and however exact the measurements were when taken, it is certain that the suit will not meet the boy's requirements at the time of delivery. So it is with a system for an organization. In the first place, why should users know exactly what they want, especially when they have never had a computer system before? In the second place, they, their functions, their immediate management, their senior management, and their organization will all have undergone changes, some of them extensive, during the period of the project.

Thus, for large projects, there is in the waterfall model an inherent impediment to achieving an effective product. When there is a lack of participation of the customer and users in the project, the problem is exacerbated.


## 5.4    THE CERTAINTY OF CHANGE

Change forms the context within which we exist. Nothing stands still; not only do things change, but everything is changing all the time. The requirements which were complete and correct (if that is ever possible) at the time of approval are now neither complete nor correct. The idea that, 'If I can just put this right, all will be well', is an illusion. Our problem is not that things change, but that we do not accept that they must. If your intention has been to hold things stable, recognize that you cannot. Recognize too that implicit in the desire to halt change within a project is a human psychological factor which predisposes us to develop the wrong product

The reason for the challenge of software engineering is change. If all were stable, software engineering, like other jobs, would be a hum-drum activity: we would simply follow the waterfall model and, if we got the specification right, all would be well. But because of the inevitability of change, the process of developing a system is a perpetual challenge, one which calls for attention and initiative throughout.

Things done will be undone, control which we have achieved will be lost, and assumptions which were (or seemed) valid will in time become invalid. Things do not fall into place once and for all, and even when they do fall into place, it is not long before something seems to be askew, not necessarily because it has itself fallen out of place, but perhaps because its relevance or context has changed. This should leave us wanting to understand change, to understand the risks which are implicit in change, and to learn how to cope with, if not control, the risks. But too often we ignore the inescapability of change, neglect to consider its concomitant risks, and place our faith in the coming of stability.

Development projects involve a continuous struggle to keep up. Beware of believing that you can achieve the perfectly smooth path, that problems are the exception and a nuisance rather than a challenge, and that they can be eliminated once and for all. Enter the task knowing that there are and always will be problems, and that your job cannot be to achieve a problemless condition but to overcome the problems as they occur and to meet your targets of time, budget and customer satisfaction in spite of them.

This is not to suggest that problems cannot be avoided. They can be foreseen and measures taken to avoid or mitigate them, for example, by putting a suitable project infrastructure in place during the initiation stage of the project.

Given the inevitability of change, the implicit assumption of the waterfall model — that a correct specification can be prepared on which to base the entire project — is a predisposition to the development of a product which will not meet the needs of its users. In many waterfall model projects, change has not been allowed for and a number of things have gone wrong.

First, it has been assumed (often unthinkingly) that the specification is correct to start with. But why should it be correct? Why should preparing a specification, which we know to be one of the most difficult tasks, be the one thing which is done flawlessly?

Second, and this is a natural consequence of the first issue, no change control procedure is agreed between the customer and the developers, so when changes do occur, they are handled inefficiently and inconsistently. Then change is uncontrolled, it is expensive, and it often leads to added complexity and error.

Third, too frequently there is no customer or user presence during development. The results of this are, first that because the users are not involved in verifying the design, the errors in the specification which should be corrected at that stage are not detected; and second, that the changes in the customer's and users' organizations are not communicated fully, if at all, to the developers.

The longer the project, the greater the influence of these issues. Then, at the end of the project, even if the developers have done a good job and produced a system in conformity to its specification, the system will almost certainly not meet the users' requirements as they exist at the time of delivery. The developers may win the legal battle of having met the specification according to the contract, but they lose the war of retaining the customer's confidence and future business.

So it is in the project manager's interest not merely to meet the specification but to deliver a system which is useful to its purchaser. This means that he must discover the changes which need to be made to the requirements in order for them to keep up with the customer's changing needs. Doing so is not prescribed in the waterfall model, but it is one of the principal purposes and advantages of evolutionary delivery.


## 5.5   COMPARING LIKE WITH LIKE

Evolutionary delivery does not of itself solve all the ills of software development. Many of the issues discussed in Chapters 3 and 4 are independent of development models, and we need to resolve them ourselves by understanding them and coping with them in the management of our projects. The prerequisites to the success of a project may therefore be said to be:

- Top-down business planning as the basis of the project;
- Good requirements elicitation and specification;
- Sound project management;
- Sound development management;
- Realistic estimating;
- Customer and user involvement throughout the project;
- Managing change and its consequential risks throughout the project.

Given these fundamentals, there is a 'level playing field' on which to compare one development model with another. The disparagers of the waterfall model in the 1980s had ignored management, and this is the most crucial factor to project success.

In comparing evolutionary delivery with the waterfall model and big-bang delivery, we need to consider the two principal deficiencies of the latter, and we find that evolutionary delivery can overcome them (whether it does so in practice depends on how it is applied and managed). It does not assume a perfect specification to start with, and it does not deliver a single big-bang product.

However, evolutionary delivery does not obviate the need for good project management. As we shall see in the next chapter and in Part 2, it throws up new project management problems which have to be overcome if it is to be successful. Moreover, of the three project management goals (time, budget, and conformity to specification), its natural tendency is to facilitate the achievement of the third — at the expense of the other two! In iterating towards a final product, evolutionary delivery incorporates change into the development process, but in doing so it opens the door to the possibility of a perpetual project which exceeds its original time and budget. The subject of terminating criteria is discussed in Chapter 15.

Evolutionary delivery is not a universal panacea. I emphasize that it does not merely fail to cope with some of the traditional development problems; it gives rise to new problems of its own.

## 5.6   LONG LIVE THE WATERFALL MODEL

In spite of its two great disadvantages, many of the problems for which the waterfall model has been blamed are due to a lack of management of the software development process rather than to the development model in use. Project failures are our failures, and it is we who are responsible for them.

In spite of the assertions of its demise, the waterfall model lives on. As we saw in Chapter 2, it represents a natural order of events. It is still the basis of the majority of development projects (many of which still go wrong). Even when a process such as evolutionary delivery is employed, the waterfall model still plays a prominent part, for each delivery needs to be specified, designed, built, validated, and delivered — in that order. Indeed, each delivery is a project (call it a mini-project if you like) in its own right, one for which the waterfall model is used. Making a delivery on time depends, therefore, not on avoiding the waterfall model but on avoiding or dealing satisfactorily with the problems outlined in Chapters 3 and 4.

As we shall see in Part 2, evolutionary delivery incurs significant overheads, and the waterfall model (which includes the V model, as discussed in Chapter 2) is likely to produce a cheaper and quicker solution, given that:

- The project is relatively short (less than one year of elapsed time);
- There is a good specification to begin with;
- The scope of the project is well understood;
- There is a defined change control procedure;
- The project risks have been assessed and are considered to be low;
- The customer and users are involved in the project.

In gaining confidence in the specification it may be wise to use prototyping in the early stages of the project. But the waterfall model lives on, and will continue to do so, for it represents basic engineering practice.

## 5.7   SUMMARY AND EXTRACTS

This chapter has considered the suggestion that the waterfall model is obsolete. The model's deficiencies have been identified and the potential of evolutionary delivery to overcome them has been examined. At the same time, the basis of the waterfall model in sound engineering practice was noted, as well as its appropriateness to certain types of project. The inevitability and the challenge of change were also discussed. The following extracts make some of the points of the chapter.

* Beware of 'consultants' who wish to sell you, or train you in, a 'methodology' regardless of your problem. Such people are likely to leave you with an unusable tool or inapplicable knowledge, less liquidity than you started with, and your problem still to be considered.

* For large projects, there is in the waterfall model an inherent impediment to achieving an effective product. When there is a lack of participation of the customer and users in the project, the problem is exacerbated.

* Our problem is not that things change, but that we do not accept that they must. If your intention has been to hold things stable, recognize that you cannot.

* The reason for the challenge of software engineering is change ... because of the inevitability of change, the process of developing a system is a perpetual challenge, one which calls for attention and initiative throughout.

* The implicit assumption of the waterfall model — that a correct specification can be prepared on which to base the entire project — is a predisposition to the development of a product which will not meet the needs of its users.

* Why should preparing a specification, which we know to be one of the most difficult tasks, be the one thing which is done flawlessly?

* It [evolutionary delivery] does not assume a perfect specification to start with, and it does not deliver a single big-bang product.

* Of the three project management goals (time, budget, and conformity to specification), its [evolutionary delivery's] natural tendency is to facilitate the achievement of the third — at the expense of the other two!

# 6

# Enter
# Evolutionary Delivery
# — with its own Problems

## 6.1  WE GO FOR IT — OR GET PUSHED

Summarizing the discussion of earlier chapters, the situation was like this: continuing problems in software development led to condemnation of the waterfall model. 'The waterfall model is dead,' said its critics. I did not accept the finality of this assertion, nor did I believe that the accusations against the model were all fair, but I did not have to look far to see that software development was not under control, that the products of software development had a reputation for poor quality and did not satisfy the customers, and that things did not seem to be improving.

As seen in the previous chapter, an inherent aspect of the waterfall model is big-bang delivery, and this is a significant contributor to the problem of delivered systems not being what their users want. In the light of this and other software development problems, we were pondering when and how to try an evolutionary method when something happened which escalated the decision. We were called on to carry out two large development projects, with business objectives for both to be completed in two years. Feasibility studies, however, revealed that with the resources available it would not be possible to achieve this target — or anything like it. Indeed, the evidence suggested that about five years would be required. But the systems were strategic imperatives, and business targets were uninfluenced by our estimates. We started work on the detailed specifications.

Systems analysis confirmed the conclusions of the feasibility studies. Indeed, it revealed that when the two systems had been developed to the specifications then being documented they would need to be extended to provide further functions and to be integrated with other systems not yet planned.

There was no way in which the two systems could be provided within two years, even if our resources were greatly increased. Nevertheless, we completed the specifications, planned the development projects, and commenced the design. By then more than a year had passed, and we were left with a mere nine months in which to carry out two large projects. Impossible. We were caught in the perennial developers' trap described in Chapter 3 — being expected to meet unrealistic timescales and likely to be blamed for failing to do so.

Using the traditional (waterfall model) development process, we could not expect to meet the specifications even within three years — more than two years late. What could we do? The time had come for us to use an evolutionary approach. This, we thought, would allow us to install a part of each system in the nine months which remained of the initial two years, thus salvaging something of our honour. But it did not work out quite as neatly as that. We soon realized that before commencing development, we needed to replan the work. In the event, we managed to get the hardware and the first software increment into service two and a half years into the project — six months late, according to the objectives. Given the original omens, this was not a bad start. Indeed, astonishingly, we were seen by some to be successful when that first (and very limited) version of the system went live. But we could have planned it better, and there were many problems ahead. We had a lot to learn.

The academic papers advising us to depart from the waterfall model were theoretical. It is doubtful if any of their authors had had any practical experience of the methods which they advocated, and without that experience they could not alert us to the fact that there were problems inherent in evolutionary delivery (ED). ED does not simply fail to overcome the obstacles erected by big bang, or those discussed in Chapters 3 and 4; the fact is that it introduces new problems of its own.

When we came to apply ED to our projects, we were unaware that it would take us many experiences and a long learning period before we could claim to employ it effectively. Naturally, we discovered the problems, and reported on them [Redmill 89]. And naturally we lost time in having to solve them — and then re-solve them or refine the solutions. The result is this book, which is intended to alert developers who employ ED of the dangers ahead.

I should emphasize, however, that documenting its problems does not imply condemnation of ED. I am in favour of it; I recommend it — except in short projects. Its advantages are valid, but it needs to be well managed. If it is not, it can (and almost certainly will) become confused, uncontrolled, and very costly. Advantages seldom come without difficulties. Gain has its cost. So my writing is to promote an understanding of its difficulties.

The problems thrown up by ED are briefly introduced in this chapter and are the subject of Part 2 of the book. The main purpose is to draw them to the attention of developers and so avert the inefficiency of their having to discover them for themselves. Often, identifying and defining a problem is more difficult that devising a solution, so in many instances a resolution may become apparent to the reader simply as a result of being made aware of the problem. The solutions which I propose are based on those which we developed (or evolved) to meet our needs as the problems became apparent, and in some cases extended as a result of later experience. They are, in the main, generally applicable to ED. At the same time, a solution must fit its context, so developers may wish to refine those proposed here in order to make them appropriate to their own circumstances.

## 6.2   WHAT IS EVOLUTIONARY DELIVERY?

### 6.2.1  Evolution

Evolutionary delivery, as considered in this book, is the provision of the functionality of a system in a number of deliveries over a period of time. The system does not merely grow with each delivery, for each delivery is not simply a new increment to be added to the existing system but a new version of the system. A version may change from its predecessor in one or more of several respects. The first type of change to the existing system is the addition of functions as per the original specification. The second type is change to what has already been delivered as the result of use and assessment. The third type consists of new requirements which emerge as the result of the users now being better placed to consider what they want from the system and how the system could best aid them. In this sense, deliveries perform the same function as prototypes, with changes arising as the result of feedback from users and other members of the customer's organization. The fourth type of change consists of corrective maintenance.

With each delivery, the system evolves, not only in size but also towards its full functionality.

### 6.2.2 Delivery

Feedback is an engineering necessity. Indeed, it is a fundamental requirement in all aspects of life. For example, in driving a car we use feedback received by our visual and audio senses, as well as that received via our sense of touch, to determine the extent to which the vehicle is under our control.

The principal problem with big-bang delivery, particularly when it is compounded by the self-imposed difficulty of a lack of contact with the proposed system users, is that the effectiveness of the system is not tested by its users until the entire system has been built and delivered, so there is no feedback to the developers. The principal advantage of ED is that it allows feedback from users from an early stage of development. What promotes customer and user feedback and, therefore, leads (ideally) to a more effective system, is early *delivery* rather than the evolution of development. Indeed, all development is evolutionary!

It is thus delivery of the system while it is still being developed, and the changes to it which result from the users' feedback, which distinguishes ED from the big bang.

## 6.3   ADVANTAGES OF EVOLUTIONARY DELIVERY

It is possible to speculate on many advantages which ED might, in theory, offer. The following are those which experience verified.

## 6.3.1 Early Feedback

As discussed in earlier chapters, a correct (and thus complete) specification is almost impossible to achieve. Further, even if it were achieved, it would not be either correct or complete for long because of the many changes taking place in the personnel, management, objectives, and ways of working in the customer's and users' organizations. Thus, successful development does not depend on producing a system which meets a 'frozen' specification, but also on identifying and understanding the changes to those requirements as they arise (during the course of the project).

Making an early delivery of a functional and useful part of the system offers its users an opportunity to assess what has been delivered, to discover how it responds to their commands and how it presents information, and to reappraise their requirements on the system. Feedback to the developers as a result of experience of the system is a control mechanism to keep the product being developed in line with what the users require at the time of development rather than with what they thought they required at the time of preparing a specification.

This feedback, this demand for change, needs to be controlled. If it is not, the door is opened to a project of unlimited temporal and budgetary demands. But feedback to the developers as a result of experience of the system is the first and main advantage of ED.

## 6.3.2 An Early Working System

ED provides the customer and users with a working system much earlier than otherwise. As well as the users putting the system to the test and providing feedback to improve it, the customer and users can and should derive benefit from its use. Indeed, if useful feedback is to be derived from the users' experience of the system, they need to put it to use — so they need to find it useful.

At first, there is a limited number of functions. However, if planning is sensible, the usefulness of the system can be optimized by prioritizing the functions in order of their benefit to the customer or users and developing at each delivery those functions of highest priority. This is not always possible, as other practical issues affect the planning of deliveries (see Chapters 9 and 12), but it is a principle which should inform planning and which gives rise to a significant advantage of ED.

### 6.3.3 Customer Confidence

A perennial problem for software developers is that they find it almost impossible to attract the confidence of customers and users. First of all, during the project it seems to the customer and users that the system will never be completed. Then, when it is finally delivered, they find that it does not meet their current requirements.

During the project, the customer is (ideally) involved in the planning and therefore recognizes the steps along the way, but frequently the users are not aware of the project details and only see a long delay in meeting their needs. Then, even though the customer and users may be largely to blame for many of the delays, this does not much influence their attitude towards the developers. Indeed, a recognition of their own culpability often stiffens their defence of themselves; why didn't the developers, knowing how busy they were, or knowing their inexperience in these matters, do something to help them? To make a bad situation worse, when the system fails to meet the users' current requirements, the fact that it meets its specification does not impress them.

With ED, the first delivery does impress the users. They did not expect it so soon. They did not expect it to work. So they are pleased to have it. The interface is not as they would like it; there are too few functions; they can immediately see where changes are needed; but a system has been delivered, and if the developers display a willingness to improve what they find unsatisfactory, the users are indeed impressed. Their experiences of previous development projects were of long waits aggravated by implausible or unacceptable excuses, and then unsuitable systems and longer waits while the problems were rectified (if they ever were). These developers aren't so bad!

Achieving customer and user approbation by the developers is a significant bonus of ED.

### 6.3.4 Development Team Morale

We all seek achievement. When the developers make the first delivery, and each subsequent one, they achieve something and their morale is raised. To find that they are not despised or resented but, on the contrary, appreciated by the users — and even by the customer — is a further boost to their self esteem. They work harder and are more effective in their work. The psychological 'strokes' generated by their own achievement and the appreciation of the users lead to increased morale, effort and effectiveness.

## 6.4 A SUMMARY OF THE PROBLEMS CREATED BY EVOLUTIONARY DELIVERY

ED is not a solution in itself. It points the way to improved effectiveness of the product, but the efficiency with which we achieve this, or indeed whether we achieve it at all, depends on applying the best planning and management principles. Without them, ED is a recipe for an infinite project.

ED is not immune to the problems traditionally associated with software development (outlined in Chapters 3 and 4). Indeed, it was pointed out in the previous chapter that of the three project problems as seen from the customer's point of view (over-budget, over-time, and not what is required), the only one whose solution is inherent in ED is the third. If we are to address the other two issues, we must start by putting in place those mechanisms which we have learnt are necessary for avoiding hazardous development — such as good project management (including a sound project infrastructure), strategic planning, and communication between the developers and the customer and users.

If the problems of ED were simply those traditionally associated with software development projects, there would be no need for Part 2 of this book, for they have already been discussed in Chapters 3 and 4. But the fact is that ED throws up problems of its own. In the following brief introductions to them, a number of issues are grouped under common headings. There is considerable interrelationship between the various issues, and any one could be classified under a number of headings. Indeed, if examined from different viewpoints, different groupings, with such titles as 'Budget Management', 'Strategy', and 'Customer Involvement', could have been formed. In the end, however, they all come under the general heading of controlling, or managing, the process, which is to say: 'Project Management'.

### 6.4.1 Initial Planning

(a)    *Specification.* Because development is to be incremental and delivery evolutionary, customers and users are tempted to specify only the initial delivery at the beginning of the project, believing that other deliveries can be specified at their leisure. But without a good initial specification, system design would suffer and the ease with which it can be modified would be compromised. Further, lack of an adequate specification precludes accurate estimation of resource and time requirements — and estimating is crucial to the allocation of a budget, to project authorization, and to the control of the project. This subject is considered in detail in Chapter 9.

*(b)    Development System.* In a big-bang project, it is not unusual for the expense of a separate development system to be avoided, with the target hardware and system software being used for development. In an ED project, continued development after the first delivery depends on the availability of a development system, which needs to be planned and budgeted for at the initiation of the project. This can add substantially to the project cost.

## 6.4.2 Control of Change

*(a)    Procedures.* ED invites change. The purpose of ED is to receive early feedback and use it to refine the evolving product so that it meets business objectives and users' requirements earlier than would have been the case with big bang. Yet, change needs to be controlled. The tendency is for users, having experienced the system, to request numerous changes, many of them trivial. While it is important to optimize the system for user efficiency, implementing all requested changes can preclude the development intended to meet business objectives; it can also be non-cost-effective. A balance must be struck. Procedures for all stages of the process of submitting, vetting and authorizing requests for change need to be developed and adhered to (see Chapter 11 for a detailed procedure).

*(b)    Requests for Change. The* inclination of developers to implement changes at the verbal request of users must be curbed. Only documented and authorized changes should be implemented. ED is not the same as rapid application development. The latter is appropriate to short projects for the development of user-based rather than strategically-based systems; the former is appropriate to longer projects. Moreover, rapid application development does not involve the concurrent management of several versions of the system; evolutionary delivery does, and will become confused and inefficient unless its processes are methodical and carefully controlled.

*(c)    Strategic Concurrence.* A system whose specification initially meets business objectives and strategic plans can, as the result of numerous changes, eventually meet none of them and only satisfy the end users' requirements.

Given the volume of requests for change which may arise in an ED project, the chance of this happening is increased. Included in the change control procedures, there needs to be a process for vetting proposed changes against business strategy. This is explained in Chapter 11.

*(d)    Budget.* A major problem is project definition. Typically, a project is seen as the means of meeting a *specification*; and, given the big-bang tradition, this may allow for no more than a 10% deviation in budget from the authorized figure. Can such a constraint be made to cover the case of a changing specification? Should it? Budget control in an ED project is not trivial. Developers need separately to record the time and other resources devoted to the original specification, to changes, and to maintenance. See Chapter 15 for a discussion of these issues.

### 6.4.3 Planning Deliveries

*(a)    Frequency of Deliveries.* The development of a delivery is a project in itself, and it carries with it the overheads of a project. Planning and preparing a delivery is time-consuming (see Chapter 12). Too high a frequency of deliveries takes too much effort away from development. Further, the rate of delivery is restricted by the time it takes to test the system (see Section 6.4.5 below and Chapter 13).

*(b)    Prioritizing Functions.* An advantage of early delivery is getting crucial functions into service. If non-essential parts of the system are delivered to the exclusion of important functions, this advantage is lost. With changes being made to the specification and to earlier plans as a result of feedback, constant re-prioritization of work is necessary. This is non-trivial and is an added overhead in the planning of every delivery. It is the subject of Chapter 12.

*(c)    Customer Involvement in Planning.* If re-prioritization is to achieve its aim, the customer must be involved in planning deliveries. This is often not easy to achieve.

*(d)    Changing Plans.* Typically a delivery consists of a mixture of work defined in the original specification and new work resulting from feedback. As mentioned above, plans are therefore always subject to change. Procedures

need to be in place for replanning during the development of every delivery (see Chapter 12).

### 6.4.4 Configuration Management

Control of ED depends in great measure on a good configuration management system. In a waterfall model project, in which only one version of the system is being developed, configuration management is crucial. In ED, it is even more important: once the first delivery has been made, a number of versions of the system are in existence, with at least two and probably three being under development at any time.

It may be expected that at least four versions of the target system software are at various stages of operation and development. In a large project, when development has been proceeding for some time, there are also likely to be a number of historic versions to be accounted for. To make the configuration management system effective, not only must rules and procedures for its operation be created, but as these on their own cannot provide a total solution, a management system for controlling it must also be put in place. Smooth operation always depends to some extent on individuals. Leadership to inspire motivation is important.

A configuration management system appropriate to ED is the subject of Chapter 10.

### 6.4.5 Testing

(a)     *Revalidation.* Ideally, revalidation of the system prior to a new delivery should be carried out under operational conditions. However, once the users have an operational system, they do not want it taken out of service for perhaps lengthy testing. Carrying out revalidation on the development system is convenient to users, but it may compromise confidence in the tests. The continued availability of the operational system for revalidation versus confidence in the test results is a trade-off which needs to be considered in contracting with the customer and planning with the users. Validation and other aspects of testing in an ED project are the subject of Chapter 13.

(b)     *What is Validated?* As the operational system grows, so revalidation time increases. Thorough revalidation requires that the total system is tested, including those functions already in operation. For a non-critical system, a compromise may be made by only carrying out selective tests — perhaps only on new functions and those which have been changed. For a critical system, full revalidation may be necessary, and for a large system this can require considerable time. Compromises may need to be made, and these must be agreed with the customer.

*(c)      Frequency of Deliveries.* The interval between deliveries cannot be shorter than the time to revalidate the system. The suggestion that we can make 'a delivery per week' is therefore glib and impractical if sound engineering practice is to be followed.

*(d)      Acceptance Testing.* There is a temptation for users to perceive only the first delivery (which may be no more than 10% of the final system) as the system to be accepted, and they may regard subsequent deliveries merely as changes to an existing system. Customers and users need to develop a new culture to deal with ED (see Chapter 15 for a discussion of this), with each delivery being recognized as a system to undergo acceptance testing. All approved requests for change should include measurable attributes and acceptance test criteria.

### 6.4.6 Maintenance

If the traditional definition of software maintenance (all work carried out after delivery of the system) is applied to ED, all development after the first delivery would be maintenance. Given that only a small proportion of the software is installed in the first delivery, this would lead to the majority of development being classified as maintenance. In ED, only corrective work should be considered as maintenance, and records should be kept of new development, redevelopment (change to what has already been done), and maintenance (corrections due to a failure of the system to meet its specification) so that the effort invested in each can be accounted for. Maintenance is the subject of Chapter 14.

### 6.4.7 Philosophy and Culture

*(a)      Management Attitude.* While the developers quickly evolve their techniques and thinking to cope effectively with ED, the rest of the business,

particularly senior management, are likely to continue to think in terms of big-bang projects. They are likely to judge progress not in terms of the effectiveness of the functions already delivered and the gains achieved by early delivery, but in terms of the originally estimated budget and completion date. A new culture is required for ED (see Chapter 15), and it may need to be the development manager or the project manager who sets out to engender it. However, while it is evolving (if it evolves), records of the work done as a result of feedback, change and re-prioritization need to be kept — otherwise, when success is judged against traditional criteria, the developers will be seen in a poor light.

(b)    *Budget.* If senior management are accustomed to think in terms of waterfall model projects, they are likely to demand that the project budget should remain within 10% of its original estimate. It takes a new management attitude to allow a fluid budget for a project. At the same time, however, even the advantages of early change do not justify unlimited expenditure. Whereas management need to adjust their thinking to get the best from ED, the developers need to plan their projects with an eye on the cost of change. Their proposed budget should include change, and they should be prepared to be held to it.

## 6.5    SUMMARY AND EXTRACTS

Evolutionary delivery increases project and process complexity over that of big bang. To get the best from ED, to operate it efficiently, to achieve effectiveness, and to avoid being swamped by change, project management of a high order is required and a number of new problems need to be understood and overcome. The effectiveness of the product depends on a strategic plan to start with, strategic involvement throughout, and a great deal of tactical planning and replanning during the project. New criteria for terminating the project and for judging its success are needed.

The recognition and understanding of many of the issues introduced in this chapter lead fairly readily to ideas for solutions. For others, a great deal of thought and pragmatism are called for. In all cases, an understanding of technical and theoretical solutions is not enough: setting up procedures, managing them effectively, and evolving and improving them are essential components of success, as are setting the right goals, understanding the processes, ensuring the necessary training, and maintaining the resolve to manage considerable change. The issues described above, and the ways in which they may be tackled, form the basis of the subsequent chapters in this book, and pointers to the appropriate chapters are included in the above text

The following extracts make some of the points of the chapter.

- When we came to apply ED to our projects, we were unaware that it would take us many experiences and a long learning period before we could claim to employ it effectively ... we discovered the problems, and we lost time in having to solve them — and then re-solve them or refine the solutions.

- It is delivery of the system while it is still being developed, and the changes to it which result from the users' feedback, which distinguishes ED from the big bang.

- The usefulness of the system can be optimized by prioritizing the functions and developing at each delivery those of highest priority.

- During the project, the customer is (ideally) involved in the planning, but frequently the users are not aware of the project details and only see a long delay in meeting their needs.

- When the developers make the first delivery, and each subsequent one ... the psychological 'strokes' generated by their own achievement and the appreciation of the users lead to increased morale, effort and effectiveness.

- ED is not a solution in itself. It points the way to improved effectiveness of the product, but the efficiency with which we achieve this, or indeed whether we achieve it at all, depends on applying the best planning and management principles.

- Without a good initial specification, system design would suffer and the ease with which it can be modified would be compromised. Further, lack of an adequate specification precludes accurate estimation of resource and time requirements.

- In an ED project, continued development after the first delivery depends on the availability of a development system.

- A system whose specification initially meets business objectives and strategic plans can, as the result of numerous changes, eventually meet none of them and only satisfy the end users' requirements.

- Too high a frequency of deliveries takes too much effort away from development. Further, the rate of delivery is restricted by the time it takes to test the system.

- Once the first delivery has been made, a number of versions of the system are in existence, with at least two and probably three being under development at any time.

- To make the configuration management system effective, not only must rules and procedures for its operation be created, but as these on their own cannot provide a total solution, a management system for controlling it must also be put in place.

- Customers and users need to develop a new culture to deal with ED

- If the traditional definition of software maintenance (all work carried out after delivery of the system) is applied to ED, all development after the first delivery would be maintenance ... In ED, only corrective work should be considered as maintenance.

- Whereas management need to adjust their thinking to get the best from ED, the developers need to plan their projects with an eye on the cost of change.

# Two

## The path through evolutionary delivery

# 7

# The Importance of Strategy

## 7.1  THE ISSUES

In many companies, perhaps in most, information system planning does not
descend from a business strategy. Indeed, in many companies, there is no
obvious business strategy at all.

Frequently, systematic planning of information systems does not occur at
all, the need for a system being first stated not in a strategic assessment of the
company's needs, but by the users or potential users of the proposed system.
From this 'bottom-up management', the scope of the system to be developed
is not defined by a plan which places constraints on it, but only by a
specification of requirements, which may expand and otherwise change at the
whim of intended users of the proposed system. The fact is that clear strategic
plans are seldom drawn up at the most senior levels of a business, and even

when they are, they are not used as the basis of lower-level planning and determining the organization's information system needs.

As a project manager, I was forced to recognize the importance of strategic planning when I found myself unable to control change to a specification of requirements, even when development was already far advanced. New users kept turning up with new requirements. If there had been a strategic plan, it would have defined the boundary, or scope, of the system, and this would have provided a basis for determining whether the new users' needs should be met by this system, by some other, or perhaps not at all. In the first place it would have assisted in identifying the future users of the system, and in the second place it would have provided me with the basis of declining to accept requirements which were inappropriate to the system. In the event, the only available definition of the system's scope was that which I was able to derive from the specification of the users' requirements, and as these changed so did the system's boundary.

In summary, the system's boundary could not be used as a means of identifying the users or controlling their requirements because it was defined only by the users themselves, and it changed as they redefined themselves. We had a recipe for an indefinite project. It was inevitable that the time and budget planned for the project would be exceeded, that the developers would become dispirited by persistent and uncontrolled change, and that the system would almost certainly not meet the business' strategic needs, whatever they might be.

Although a project manager's terms of reference do not normally include strategic planning, it is crucial that he understands its importance to the success of a project. With such understanding he will certainly enquire, at the very beginning of the project, into the source of the proposal for the system. If the source is shown to be a top-down strategic plan, the project manager may reasonably expect to be able to define the project boundary with some clarity. There is no guarantee that this will not change, but at least it gives the project a clear definition, and this is a good — indeed a necessary — starting point. It is also a point of reference against which to evaluate proposed changes and to judge the claims of self-defined new users.

If, on the other hand, it turns out that the proposal for the system arose only out of users' requirements, and that it is not defined or supported by a strategic plan, the astute project manager will certainly sense danger. He will know that the scope of the project can at best be ill-defined, that there is a greater likelihood of change to the requirements, that he will have no basis for challenging the proposed changes, and that he will experience greater difficulty in controlling them. He may not have the option of declining to manage the project, but he should certainly inform the customer and his own senior management of his reservations and anticipated difficulties, and he should make allowance for them in his time and budget estimates for the project. He should also assess the risks which the uncertainty throws up, document them, discuss them with the customer, and take steps to mitigate them (see [Redmill 97]).

In ED, a prime intention is to invite change to the system so far developed so as persistently to tailor it to meet the customer's and users' real needs. But changes should not be implemented unless they fall within the defined scope of the project and have been vetted and approved by the customer. Not to apply these criteria is to run a serious risk of losing control of the project. Strategic planning and the resulting definition of the project boundary and scope are of increased importance in ED projects.

There are two purposes to this chapter. The first is to advise project managers, senior managers, customers, and all who are involved in management and in projects, on how and why a strategic basis is important to a project. The second purpose is to offer a brief overview of the steps in the strategic planning of information systems.

## 7.2 STRATEGIC PLANNING

Strategy suggests a certain clarity of intention, a definition and understanding of the goal to be aimed at, and a statement of the direction to be taken in attempting to attain it. A business strategy provides a definition of the organization's goals, such as its products and its markets. Strategic planning, derived from the business strategy, should then define the achievements to be striven for by the departments of the organization and their managers, and indicate the directions to be followed and, importantly, the constraints on what is to be done and how it is to be done.

Like every plan, strategy must be dynamic. It should not be (and is sure to be counter-productive if it is defined as) a rigid blueprint for the indefinite future. It should be reviewed periodically and when a change in the organization's direction is indicated, such as when a competitor is about to introduce a new product. But while it is in force, the constraints imposed by a strategy should be observed, though they should not be seen as definitively blocking all changes of direction. If a manager is taking, or wishes to take, a course outside the strategy, either that course should be abandoned or the strategy should be reviewed. To take such a course in the face of the organization's strategy is economic waste (given that the strategy has been properly devised).

Determining the details of the course to be taken requires further planning, for a strategy is typically brief, defining goals but not every step of the way. Strategic planning requires input from the organization's strategy department (if one exists) and from its senior and middle managers. The senior strategists should have a clear perception of both the strategy and its interpretation in the context of each department, and the organization's managers should understand the details of the strategic goals, the technologies, methods and tools necessary for achieving them, and the options available and the decisions to be taken along the way.

Too often, however, there is no concept of strategic planning within an organization. To be fair, the need for it is frequently not apparent because the strategy itself, the basis of further planning, is absent — either not documented or even carefully thought through (which is usually the case) or merely a vague and hastily drawn up statement not communicated to the managers or planners in the organization. But whatever the reason for its lack, without strategic planning there are significant disadvantages, such as:

- Aiming at goals which are not strategically useful, which leads to inappropriate and wasteful effort;
- Failure to aim at some strategically advantageous goals, which leads to lost opportunities;
- Inconsistency in approach across the organization, which leads to waste and confusion;
- Uneconomic methods;
- Lack of coordination of suppliers and the making of uneconomic purchases;
- Bottom-up management.

Strategic planning achieves (or should achieve) two ends in particular. It should add clarity and visibility to the strategic goals, and it should provide an outline plan for achieving them. In carrying it out, three questions need to be answered.

- Where do we want to get to? This is often the easiest question to answer, for it can take no more than a 'vision' to resolve the issue. Yet, in its fullest form, the answer must depend on such issues as what competitors are doing, what technologies are available, and what market niche we should aim at. The answer to this question is the strategic goal.

- Where are we now? This is usually the most difficult question to answer, for answering it requires measurement, and most managers guess their position rather than measure it. For example, if we define a strategic goal as being to increase our market share of a given product, knowing that we achieve it depends on knowing our current market share.

- How do we get there? Although some answers may readily suggest themselves, the route to the strategic goal needs careful planning. Some routes are more expensive or more difficult than others, some offer tactical advantages on the way, and some do not. Some offer longer-term advantage and some may offer short-term gain. The longer-term benefits may depend on employing technology which we are not yet ready for, and we may be better off taking a different route in the short term and gradually developing the skills and confidence necessary for later strategic positioning. Computer systems are usually support mechanisms on a strategic path rather than strategic goals (i.e., the means of providing a service and not the service itself). In planning the route one needs to recognise that it must start from where we are now.

As strategic planning is carried out, it begins to become clear what computing needs the organization will have over a defined period of time. The next step is then to convert the statement of computing needs into a plan for specific computer systems.

## 7.3 INFORMATION SYSTEMS PLANNING

If each system is defined independently of all others, an organization is almost certain to end up with: a miscellany of systems which do not communicate with each other, the inefficient use of data, uncoordinated maintenance, and significant over-staffing. It is not uncommon for such deficiencies to become apparent during a development project, giving rise to changes in requirements and the resulting increased costs to the customer and difficulties for the project manager and development team. It is therefore important to a project manager not only that the need for a system has been derived from strategic thinking, but also that the requirements on the system have been founded on coordinated information systems planning.

Coordinated systems planning implies assessing an organization's total data and information requirements and integrating them into a 'grand plan'. The alternative is for small sections of the organization to identify the requirements on specific systems, but this leads to the lack of coordination of systems referred to above. Data and information planning should precede system planning.

Within the scope of an organization's overall needs, a systems plan, or architecture, may be produced, not for a single information system but (ideally) for all the systems needed, or thought to be needed, by the business in meeting its strategic goals. The interconnections between systems should also be included. The scope of each system is thus implicitly defined and can be explicitly described. The users and potential users of each system are also identified, or at lease are identifiable, and this, as has been shown, is of considerable importance to a project manager in controlling a project. This is top-down planning which supports both the management of the business and the cost-effective implementation of tools (such as computer systems) to support the business.

From the systems plan, too, the strategic constraints on any given system, which may be vital during its development, can be identified. For example, if a new product is estimated only to be viable if it can be brought onto the market within two years (say, because it needs to precede its competition), the implication on a computer system intended to be a part of that product could be that it needs to be developed within (say) one year. Then time, rather than budget, may be the crucial factor in the development of the system. Business objectives for the system and the development project can be set accordingly, with the project manager taking them into consideration in planning and managing the project. Indeed, in an ED project, the strategic objectives will define the priorities of business functions and thus contribute to maximizing the effectiveness of each successive delivery.

Once the users (or intended users) of a proposed system are known, the requirements capture for the preparation of its specification of requirements can be planned. This is not to say that the initially identified users will be the only users, or even that they will have all been correctly identified, but at least the starting point for the systems analysis will have been determined. Systems analysis depends on following clues, and if competent analysts are clear about where to begin, what the scope of the system is, and what constraints apply, the chance of identifying all relevant viewpoints on the system and thus developing a good specification of requirements is enhanced.

It is often the case that a number of the functions identified in the systems plan are already being carried out. The ideal plan, showing all required systems, thus needs to be assessed against the systems already in existence. From this comparison, the following may be deduced:

- Existing systems possessing functions which fulfil a current need;
- Existing systems possessing functions which are obsolete and do not meet a current need;
- Existing systems which are in their entirety redundant or obsolete and should be abolished;
- Existing systems which could be adapted to meet current or anticipated needs;
- Proposed systems which need to be developed;
- Connections between systems which need to be put in place.

Given these deductions, projects may be proposed for the development of new systems and the modification or phasing out of old ones. Strategic necessities may impose time constraints on the projects, which would allow an initial prioritization to be carried out and timescales to be set.

Thus we arrive at an information systems development plan (or strategy) which shows how the business' information system requirements should be met and over what period. This aids not only the business as a whole, but also staff and skills planning for the development of the systems.

When the technical aspects of the information systems strategy (such as hardware and software standards and purchasing policy) are applied to the systems to be developed, an integrated plan of the business' information systems may be generated. This should ensure optimized data storage and updating, standardized communication between systems, and cost-effective maintenance. It also should ensure that the boundaries of systems are clearly defined, and this is important for the project managers of the various system development projects.

## 7.4    NOTES ON STRATEGY AND PLANNING

Planning in an organization should be a continuous, seamless process. It should be continuous through time, for every plan needs to be reviewed periodically and adjusted in response to changing circumstances. It should be seamless from the definition of strategy, through strategic planning, right down to the detailed planning of projects and day-to-day tasks, with higher-level plans defining the criteria to be met by, and the constraints on, the lower-level plans. Thus, the line between strategic planning in a business sense and information systems planning is a blurred one. What is important is that the planning continuum exists. At the same time, it is also important to define certain points at which the nature of planning (or at least the basis of the planning process) changes. At some point, planning which is strategically relevant to an organization as a whole gives way to the more detailed planning of the tactics to meet the strategically defined goals.

Much has been made of 'information systems strategy', and the impression is often given, or received, that it is an end in itself. This has led enthusiastic systems managers to define 'strategies' which call for the latest technologies and tools because they are in vogue, or because of exaggerated advertisements. But the latest technologies and tools, even if they are indeed true to their advertisements, may not be cost-effective or practical in a given organization, perhaps because no one is trained to use them, or perhaps because they are incompatible with the existing technologies and tools within the business.

It is important to recognize that an information systems strategy is not an end in itself. It has no real existence other than in support of the business, and should be derived with reference to the business' strategic goals. While it should include such things as standards for hardware, software, tools and the interconnections between systems, these should be practical and attainable in the context of the business.

## 7.5    SENSITIVITY TO CHANGE

When a system is planned bottom-up, that is, only from users' requirements, it is highly sensitive to changes made to the strategic direction of the business. When a system is based on a strategic plan, it is less sensitive to business changes. To understand these statements, consider the three-tier (simplified) model of a business shown in Figure 7.1. The bottom layer represents the 'workers', who usually include the users of the system. Typically, the users are those who prepare the input data, use the output data, and operate and maintain the system. The middle layer represents the users' managers, and the top layer represents senior management.

The workers on the bottom tier are most numerous, and among them there are frequent staff changes. Individuals make career moves, are promoted, and leave the company. In addition, there is the arrival of new recruits and staff transferred from other parts of the organization. With each arrival and departure there is a small change in working practice, and these take effect as changes to the requirements on a system. However, the influence of staff at this level is small, so the changes, though many, are typically not far-reaching.

The managers on the middle tier are the users' managers. They define working practices, the distribution of work, and the relationships between individuals and teams. As managers leave and are replaced, and as they initiate changes in work allocation and in procedures, they affect not merely the end-users' requirements on a system, but the functions of the system. Their changes are more far-reaching than those of the users.

Senior managers on the top layer are responsible for the direction of the business. They determine when new products are to be introduced and old ones phased out, they define the budget and the staffing levels for the business as a whole and for each department. Such decisions are fundamental to the definition of functions and the staff structures at the lower levels. Even small

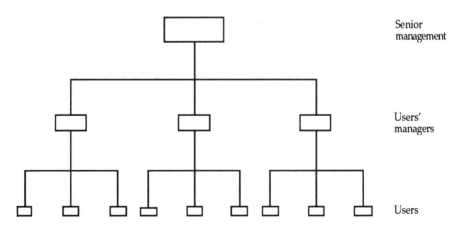

**Figure 7.1** A simple three-tier model of a business hierarchy

changes at the top can have significant effects at the lower levels. It is the top-level decisions which determine the need for systems in the business and the uses to which the systems should be put.

Thus, changes on the bottom tier are at the data level, those on the middle tier are at the function level, and those on the top tier are at the system level. Systems planned at the top tier are more likely to match the needs of the business and support the direction of the business, are better understood by the strategists and so are more readily adapted to meet changing business needs, and can tolerate changes at the two lower tiers. Systems planned at the middle tier can tolerate changes at the lowest level, but are more likely to become obsolete in the face of changes at the top level and are less easily adapted to meet them. Systems planned only at the bottom tier are less likely to match the real business needs in the first place, will be most sensitive to top-tier changes in business direction, and least easily adapted to meet changing strategic demands. Numerous systems built only to meet users' needs have been abandoned because of the difficulty (and sometimes the impossibility) of changing them in response to adjustments in business direction. A great deal of money has been squandered in this way. The importance of strategic planning prior to the definition of projects cannot be too strongly emphasized.

When it comes to ED projects, establishing basic criteria for the system, against which all proposed changes can and must be assessed, is crucial. One of the principles of ED is that it offers users and customers an early opportunity to assess the system. One of its great advantages is that changes proposed by users can be implemented early so that the system, as it is developed, meets their real requirements. But change can easily get out of hand and therefore needs to be controlled. If there are no stated business objectives for the system, and if the system's scope is not defined, there are no criteria against which to assess and control change. Strategic planning is particularly important as a basis for ED projects.

## 7.6   STRATEGIC CONCURRENCE

A sound planning process should result in the identification of the data flows to, through and from the system, and the identification of the intended system's users — which should lead to the capture and analysis of the users' requirements.

Ideally the requirements should be within the defined system scope, but numerous influences result in this seldom being the case. Among them are the facts that in practice the users are unlikely to be familiar with the business planning process, the objectives for the system or the constraints on it, or the changes which will be made to working practices and skill requirements as a result of the introduction of the system. Typically, the systems analysts interviewing the users simply enquire what their requirements are. Naturally, the users take an idealistic view and define requirements which would seem to suit their present needs rather than trying to visualize those which would suit the business as a whole or which would be appropriate to a system in a reorganized way of working.

Therefore, if there is to be any confidence that the system conforms to its strategic objectives, the requirements need to be validated against the strategic plan for the system. This needs to be done by a senior manager involved in the organization's strategic planning and conversant with its information systems strategy. The process of authorizing the requirements by strategic validation may be referred to as giving 'strategic concurrence'.

Initial strategic concurrence is not sufficient, however, to ensure the effectiveness of a system. It has already been observed that almost certainly there will be numerous changes to the requirements during the development of any system. In theory, at least, an abundance of changes outside the defined scope of the system can lead a strategically approved specification to end up as a strategically ineffective system. It is therefore imperative for a business strategist to remain responsible throughout the project for the concurrence (or rejection) of proposed changes to the requirements. It should not be expected that the strategic representative is involved in all the detail of analysing the users' requirements, but only in validating those which have been approved by the customer for development (see Chapters 8 and 11 for more information on the strategic representative's role).

The permanent involvement in the project of a business strategist, and the existence of procedures for the strategic concurrence of both the original specification and any intended changes, offer comfort to the project manager. But the project needs to be based on a strategic plan to start with; strategic concurrence to changes is hardly worthwhile otherwise.

Even strategic plans can change. Businesses react to changes in customers' needs, in competition, and in national and international conditions; they enter new lines of business, initiate new products and discontinue old ones. These adjustments change the business' goals, whether or not they are formally reflected in documented strategy statements. But they should be. Numerous systems have been developed unnecessarily, often at considerable expense, because senior management were not sufficiently aware of the relationships between the projects and the organization's strategy to cancel them when the systems under development were no longer needed. The strategic representative on the project should therefore vet not only the proposed changes to the users' requirements for concurrence with the business strategy but also the project as a whole for concurrence with any changes to the business strategy. He should keep the project board (see Chapter 8) informed of changes to the strategy and, in consultation with the other board members, deduce their effects on the project and the requirements specification.

When strategic changes which affect the project take place, the following questions, among others, should be raised:

- Does the business still need this system?
- Does the business require all the functions of the system?
- Should the levels of system attributes (such as security, reliability and availability) remain the same?

A 'no' answer to any of these questions should result in a review of the project plans and of the work already carried out on the project. A project with changed goals is a new project which requires new plans and a new definition of its purpose, its constraints and its product. If these are significantly different from before, development should be halted and systems analysis resumed. Although the inclination of senior managers is often to carry on the project according to the current schedule — because, they argue, changing now would make the system late — such a decision leads to the development of the wrong system, with a great deal of waste. What is the value of a system on time if it is the wrong system? Often the most effective option is to cancel the project, and this takes courage — but it is the business of senior managers to determine the best option and have the courage to take it. Yet it is senior management who in the past have led to many of the delays in projects and the ineffectiveness of developed systems, mainly because they have not discharged their duty to think, plan and, importantly, act strategically.

As we shall see in Chapters 11, 12 and 15, the effective control of change in ED is strongly dependent on strategic planning — and, indeed, on understanding and using the strategic plans. The role of a strategic representative to the project is crucial.

## 7.7 SUMMARY AND EXTRACTS

In many, if not most, organizations, strategic planning is nonexistent, inadequately carried out, or not communicated. Yet, business objectives for systems to be developed should be derived from strategic planning.

This chapter offers brief guidance on the strategic planning process and on how it should be used to inform the planning of information systems and development projects. It describes the role of senior management in strategic planning and the importance of strategy to project managers.

The following extracts make some of the points of the chapter.

- In the first place it [a strategic plan] would have assisted in identifying the future users of the system, and in the second place it would have provided me with the basis of declining to accept requirements which were inappropriate to the system.

- Although a project manager's terms of reference do not normally include strategic planning, it is crucial that he understands its importance to the success of a project ... If it turns out that the proposal for the system arose only out of users' requirements, and that it is not defined or supported by a strategic plan, the astute project manager will certainly sense danger.

- Strategy suggests a certain clarity of intention, a definition and understanding of the goal to be aimed at, and a statement of the direction to be taken in attempting to attain it.

- Like every plan, strategy must be dynamic. It should not be (and is sure to be counter-productive if it is defined as) a rigid blueprint for the indefinite future.

- Strategic planning ... should add clarity and visibility to the strategic goals, and it should provide an outline plan for achieving them.

- Coordinated systems planning implies assessing an organization's total data and information requirements and integrating them into a 'grand plan'.

- Within the scope of an organization's overall needs, a systems plan, or architecture, may be produced, not for a single information system but (ideally) for all the systems needed, or thought to be needed, by the business in meeting its strategic goals.

- If competent analysts are clear about where to begin, what the scope of the system is, and what constraints apply, the chance of identifying all relevant viewpoints on the system and thus developing a good specification of requirements is enhanced.

- Planning should be a continuous, seamless process.

- An information systems strategy is not an end in itself. It has no real existence other than in support of the business, and should be derived with reference to the business' strategic goals.

- If there are no stated business objectives for the system, and if the system's scope is not defined, there are no criteria against which to assess and control change.

- The users are unlikely to be familiar with the business planning process, the objectives for the system or the constraints on it, or the changes which will be made to working practices and skill requirements as a result of the introduction of the system.

- The requirements need to be validated against the strategic plan for the system.

- In theory, at least, an abundance of changes outside the defined scope of the system can lead a strategically approved specification to end up as a strategically ineffective system.

- Numerous systems have been developed unnecessarily, often at considerable expense, because senior management were not sufficiently aware of the relationships between the projects and the organization's strategy to cancel them when the systems under development were no longer needed.

- A project with changed goals is a new project which requires new plans and a new definition of its purpose, its constraints and its product.

# 8

# Project Infrastructure

## 8.1  THE ISSUES

The heart of a project is the development of the product — the system. Yet, if consideration is only given to technical development, without planning, coordinating and monitoring the effort invested, the project is almost certain to run into difficulty. When a number of people work together, there is a need for communication between them and coordination of their efforts.

The project manager's purpose is to control the project and thus ensure that it is completed on time, within budget, and to the customer's satisfaction. At the best of times, control of a software development project is difficult. Without having appropriate teams, communication channels, reporting procedures, and other infrastructure components in place, it can be almost impossible. The communication and coordination are sometimes thought of as overheads on the basic development process, but they are essential to the success of the project. They must be efficient in their functioning and effective in achieving their purpose.

In spite of their importance, they do not occur naturally. Typically, the project participants can be likened to the musicians in an orchestra: they may be conscientious in discharging their own responsibilities, but not necessarily concerned with what it takes to blend the individual performances into an harmonious symphony. The project manager, on the other hand, may be likened to the conductor who must take a 'system view', appreciating the detail of each component but at the same time not losing the vision of the complete work. He must understand how each component needs to be integrated into the whole, what it takes to bring about the integration, and how he is going to achieve it.

In order to facilitate communication and to coordinate the efforts of the various participants during the project, the means of doing so must be planned and put in place before development commences. A 'project infrastructure' must be created. The three most important aspects of creating it are:

- Identifying the project participants and ensuring that they understand and accept their roles;
- Creating a communications infrastructure (including committees, meetings, and reporting mechanisms) for ensuring that the participants provide and receive the necessary information and that appropriate actions are taken when necessary;
- Defining and putting in place a document infrastructure.

In addition to these three 'management' infrastructure components, there also needs to be a 'technical' infrastructure in place. This is introduced in Section 8.7 below and its components are discussed in detail in subsequent chapters.

It is important to have an 'initiation' stage of a project, with its principle purpose defined as being the creation of the project infrastructure. Yet all too frequently there is no initiation stage. Why? Because the project manager does not appreciate the importance of the project infrastructure. And why not? Because even today those things which are seen as important in a project are the technical activities—the 'doing' activities, such as designing, programming, and sometimes even testing. Preparing for 'doing', attempting to make sure that when the 'doing' is carried out it is effective and efficient, is often neglected, and when considered, is perceived as something to be got out of the way quickly so that the doing can begin. In many ways, things have not changed a great deal in projects since the early days.

If senior management want successful projects, they must install the right people as project managers, train them appropriately, counsel them in what is required, and monitor their progress and achievement. In other words, senior management need to understand project management and what it takes to make a project successful, and to subject their project managers to the same scrutiny to which they subject other managers.

If a project infrastructure has not been created, it is inevitable that problems will occur later in the project. When they do, the connection between them and the lack of an infrastructure is seldom made. They are not seen to have been avoidable, or even foreseeable, because the project manager did not recognize the need for an infrastructure in the first place. It is likely that the time taken to resolve the problems is excessive, for the means of coping with them is not defined, and frequently the people necessary to solving them are not available when needed. Then the problems recur because, without the means of their resolution, time is short, and the root causes are not traced and removed. Almost certainly, the time spent on them will not have been allowed for in the project plans, so they cause the project to go late and over budget. Then, because the problems are to do with human issues — failures in communication and a lack of coordination of effort — they are perceived as unfortunate incidents which can occur at any time without warning. Their persistence is attributed to a run of bad luck, to the lack of cooperation of this or that project participant, or to 'uncontrollable forces'. The project manager does not recognize that he could (and should) have created a run of good luck, and facilitated cooperation, by putting a sound infrastructure in place at the commencement of the project — and thereafter devoting a proportion of his own time to maintaining it. People are capricious and individualistic and often uncommunicative and uncooperative, but they can be the opposites of these if the project manager creates a supportive environment for them to work in.

Project managers would usually accept the notion that the success of a project depends on their planning. But frequently planning is perceived only as scheduling the technical activities involved in development. Only occasionally is there an awareness of the need to plan the 'people' aspects of the project, or does the project manager possess experience and competence in doing so. But if a project infrastructure is put in place early, and the project manager invests time and effort in maintaining it and inculcating its principles and procedures into the culture of the project, the probability of smooth running is greatly enhanced, and the project manager stands to reap the rewards — in the lack of major problems, in the relative ease of resolving problems when they do occur, and in the resulting success of the project.

## 8.2  PROJECT COMPONENTS

The first step in the creation of a project infrastructure is the identification of the principal participants, for it is these who must make the major decisions within the project and solve significant problems when they occur. Their roles must therefore be clearly defined; they must be available when needed and so must understand their own roles in the project. It is they who will need to be kept up-to-date on the progress of the project, technically and with respect to time and budget, so they will require appropriate information delivered to them promptly.

There are four principal roles in a project. The following paragraphs treat the roles as though they were played by separate individuals or teams, but in small projects it is possible for roles to be combined — for example, for an individual to perform the roles of project manager and development manager, or customer representative and strategic representative — and thus make the number of participants commensurate with the project size. But it is always important to recognize the roles which are being enacted, for by understanding the roles we become aware of the activities which need to be carried out if the project is to be successful.

### 8.2.1  Project Management Team

A project manager needs not only to coordinate the work of a project but also to be involved in it. Doing all the 'right' things (planning, delegating, monitoring, reporting, and so on) should provide the basis of control, but usually the first clues of something going wrong are there to be detected long before they are made available through the formal reporting channels. If a project manager wishes to detect them early (if he wishes to sense the spirit of problems before they materialize — see Section 4.6 of Chapter 4), he needs to know and regularly talk to the people on the project. But in any but the smallest projects, the load of planning, delegating and coordinating work, monitoring progress, reporting to the customer, senior management, and the project team, taking corrective action, and providing the leadership necessary for inculcating a 'good' project culture, is already more than a full-time job for one person. The project manager needs assistance. In too many projects the full load falls to one person, often with the result that the 'standard' tasks receive all the attention and taking corrective action receives none — with the result that the project runs into difficulty. It is not enough for the project manager to have the information on what is wrong in the project, he also needs both the time and the resources to do something about it.

The size of the project manager's team depends on the size and complexity of the project. It also depends on whether the project manager is able to delegate 'project management' tasks to others. Let us here assume at least one assistant whom we will refer to as the project management assistant (PMA).

## 8.2.2 The Development Team

In Chapter 4, the distinction was drawn between the management of the project and that of the development of the product. Managing the project involves maintaining overall control, not only of the development process but also of such essentials as the production of documentation and training materials for the customer, of the purchase of necessary equipment, controlling the budget, and communication both within the project and across the project boundary. At the same time, the development of the system is not only the main purpose of the project but also the most significant task within it. Without the developers there would be no product and therefore no project. Whereas in small projects it is feasible for the development manager also to be the project manager, in practice the person taking on both roles needs to understand both as well as the difference between them. Too often such a person is of purely technical background, with the result that project control is ignored (see Chapter 4). The separate definition of the project management and development management functions is a necessary step in any project. Then, if the project is indeed small and the two roles are assumed by the same person, they can be discharged separately, with reports to senior management clearly distinguishing between the control of the project and the progress of the development of the product.

In an ED project, it is unlikely to be practical to integrate the two roles. Each is a heavy load, as we shall see in subsequent chapters. The second principal component of the project is therefore the development team, the structure of which is discussed in Section 8.4.

### 8.2.3  Customers and Users

In Chapter 3 the problems arising from the absence of the customer from the project were discussed. The customer's involvement throughout the project is crucial, but 'customer' is a vague word in this context. There are three categories of people in the customer's domain with interests in the project:

- The intended users of the system and their managers. They will have functional requirements on the system, mostly taking the form of what it should do, how it should respond to their commands, and what the screens and other outputs should look like. They are the intended 'users' of the system.
- The senior managers who will 'own' the proposed system and who have commissioned the project. They are the developers' 'customers'. They may be the heads of the users' departments and should determine the business functions which the system should support. They should define their criteria for measuring the success of the development project and the acceptability of the system.
- The organization as a whole, as represented by its business strategy and its information systems strategy (see Chapter 7). Ideally, plans for the system based on the organization's business strategy should determine the business objectives for the system, and the information systems strategy should place constraints on the system's design. Strategic constraints on the system are particularly important in ED because of the number of changes which are likely to be requested during development. These aspects are the responsibility of the strategic representative (see Section 8.2.4).

Both users and their senior managers should be consulted during the preparation of the original specification, both are likely to desire changes to the system as deliveries are made, and both should be involved in the project throughout. The 'customer representative' should be one of the senior managers, and his team should include at least one 'user representative'. The manner in which both are represented on the project is discussed in Section 8.3.1.

### 8.2.4  The Strategic Representative

In the previous chapter the need for strategic concurrence to all requirements was established, and this implied the need for someone familiar with the business and information systems strategies of the customer's organisation to vet not only the initial requirements but also any changes to them. The need for a strategic representative throughout the project was thus defined.

It is true that the strategic representative could function entirely within the customer's organization and not be visible within the project. In a contracted-out project this may be the case, and any changes introduced by the customer representative would already have been vetted for strategic concurrence. However, in order to explain the appropriate responsibilities, the strategic representative will in this book be defined as a project participant.

## 8.3   PROJECT RELATIONSHIPS

### 8.3.1 The Customer Council

A system is frequently planned to support a number of parts (for example, departments) of an organization. There are then a number of senior managers of equal rank who will make demands on the system, will therefore have some responsibility for it, and who perhaps will consider themselves to be owners of it. Typically, such managers have different, and often conflicting, objectives for the system. Yet, typically they do not take time, at least not sufficient time, to meet and discuss their objectives for it, their ideas about it, their claims on it, and their plans for its development. Without coming together to discuss these matters, the managers are unlikely to arrive at a consensus, and without a consensus there will be conflicting demands not only on the system once it is in operation, but also on many aspects of its development, such as the budget and where the money should come from, the availability of support from the customer, and the priorities of delivery of system functions.

It is a fundamental requirement of a project that all that is done within it should be towards a common goal. If there are conflicting goals, there is bound to be trouble. Indeed, lack of a common goal suggests either that the project should be halted until the diversity is focused into a single goal or that there should be more than one project.

It is therefore in the interest of everyone on the project for the managers to agree among themselves on their objectives and expectations for the system and the project, so there needs to be a process to facilitate their doing so. The following is such a process. Although it may be argued that the customer's responsibilities should not be the concern of the project manager, the latter will suffer increased difficulty in controlling the project if there is a lack of consensus and so needs to include the creation of a 'customer council' in the setting up of the project infrastructure.

The customer council should consist of all the senior managers who have a responsibility for the intended system. The first three tasks for this body to perform are to arrive at agreement on their objectives for the system, to elect one of their number to represent them on the project (to be the 'customer representative'), and to arrange for user participation in the project.

Arriving at a consensus is seldom easy for such a body, not least because they may have no understanding to start with of each other's (or even their own) objectives for the system. The most efficient way of overcoming this barrier is via a facilitated meeting, or series of meetings. This is particularly effective if the facilitator employs a tool (for example, the Soft Systems Methodology [Checkland 90]) designed to aid both the identification of a common purpose in the different managers' views and the arrival at a consensus on a set of objectives.

When the customer council has arrived at and documented a common set of objectives for the system, its next task is to elect from among its members a representative to the project. The customer representative will be a member of the project board (see Section 8.3.2) and so should have the authority to take major decisions on the development project and the system being developed.

Choosing a customer representative does not discharge the other senior managers from further responsibility for the proposed system or the project. The customer council should meet at regular intervals to receive reports from the customer representative and review the progress of the project and the extent to which it continues to meet their objectives for it. In an ED project, the many proposals for change will occasionally either explicitly or implicitly seek to alter some fundamental purpose of the system, and the customer council will need to decide whether to permit such changes. If they do, they may then have to consider whether to change their objectives for the system. There needs to be a perpetual review of their own demands on the system, both because it will be changing as a result of other influences and because of changes in their own organizations. The customer council therefore has a major role to play in ensuring that ED is successful — that is, that the changes made to its requirements do indeed keep it on course to satisfy the true needs for it.

Being a senior manager, the customer representative is unlikely to be able to spend a great deal of time on the day-to-day affairs of the project. Yet it is important that there is a continuous customer presence on the project and that the communication between the customer and the supplier is harmonious. A support team is therefore required for the customer representative, in the form of a (or more than one) 'user coordinator'. The user coordinator should be assigned to the project to liaise with the developers, to assist in regular progress and quality reviews, and to provide regular feedback to the customer representative and thus to the customer council. Some of the functions of the user coordinator are included in his membership of the 'coordination team' (see Section 8.3.3).

I think that the user coordinator should be involved in activities intended to assure or check the quality of the emerging product, such as design reviews and quality assurance. This provides the supplier with an 'extra pair of hands' at no cost, and it provides the basis of reassuring feedback to the customer. Yet, many suppliers (and project managers) do not like this level of customer involvement, perhaps because they are not confident that the feedback to the customer will indeed be reassuring. But gaining the customer's confidence in a project is a great prize. Further, if having a user coordinator present means that we must put our house in order, then his presence is invaluable. I believe that suppliers should put their houses in order by adopting quality practices, that they should welcome the user coordinator, and that, if he finds the occasion to criticize, they should accept the criticism with gratitude and use it to bring about improvement.

### 8.3.2 The Project Board

The project board comprises those senior participants who have the authority to take consequential decisions. They are: the project manager, the development manager, the customer representative, and the strategic representative (see Figure 8.1). The purpose of the project board is to review project progress and continually to take decisions on the project's direction — whether it should continue on its present course, whether it should change direction and, if so, what its new course should be, and in some cases even whether it should be terminated.

The first thing which the project manager needs to ensure is that each of the project board members knows, understands and accepts his role. As already mentioned, a major problem in many projects is not merely the lack of participation of senior managers but the time which it takes them to become effective when they do become involved. Rapid resolution of problems demands familiarity through constant active involvement.

For the project board's decision-making process to be continuous rather than intermittent, the project manager needs to ensure that the members are kept well informed and that they meet regularly so as to be in the habit of working as a team. Yet, given that the project board is composed of senior managers who are unlikely to be involved in the daily running of the project, 'regular' may imply every two or three months on a large project, if things are going well.

At the same time, arrangements need to be in place to call a meeting at short notice if a significant problem makes this necessary. Meetings should be planned well in advance (we had a rolling one-year schedule) and board members should be encouraged to apply peer pressure on each other to ensure that reliability is the norm and cancellations are frowned on. Nor should substitutes for members at meetings be acceptable, if they are not empowered with the authority to take consequential decisions. A great deal of time is wasted by substitutes having to 'refer back' to their managers before a decision can be taken, and by board members reversing decisions taken by their substitutes at previous meetings. If the project is to run smoothly, the right people (with the right level of authority) must sit on the board and they must

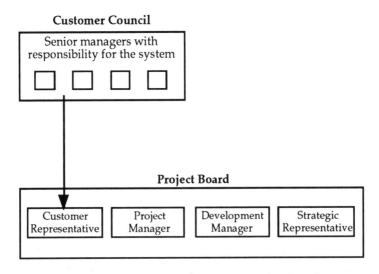

**Figure 8.1** Customer council and project board

understand their roles and discharge them conscientiously.

The project board serves not only to bring the right people together, but also to remind them of their responsibilities to the project. The meetings retain their awareness of their responsibilities. Thus, should a major problem occur, they will not only be accessible, but they will also be up-to-date on the project's situation and, therefore, in a position to take decisions which otherwise might take weeks or months.

If the board is to function efficiently, and if its members are to not to be alienated by their time being wasted, discussion must be at a decision-taking level. Too frequently senior managers squander their time at meetings on trivia and then regret attending the meetings. It is they who should recognize, demand and assure the level of discussion appropriate to their positions. But given that they seldom do so, the project manager must define an appropriate agenda and ensure not only that the right information is presented to the project board, but also that it is presented in the right form.

If senior managers are presented with raw data and invited to analyse it, they often do so with great interest. But their purpose should be to make system- and project-level, rather than component- and task-level, decisions, and for this they need processed information and not raw data. Their time should only be spent on task-level detail when the evidence of poor quality, dubious results, or a lack of attention to procedure shows that it is necessary. A great deal of time is wasted by project board members being asked, for example, to examine test data rather than being presented with a final test or quality assurance report.

The project manager must therefore put procedures in place to ensure that information is processed before it is presented to the project board, that it is presented in advance of meetings, that quality has been assured, that results are clearly presented and defendable, and that signing-off procedures have been observed so that the project board can have confidence that progress of the project is being honestly reported.

Let us remember that the project board cannot prove that all is well with the project; its purpose is to derive an appropriate level of confidence that all is well.

### 8.3.3 The Coordination Team

To control the project, the project manager needs information. The acquisition of information implies monitoring the progress of development. How the

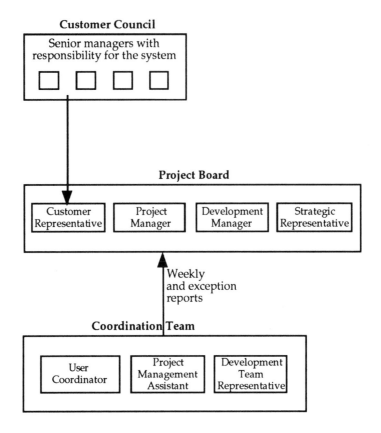

**Figure 8.2** The coordination team within the project

monitoring is carried out and by whom, and how the information gets to the project manager, are issues which need to be planned at the start and included in the infrastructure. A means which we found effective was for it to be done on a continuing basis by a working-level team, the 'coordination team', consisting of the project management assistant, the user coordinator, and a development team representative.

The various project participants have different viewpoints on the project, and they may have different short-term needs, but all of them have the same long-term goal of a quality system. What better, then, than for them to work together to monitor the progress of development?

In our projects, the three coordination team members met regularly in the course of their various individual responsibilities, but they were mandated to hold one formal coordination team meeting at a predetermined regular time each week. This was chaired by the project management assistant. The monitoring variables were defined by the project manager, and these were reported on (at the coordination team meeting) each week by the development team representative, who had previously collected the relevant information from the various parts of the development team and held discussions with the development manager. Reasons for delays were reported, and solutions to problems were discussed. Actions from the previous week's meeting were reviewed.

The principle was that local solutions should be found and implemented whenever possible. This gave the team and other working-level staff the responsibility for their work and its problems and the authority to take appropriate action to meet their targets. However, they needed to recognize the influence of their problems on the rest of the project, so they had limited time in which to resolve them. But 'limited' did not mean uncertain. From the working-level plans, they knew how much time they had to achieve solutions to their problems or to meet new targets for tasks which had fallen behind, so they needed to plan their work rather than simply decide to do it. Their plans were included in their weekly reports.

Each week a report was submitted to the project manager (and copied to the development manager and customer) — see Figure 8.2. In this, the monitored information was presented so that progress was clearly defined. Reasons for not meeting targets were also presented, along with a statement on what action was being taken. In the main, the project manager's assistance was not required, but if a problem was not resolved in the time allowed for it, or if rearranged targets were not met, he was asked for his support, or he stepped in to make appropriate decisions and use his authority to achieve the necessary results. The coordination team's weekly reports were not lengthy. They conformed to a guideline which avoided extraneous detail and made them easy to prepare but which ensured that appropriate records were kept.

This form of monitoring is effective in a number of ways. Not only does it involve all parties with an interest in the project, it also places responsibility on them for the success of the project. Working-level staff respond positively to the responsibility which it places on them. Indeed, it not only provides them with an incentive to take initiatives but it also develops their sense of responsibility. Moreover, it takes a load off the project manager's shoulders while keeping him well informed.

## 8.4   DEVELOPMENT TEAM STRUCTURE

A large development project demands a large development team, under the jurisdiction of the development manager. A large team is usually sub-divided into a number of smaller teams, each coordinated by a team leader. Often the structure of a large team remains as its manager inherited it — because he didn't think he had the authority to change it, or because he just did not stop to consider whether its structure was appropriate to the job in hand.

The project and development managers need to determine the team structure which they believe will best facilitate efficient development, from the points of view both of the efficiency of the developers and of their own control of the project. It would be possible, for example, for each team leader to take on the full responsibility for a given delivery, amending the high-level design, carrying out the detailed design, doing the programming and testing, and then delivering it. A major disadvantage of this is that it removes the dependencies between teams, and it is these dependencies which provide the peer pressure which is both an incentive to meet targets and a check on whether they are met. Other disadvantages which experience revealed were inefficiency in the use of skills, the difficulty of distributing certain skills among several teams (for all teams needed to possess the same skills), the lack of independent testing, and inefficiency in the management of the flow of work. Further, given that the content of future deliveries is uncertain, devoting teams to them can lead to a great deal of rework.

In any project, the project and development managers must make their own choice as to the most appropriate development organisation for their purposes. However, the following paragraphs briefly describe one which experience showed to be effective. As shown in Figure 8.3, the teams into which the development team was divided reflected the categories of development work. The organization of work was such that it flowed from team to team.

Considering Figure 8.3, the analysis and architecture team was responsible for the architectural and other high-level designs of the system and for dealing with the customer and users on specification matters. They produced the high-level design for each delivery, having in the first instance designed the architecture of the system. They received requests for change (RFCs), carried out the feasibility studies to analyse them, and when the RFCs were approved, compared them with the original specification, reviewed the architectural design, and produced high-level designs for the necessary changes.

The design and coding team received the high-level designs, produced detailed designs at as many levels as were needed for the application, coded the individual modules of code, and integrated the system. This team was sub-divided into two groups. The first, the program and test team, carried out the designs and programmed and tested the individual modules; the second, the integration and test team, carried out the successive stages of integration of the system, testing appropriately as they did so.

The system test team carried out validation of the system after its integration. As each delivery consisted of the complete version of the system as it existed at the time, validation was essential prior to each delivery. As the system grew with each delivery, this became a lengthy process. It is explained in Chapters 10 and 13.

The support team had two responsibilities, the first being maintenance of the delivered system. Once a version of the system was delivered, a copy of it was kept ready for testing by the support team in case the users encountered a problem. If maintenance changes were made to a live system, they had to be incorporated into all versions of the system then under development, and this added complications and increased the effort required. Thus, changes were deferred to a later delivery if possible. Chapter 14 explains the decisions involved and describes our maintenance process.

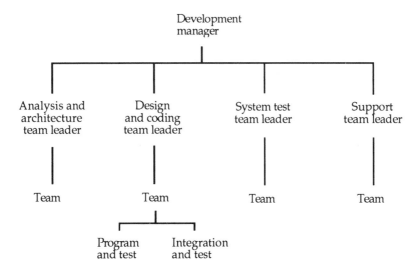

**Figure 8.3** Structure of the development team

The support team's second responsibility was to provide support to the entire development team. They serviced and maintained the development environment, received and installed new versions of system software and tools from suppliers, and instructed the other development team members in changes to their environment.

The team structure which we created enabled a smooth flow of work from team to team, in the manner suggested by the waterfall model. It also facilitated the development of team members' expertise and knowledge in particular domains and so increased their confidence and efficiency and, indeed, their professionalism. This was particularly significant in the analysis and architecture team and the support team, whose members dealt with the users. The good relationships which were of such importance to the project depended on their competence and confidence. I do not believe that any other development team structure would have been as effective in our circumstances.

## 8.5    COMMUNICATIONS

### 8.5.1  Reporting Within the Project

In order to manage something, we need information about it. Sometimes the required information exists and we merely need to find and acquire it. In other cases it may not be held by anyone in the form in which we need it, so we must identify the data and plan the analysis which will lead to the information. In all cases we must be absolutely clear as to what we need and how we are going to acquire it, so we need to follow a path of questioning which goes something like this. First we ask, What purpose do we need to achieve? For a project manager, there are many answers to this, for example, we need to produce a report to inform senior management of the progress of the project, to produce a report to give the customer confidence in the progress of the project, and most importantly, to aid us in controlling the project. The next question is, What information do I need to accomplish these purposes? That which I need to give confidence to the customer is certainly different from that which I need to convince myself that the project is on track, or that which I need if I am to detect problems early. Then, Does the required information exist in the form in which I need it and, if so, where must I get it from? And, if it does not exist as I need it, what raw data do I need in order to compose the information, and where must I get that from?

Often such a process of reasoning is neglected, and either the project manager does not collect information at all or he collects what is easy to collect. Then, useful purposes are not satisfied by the information, the project manager has no firm basis for controlling the project, and the project goes uncontrolled.

The information and data necessary to the project manager should be defined at the commencement of the project, and the monitoring mechanisms for acquiring it put in place. Then the means of analysing it and transferring the results to the project manager must be planned and set up. This implies not only monitoring but also reporting. What is more, reporting must be timely; delays in reporting lead to delays in discerning problems, delays in curing them, and thus slippage in the project. Nor does the project slippage result merely from time delays, but also, and more importantly, from the fact that the more mature is the problem when it is discovered, the more effort and time it requires for its cure. Having to deal with the material manifestation of a problem is the project manager's punishment for not sensing its spirit before it materializes.

One point that a project manager might usefully observe is that progress cannot effectively be measured in terms of effort invested but only by the achievement of goals. If you praise yourself for great effort, you will find yourself doing so for far longer than you had hoped or intended.

One further point: reporting does not necessarily mean long reports, or even written reports. The method of reporting must be appropriate to the purpose. Documentary evidence is often important, for instance in the case of quality assurance results. Eloquence is sometimes appropriate, for example in the case of reports which are to be read by senior customers. But even in these cases, brevity may not be out of place. Guidelines should be prepared at the initiation stage of the project for all types of project report, and they should make it clear that time should not be wasted on the inclusion of extraneous information.

A mistake which is often made is to believe that time would be saved by combining the reports to fulfil two purposes into one; in fact, the result is often a falling between two stools and a wasting of time. First be clear as to what is required, and then define clearly how it should be produced and by whom. Then use the result. If you find that the result does not serve the intended purpose, discontinue its production and don't waste time on it. In other words, monitor the effectiveness of your own operations.

### 8.5.2  Transfer of Information

If the large amount of information which needs to be transferred throughout the course of a project is to be communicated smoothly, formal mechanisms such as those mentioned in the previous section need to be installed and maintained. Yet, all necessary information can never be transmitted by formal routes: there are some things which people will not say openly, some which they will not say to certain people, some which they will not document, some which they do not think of saying, and some which they cannot consciously say because they are not aware that they know them.

If the project manager is to sense the spirit of problems before they materialize, he must discover the early clues. He must become *involved*. He must get to know everyone on the project and become someone in whom they are willing to confide — which means that he must win their confidence and not demand or expect it. He needs to be sensitive to body language. In order to discover from people those things which they would not think of communicating and those things which they do not know that they know, he must ask the right questions. Then he must listen to the answers: listening is an art he must learn and practise. Further, as it is only in casual or spontaneous encounters in which certain things are said, he needs to have such encounters: it is often the case that more useful information is transmitted in the corridor, in the pub and in the toilet than at meetings. Spontaneous encounters need to be planned.

### 8.5.3  Communication Across the Project Boundary

Figure 8.4 shows a number of examples of lines of communication across the project boundary. It reminds project managers (and others) that such communication is necessary. The means of achieving it must be provided as part of the project infrastructure if delays are not to occur when the need arises. For example, when staff with certain skills are needed at short notice, an established relationship with a recruitment agency can make the difference between rapid and delayed service; having a list of consultants who could provide the advice which we might need on the various technologies in use, or on our equipment and software, can save a great deal of time when we find, in the middle of the project, that we need certain problems to be resolved by the next day; establishing relationships with other projects similar to ours can result in our receiving information on problems and their solutions before

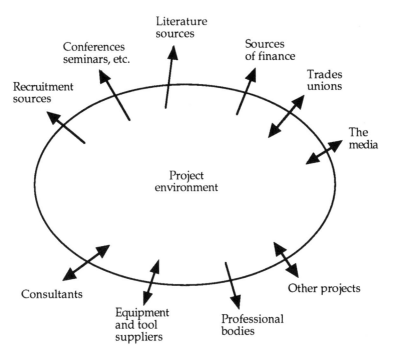

**Figure 8.4** Communications across the project boundary

they occur in our project.

If communication mechanisms have not been put in place, the likelihood is that the need has not been recognised. Then when it arises, it is not recognized that it need not have arisen, and the delay before it is satisfied will consist of three elements. The first is the time to come to the realization that external communication is necessary (or desirable), the second is the time to identify the external source with which to communicate (to do business), and the third is the time to conduct the business. Putting an infrastructure in place can seem so simple that it is overlooked; or, if it is considered it is scorned; but its absence leads to far greater problems than do the various technical concerns in which project managers often immerse themselves.

## 8.6    DOCUMENT INFRASTRUCTURE

Although the project's principal product is a computer system, and the contents of the deliveries are software, a great deal of a project is given over to the production and maintenance of documentation. Moreover, the success and smooth running of the project depends on documentation. This section is a brief indicator of what needs to be catered for in creating a sound document infrastructure (including the rules for maintaining it) at the start of a project. Some examples of the great variety of documents crucial to a project should give an idea of its importance:

- Project standards, guidelines and procedures;
- Specifications, both for initial requirements and for new requirements and changes to existing functions;
- Plans, for example technical, resource and quality plans, which may be at project, stage or task level;
- Minutes of meetings of all types within the project, for example project board meetings at the ends of stages, project board meetings for prioritization and delivery planning, and coordination team meetings;
- Correspondence;
- Reports of various sorts, for example from the coordination team to the project manager, from the project manager to the project board, and from the project manager to the customer;
- Design documents at various levels, for example architectural, sub-system and module designs;
- Test plans for all the units of software at the various integration stages;
- Test and quality assurance results;
- Manuals for the reference, training and convenience of users, such as the users' guide, and the operation and maintenance manuals.

It is not only important to write these documents. Let us remember that the purpose of a document is to convey information (or to record it for possible later conveyance). In some cases, such as with the minutes of a meeting, the information in a document, once correct, is fixed. With many documents, however, the information changes, so the document needs to be reproduced so as to convey the latest information. Control therefore needs to be exercised not only over the initial preparation of documents but also over their subsequent versions and their quality [Ferraby 91].

Frequently it is discovered in mid-project that a designer is using an out-of-date version of a specification, or test plans have been based on an obsolete design, or developers are working to an old version of a standard. Then, if it is recognized (and it may not always be) that a document control system (a document infrastructure) is lacking, reparation takes a considerable time — which had not been planned for and therefore which creates a project delay. Meanwhile, there is uncertainty as to whether the correct versions are in use throughout the project. Yet, it would have taken little time to install a document infrastructure at the start. The trouble is that it is such a simple matter that it is ignored. But its lack leads to untold trouble.

Briefly, a document infrastructure must include at least the following mechanisms:

- A definition of each type of document to be used in the project (for example, see the list earlier in this section);
- A numbering system capable of uniquely identifying each and every document and which, as a minimum, must define the document type, the number of that particular document, and the issue (or draft number);
- An information system which includes further information on each document, including the author and the date of issue;
- Identification of the individuals responsible for the production (not necessarily the author), the issuing and filing, and the signing off of the document;
- A change-control procedure for each and every type of document, including the individuals responsible for authorizing and signing off changes;
- The quality assurance method to be used for each type of document;
- The filing system for each type of document, and the individuals responsible for it;
- A distribution list for each type of document.

## 8.7   COMPONENTS OF THE TECHNICAL INFRASTRUCTURE

The three most fundamental aspects of the infrastructure for controlling the project — people, communications and documentation — have been discussed above. However, they do not represent the full extent of what must be put in place in the Initiation stage in order for the project to run smoothly. The way also needs to be paved for smooth development of the product, so a 'technical' infrastructure needs to be installed.

For example, standards on many aspects of development need to be in place in advance of work being carried out. Experience shows that even when company standards exist and are understood, it is often necessary to tailor them to the needs of the project. Or sometimes *de facto* standards exist and it suddenly becomes apparent that they need to be documented — for example, when new staff join the team, or when it is decided to employ contract programmers . Then, if the programmers are not provided with documented programming standards, information necessary for identifying and tracing programs or program versions are likely to be omitted from the documentation. As a project manager may not foresee all instances of such 'extra' work, he should not only plan the writing and tailoring of standards at the commencement of the project but also allow time in the plans for such work later on.

Further aspects of the technical infrastructure to facilitate product development which must be put in place at the start of an ED project are so important that separate chapters are devoted to them:

- The configuration management system, including its management — see Chapter 10;
- A change control procedure — see Chapter 11;
- A procedure for prioritizing development work — see Chapter 12;
- A process governing how the configuration management system is to be used to facilitate testing throughout development — see Chapter 13;
- A process for conducting and managing maintenance — see Chapter 14.

## 8.8  SUMMARY AND EXTRACTS

Creating a project infrastructure at the initiation stage is crucial to project success, and doing so is one of the project manager's most important tasks. Then, throughout the project, he must maintain the infrastructure and make it work. This chapter has explained what an infrastructure consists of and what a project manager needs to do to put it in place.

Of primary importance to project control are the three 'management' aspects of the infrastructure — people, communications and documentation — and the chapter considered these in detail. But certain 'technical' aspects need also to be installed to facilitate the development of the product. These were briefly introduced and will be described in detail in subsequent chapters.

The following extracts from the text make some of the chapter's points.

- At the best of times, control of a software development project is difficult. Without having appropriate teams, communication channels, reporting procedures, and other infrastructure components in place, it can be almost impossible.

- People are capricious and individualistic and often uncommunicative and uncooperative, but they can be the opposites of these if the project manager creates a supportive environment for them to work in.

- If a project infrastructure is put in place early, and the project manager invests time and effort in maintaining it and inculcating its principles and procedures into the culture of the project, the probability of smooth running is greatly enhanced.

- In small projects it is possible for roles to be combined ... But it is always important to recognize the roles which are being enacted, for by understanding the roles we become aware of the activities which need to be carried out if the project is to be successful.

- It is not enough for the project manager to have the information on what is wrong in the project, he also needs both the time and the resources to do something about it.

- The customer's involvement throughout the project is crucial.

- Typically, managers have different, and often conflicting, objectives for the system.

- It is a fundamental requirement of a project that all that is done within it should be towards a common goal. If there are conflicting goals, there is bound to be trouble.

- The customer council should consist of all the senior managers who have a responsibility for the intended system.

- The user coordinator should be assigned to the project to liaise with the developers, to assist in regular progress and quality reviews, and to provide regular feedback to the customer.

- If having a user coordinator present means that we must put our house in order, then his presence is invaluable.

- A great deal of time is wasted by substitutes having to 'refer back' to their managers before a decision can be taken, and by board members reversing decisions taken by their substitutes at previous meetings.

- The project manager must put procedures in place to ensure that information is processed before it is presented to the project board, that it is presented in advance of meetings, that quality has been assured, that results are clearly presented and defendable, and that signing-off procedures have been observed.

- Often the structure of a large team remains as its manager inherited it — because he didn't think he had the authority to change it, or because he just did not stop to consider whether its structure was appropriate to the job in hand.

- The information and data necessary to the project manager should be defined at the commencement of the project, and the monitoring mechanisms for acquiring it put in place.

- Progress cannot effectively be measured in terms of effort invested but only by the achievement of goals. If you praise yourself for great effort, you will find yourself doing so for far longer than you had hoped or intended.

- There are some things which people will not say openly, some which they will not say to certain people, some which they will not document, some which they do not think of saying, and some which they cannot consciously say because they are not aware that they know them.

- It is often the case that more useful information is transmitted in the corridor, in the pub and in the toilet than at meetings. Spontaneous encounters need to be planned.

- Control needs to be exercised not only over the initial preparation of documents but also over their subsequent versions.

# 9

# Initial
# Planning

## 9.1 THE ISSUES

Creating the project infrastructure and defining the methods of working and communication were considered in the previous chapter, so the issue here is the planning of the work itself. But given that ED invites change, what confidence can we have in any plans which we draft? What assumptions can we make about the time it will take to do the job, or the required budget? We certainly cannot assume that the specification will remain constant, for this would not only contradict all experience but also negate the benefit of ED.

In a traditional development project, planning is specification-based. The tasks required to do the work to meet the specification are identified, the resources necessary to the tasks are determined, and the budget to support both is estimated. Thus the plans are laid. And in spite of overwhelming evidence to the contrary, the expectation is typically that the plans will be met

— until, within an embarrassingly short time (usually no more than a few weeks) history is vindicated and it becomes clear that the plans will not be met. Reasons are surprisingly consistent, and usually include as least some of the following:

- Many essential tasks have been omitted from the plans;
- Annual leave, sick leave and disturbances have not been allowed for (i.e., the assumption has been made that everyone will work effectively for five full days each week for the entire project);
- A project infrastructure has not been put in place;
- It has been assumed that the project team will require zero time to be assembled and to become fully productive, and then will not change;
- Differences in competence level have not been considered and training has not been allowed for;
- The project manager is both inexperienced and untrained;
- The project targets are arbitrarily imposed and are a great deal tighter than the project estimates.

Suppose we were to eliminate these problems so that we could get the plans right, stick to them, and end up with a satisfactory system! Would we then have the perfect project? Only if we had got the specification entirely correct and there were no changes in the client organization's requirements during the course of the project — almost impossible. So we introduce ED. This is intended to overcome the change problem; at least, it is expected to ensure that changes are recognized early and implemented during development instead of after a 'big-bang' system has been delivered. It should thus ensure that the final system really does meet the customer's and users' requirements and that achieving it is cheaper. But it does not solve the planning problem. In fact, it complicates it. With ED we know that the specification will not be stable throughout the development project. We can be certain that if we derive our time and cost estimates from it we will get them wrong, even if we avoid the other problems mentioned above.

So is there any point in planning? Should we simply get on with the job of development without giving any thought to how long the project will take or how much we spend? Clearly not; that would be a recipe for chaos in the project and conflict with the customer. But if we plan too rigorously, and place too much confidence in our plans, we will be disappointed and we will have wasted time and resources. Is there a middle way?

Changing from the traditional way of project planning to a way more appropriate to ED is in fact a change in culture.

## 9.2    SPECIFICATION

To plan the project we require a good understanding of what needs to be done. Traditionally in a development project, the assumption has been that this understanding must be based on a specification of the system to be developed. And this assumption has been shown to be well founded, for a plan based on a mere conception of the system, or even on the results of a feasibility study, has always been less accurate than one based on a good specification. Indeed, experience has shown that the accuracy of plans increases if they are reviewed at each stage of a project, when more information becomes available.

Yet in ED projects customers and users are inclined to minimize the time spent on preparing a specification, reasoning that if delivery of the system is to be evolutionary they need not prepare any more of the specification than is sufficient to define the first delivery. There is a certain logic to this, for by the nature of ED it is expected that the specification will change anyway. However, there are a number of reasons why this way of thinking is detrimental to the project and to accurate planning.

The first and most important point is that a specification of requirements is essential to the design of the system architecture, and the system architecture is essential to accurate planning, lower-level design and, thus, programming the software. Of what value is the perfect programme if it is the wrong programme?

A partial specification is inadequate as the basis of a sound system design. When a system is going to be very small, and its development project of relatively short duration, it may be justifiable to elicit its requirements implicitly via rapid prototyping, particularly if its purpose is mainly to meet the needs of its users rather than to satisfy business objectives. Then the design of the system and the specification evolve together. But when a large system is being developed by means of a long project, even though delivery may be evolutionary, an architectural design on which reliance may be placed needs to be established early in the development process. A high-level design is of crucial importance to the performance and dependability of a system. It allows the main system components to be identified and configured. If its fundamental properties remain constant through the development of the system, even though detail is being added to them, system attributes such as reliability, availability, maintainability, safety, security and responsiveness may all be expected to benefit. For example, if at the time of designing a database it is only partially known what data is to be stored in it (because only part of the system requirements have been specified), it is likely that later, when additions are made to it, access modes will become sub-optimum and its response times will lengthen. Under such circumstances, it is not unusual for a database to require redesign or, at least, 'tuning'.

Second, the requirements are less likely to change if the specification is produced in a thorough process in which the requirements are captured, verified and analysed and then the specification written, quality assured and validated. This implies the production of a complete specification rather than a partial one, with the time spent in preparing it having a controlling effect on later change — which can be a considerable advantage.

Third, if the project and the system have not arisen out of strategic planning, the project manager needs a good specification from which to determine the scope of the project — otherwise, how can estimates of budget and time be made? A broad specification (one with all or most of the requirements identified) is necessary for determining scope. A deep specification (one in which the requirements are defined in detail) is necessary for determining the size and nature of the system.

Fourth, if deliveries are to be tailored to provide maximum benefit to the customer and users, and if they are to be on time, they must be planned well in advance. Once the developers have got into a routine, it will be found that deliveries N+1 and N+2 are planned and their development commenced even before delivery N has been made. Such planning cannot be done if the requirements are being provided on a per delivery basis.

Fifth, prioritization of requirements in order to optimize deliveries can only be carried out if the requirements have been specified.

A good specification, as thorough as it is practicable to produce, is therefore a necessity in an ED project. Similarly, clear and well-defined business objectives for the system to be developed are crucial. To start with, the specification is less likely to change if the requirements in it are based on business objectives which were derived from strategic planning (see Chapter 7). Then, as changes to the requirements are proposed, the business objectives will form the criteria against which their validity is judged. If there are no business objectives, there will at best be improvised criteria of doubtful validity.

The project manager would therefore do well not only to ensure (if possible) that a full specification exists, but also to know the business objectives of the system and to inquire what strategic planning formed the basis of the project.

It could be argued that the business objectives for the system might change. So they might, and if they did their change would invalidate a part, perhaps a substantial part, of the users' requirements. But it is one of ED's advantages that it would respond to such a change rapidly during the system's development rather than a considerable time later during its operation, and this does not obviate the need for a good specification at the start of development.

It is false economy, and erroneous logic, to capture only a small part of the requirements at the start of the project. One of the most recurrent lessons which we have learned in software development is the importance of a good specification prior to the commencement of design or programming, but it is perhaps the lesson which we most consistently ignore.

## 9.3    PLANNING THE PROJECT

What are the constraints on the project? Do we have to deliver a final product by a certain date? Is there a defined limit on the budget? How is the budget apportioned — do we have access to what we need when we need it, or can we only spend certain amounts at certain times? We need to be clear as to the assumptions that we are making and the constraints which have been placed on the project.

In software development projects, assumptions are frequently made and financial and time constraints imposed without reference to the system to be developed and independently of the proposed development project. Inevitably the assumptions are often ill-founded and the constraints too severe. The result then is that even a well managed project which produces a well-engineered product may be perceived as a failure because it exceeds the arbitrarily imposed time and budgetary limits (consider the experiences related in Section 3.2 of Chapter 3). Ideally, the assumptions and constraints, made at a feasibility stage or earlier, should be reviewed in the light of the full specification, but this is seldom done. The specification may be used as the basis for the technical planning of the project, but often the project manager sees the previously imposed constraints as fixed and impossible to challenge.

Considering the waterfall development model, it is typical that at the end of one stage there is adequate information to allow detailed plans to be drawn up for the next, with plans based on less confident estimates being prepared for the stages beyond that. Thus, at the end of the specification stage the plans for design can be produced in detail, with less reliable estimates being used for planning the later stages of coding, integration, and validation. Knowing the tasks to be carried out and the effort which will need to be invested in them would allow not only a time profile for the project to be prepared but also a budgetary profile, with an estimate of the total necessary expenditure. One reason why this is not often done is that the project manager perceives his responsibility as being only to manage the development of the system and not either to estimate time and budgetary requirements or to question the earlier imposed constraints on them. He simply gets on with the job knowing that it is unlikely to be perceived as successful.

A process which might usefully be imposed on all development projects within an organization is as follows:

1.   Given the strategic need for a system, carry out a short feasibility study to answer any questions related to the business objectives of the system to be developed, such as: what is the likely project cost? What technology should be used for developing the system? What is the likely development time, given certain resources? 'What-if' studies could be carried out to derive answers for different scenarios.

2.   If it is decided that the system is worth developing, give authority and the necessary budget allocation for a project for the development of a specification of requirements on the proposed system. In doing so, be particularly clear about the business objectives for the system and any constraints on the intended project. Identify and analyse any risks attached to the development project, and develop action plans to eliminate or mitigate them. Identify the costs of the action plans, for these must be included in the project cost.

3.   When the specification for the system has been produced and validated, the authorized project comes to an end.

4.   Use the specification as the basis for planning the intended development project in as much detail as possible. The resulting plans may be referred to as the 'specification-based plans'. Use these for assessing the time to develop the system (using various resource options) and the cost of doing so. Compare the results of this planning study with those of the original feasibility study, reviewing the costs, development time, resource requirements, assumptions and risks of the project. Any major

discrepancies should be examined carefully to discover the reasons for inaccuracy, so that future estimating can be improved.

5.   If the new estimates are greater than those previously defined, decisions should be taken at a strategic level on what action is appropriate. Options would include abandonment of the project, authorization of the larger amounts of time and money, and the reduction of the specification. If it is decided to authorize the development project, formal authorization should now be given on a realistic basis, allowing adequate time, budget and other resources.

I strongly recommend this process for all software development (including ED) projects. Imposing restrictions, usually *ad hoc* and without strategic reasons, on a project before defining what needs to be produced is a major cause of 'failure'. So many project failures are in fact failure to meet randomly set targets! Randomly imposed restrictions cause demoralization of development staff from the start, because the staff are persistently under stress to achieve what they know to be impossible (see Section 3.2 of Chapter 3 for a discussion of this). They go from one missed deadline to another, always failing, and seldom receiving recognition for the good work that they so often do.

Remember, however, that a process such as that described in points 1-5 above provides estimates of cost and time for the development of a system according to the original specification. In an ED project, it must be assumed that the work done will not all be in accordance with the demands of that document. Yet, for the several reasons given in the previous section, it is important to have a good specification and to understand what it implies. Further, without a change in the prevailing software development culture (see Chapter 15), management is still likely to think in terms of the original specification and to judge success against it.

Because there will be many changes to both the plans and the specification, management of an ED project will not be successful if it is purely procedural. A rigorous adherence to plans can be as dangerous as having no plans, and an ED project manager needs to apply judgement in their use — see Worsley and Lee for a discussion of 'third generation project management' [Worsley 97]. Further, because of the high likelihood of change, the project manager should understand the strategic basis of the project. He should not only ensure (if possible) that an adequate specification exists, but also seek to know the business objectives of the system and to inquire what strategic planning formed the basis of the project. If he is unable to find an adequate strategic basis for the project, he may not be able to halt the project or decline to manage it, but he should then be aware that the chance of encountering problems during development is high. He should plan accordingly and, if appropriate, inform senior management in writing of his assessment of the shortcomings and their likely results.

Next, it is important in planning to make allowance for the requests for change which will be proposed — both those which lead to changes and those which do not (dealing with proposals for change which are not implemented can be time-consuming and can upset the best laid plans). The problem is that their volume and complexity are unpredictable. Thus, while a good plan is important, it is also important that it includes flexibility and that the project manager is capable of the judgement necessary in applying flexibility. The organization's culture (see Chapter 15) needs to be such that management accepts the inevitability of change and the need for flexibility both in planning and in the requirements on the system.

Though not based on certainty, a plan needs to be realistic, so there are factors which the project manager may need to consider.

- If the project budget was defined at the feasibility study stage, it now needs to be reviewed in the light of the specification-based estimate. If the reviewed estimate is greater than the earlier one, the project may need to be re-authorized. Now is the time to raise the matter with senior management.

- In allowing for later change, it is of course possible that the extra work generated by changes will be counteracted by the cancellation of some of the requirements in the specification, but this balance cannot be guaranteed, and is improbable. There is also a chance that there will not be a great deal of change arising during the project, but don't count on that. Our experience was that once offered the opportunity to request changes, the users had to be restrained rather than encouraged.

## 9.4   MODELLING THE PROJECT

Many people want a clear statement of what development model (see Chapter 2) they should work to, so the question often arises: What model is appropriate to ED? Rather than present an ED model which is more complex than valuable,

I would like to offer an answer to this question in several parts.

First, it is important not to be a slave to any model. A model may be a guide to what to do, but it should be quite clear what it is a model of, and it should not be employed outside its intended use (see Section 2.5 of Chapter 2). Further, blind adherence to a model is almost certain to lead to false assumptions being made about its applicability. So derive benefit from models, but employ them only as far as their benefits extend.

Second, let us consider the project as a whole. The feedback from the customer and users following deliveries provides opportunities for changes in direction in the project. A major change in direction may not often be necessary, but there needs to be replanning (and re-specification) after each delivery (see Section 9.5). Replanning offers a formal opportunity for the reassessment of the value of what has been done, the value of what is scheduled to be done, the options for what might be done, and the risks associated with the various courses of action. This process is very much in accordance with the spiral model (see Section 2.3 of Chapter 2). So, the course of the project as a whole can be mapped onto the spiral model, with one loop of the spiral being equivalent to a delivery.

At the review point in each loop, do not forget to review the business objectives for the project, the constraints imposed, and the assumptions made. Remember that if a project's objectives change, it in effect becomes a new project. What do I mean by this? In the first place, I have in previous chapters emphasised the importance of the project objectives and the fact that these should define the scope of the project. Then, the specified requirements should lie within the scope. Thus, if the objectives are changed, it is almost certain that the scope of the project is also changed, and this must render the specification in need of review. Some specified requirements will no longer be valid, and some (new) requirements on the system will not have been specified. In the second place, the objectives are likely to have influenced both the project budget and the time allowed for the production of the system, so both of these targets will need review. If new objectives relax the time within which the system is required, it would be folly not to replan the project with this as a factor. Similarly, if either the budget or the development time is to be cut, replanning should take place with the project manager seeking to reduce the system's functionality so as to make the new project viable.

So the project board must recognize that new objectives create a new project and ensure that the customer does too. New requirements, assumptions, constraints and risks may accompany the new objectives, and these should not be accepted by default, but rather assessed for their implications. Replanning and re-authorisation of new plans may also be necessary.

Third, let us consider the development of one delivery. This is a mini project of relatively short duration. As such, it requires the application of the good engineering principles imposed by the waterfall model (see Section 2.1 of Chapter 2), which is most beneficial as a management tool. It is simple, and it invites detailed plans for each stage (each delivery) of the project. Based on such plans, the project board can determine the schedule of their meetings, the production and signing off of stage products, and the critical points at which action would need to be taken to keep the delivery on schedule. So the waterfall model is useful for the management control (by the project manager and the project board) of the development of individual deliveries.

Fourth, let us recognize that the additions which the V model (see Section 2.2 of Chapter 2) brings to the waterfall model are of particular use to the developers. It defines the successive levels not only of the system's description but also of its composition. It also provides a sound basis for the testing process. Thus, the V model is a useful guide to the details of the development of each delivery and, as such, is appropriate for the use of the development manager and the development team.

Fifth, in order to develop a better understanding of ED projects and to improve our estimating of them, we should develop a profile of the effort spent on each project activity. A model appropriate to recording and displaying an effort profile is the matrix model (see Section 2.4 of Chapter 2). But in its presentation in Chapter 2, the rows were dedicated to the stages of the project in the manner defined by (but extended beyond) the waterfall model, and in ED these stages apply not to the whole project but to each delivery. It is possible to use the matrix model in two ways in monitoring an ED project.

On the one hand, we may use it for monitoring a delivery. A delivery may be considered to be a mini project, but its life cycle does not merely cover an inter-delivery period. Planning for a delivery may commence a year or more before the delivery takes place, so applying the matrix model to it implies dedicating a matrix to recording the effort which is invested in the activities over the delivery's life cycle, including maintenance.

On the other hand, a matrix may be dedicated to the interval between two deliveries. This period typically includes almost every type of activity, from strategic planning (or at least strategic involvement) to maintenance (after the first delivery). We notice, however, that with three deliveries being developed concurrently, their activities are carried out in parallel, so each period between deliveries cannot be divided into chronologically sequential stages, beginning with strategy and ending with maintenance. The data being recorded will therefore be over three life-cycle stages, one for each delivery in preparation, and one for the maintenance of the system in operation.

At the end of the project, a number of matrices will exist, and these can be combined to provide information on three types of project profile:

- The profiles of the life cycles of the deliveries;
- The profiles of the inter-delivery periods;
- The profile of the project as a whole.

During the project the evolving matrix can be analysed and its value as a predictor of the future delivery and inter-delivery period profiles of the project put to the test. At the end of the project, the profiles derived from the matrix will be available for inclusion in the end-of-project report, and the total amounts of effort expended on the various project activities calculated and used as guides to estimating on future projects.

Thus, not one but four models are of value in an ED project. Each is appropriate to a different viewpoint, each satisfies a different purpose, and each should be used within its constraints and to provide its particular benefits. None should be followed slavishly.


## 9.5   PLANNING THE FIRST DELIVERY

Something of huge importance in ED is to attract the confidence of the customer and the users of the system. It is therefore crucial that ambitious promises are not made before there is sound evidence that they can be kept. Too often project and development managers make rods for their own backs by allowing a desire to please to lead them into making wild and extravagant commitments. This not only affects the development manager, but, perhaps more importantly, it is a cause of demotivation of the development staff, for they know from the start that they have no chance of success. ED offers the developers a good opportunity to please the users by providing them with an operational system long before they might otherwise have expected it. If it is offered at the end of seven months rather than six, there may be small initial disappointment, but the advantage of early delivery has not been affected. When the delivery is made, the users will not only be pleased with it (if it meets their needs) but also gain confidence in the developers for doing a good job and keeping their word. The resulting feedback from the users will boost the morale of the developers, which is an unusual prize and one of great value to the project and development managers. But the users' confidence will not be gained if the delivery is not made on time or if the system is unreliable or does not include useful functions. Adequate time must therefore be allowed for planning and developing the first delivery and assuring its quality.

### 9.5.1  Project Infrastructure

Once the specification has been prepared, a project manager is often tempted to 'get on with the development' and neglect the crucial initiation stage of the project. Be reminded, therefore, of the need not only to carry out the tasks necessary to setting the project on a sound course, but also to plan the time to do so in the period between receiving the specification and making the first delivery. Reference should be made to Chapter 8 for consideration of what needs to be done in creating the project infrastructure.

In addition to the 'people', communications and document infrastructures, the structures and rules for managing them also need to be initiated. The following (which are discussed at length in later chapters) are examples of aspects of the infrastructure which are crucial to the success of an ED project:

- The structure and management of the configuration management system (see Chapter 10);
- The change control system (see Chapter 11);
- The means of planning deliveries (see above and Chapter 12);
- The way in which the configuration management system is to be used for testing (see Chapter 13);
- The rules governing maintenance and the way in which the configuration management system will facilitate and control it (see Chapter 14).

The project manager should understand the problems likely to arise if sound plans are not in place. At the beginning of the project he needs to define and install detailed control procedures, and subsequently he needs to ensure adherence to them.

### 9.5.2  Architectural Design

In the first place, a thorough high-level design of the system needs to be prepared, verified against the system specification, and validated against the strategic objectives for the system. So often this system architecture is neglected, so often it is drawn up only sketchily, and so seldom is it validated by the customer against business objectives. But the larger or more complex the system, the more important it is to be absolutely clear on its design principles.

The architecture is of great importance. It sets the direction of the more detailed design and it provides the context for all future design decisions. This point is important, for in ED proposed changes are likely to give rise to numerous design decisions. Moreover, the high-level design is essential at the beginning of the project to deciding what hardware the system should be based on and what system software and tools to use in supporting the applications. If non-optimum design decisions are made at this stage, the repercussions can be disastrous and extensive: development and testing can be made difficult and inefficient, and system performance can be unsatisfactory for the life of the system. In the extreme, major redesign may be necessary, perhaps late in the project, with the disposal and re-programming of a great deal of software — and if this is necessary, what has become of ED's advantages of keeping the system in line with the users' requirements and avoiding major re-work late in the project?

Designing a system architecture is usually an iterative process, and the initial effort cannot be assumed to be stable. Typically, it is only after a number of designers have challenged each other over various (perhaps numerous) points that the principles begin to be established. Even then, there is usually a lengthy period of change as ideas crystallize, deficiencies become appreciated, and the architecture begins to be perceived as an integrated whole rather than as a number of disjoint parts. So the short cut of a single designer rapidly drawing up a system architecture 'so that the more important business of detailed design and coding can be done' is likely to be a dangerous illusion. Time should be allowed for the natural process of iterative design; the future of the project depends on it.

The ability to plan which functions can be included in any given delivery also depends on it. Dependencies between functions are only likely to be identified with confidence in the context of the system architecture, when the way in which they will be provided can be seen. There is no point in promising, or trying to provide, a function which is dependent on another if the latter has not been or is not scheduled to be implemented. It can be even more disastrous if the dependency is not even recognized.

### 9.5.3 Detailed Design

It is useful not to carry out any unnecessary design in case it has to be changed later. But how much detailed design should be carried out in advance of the first delivery? Certainly, any functions to be included in the next (in this case, the first) delivery must be designed in detail. But the amount of further design necessary to support or substantiate the design of the functions to be delivered varies according to the project, and the judgement of the project and development managers is always required.

In the first place, the architectural design should show the decomposition of the system into sub-systems. Then, it must be clear how the functions (as perceived by the users) are distributed across the sub-systems. This understanding of how each function is catered for in the system architecture and how it is integrated with the other functions is crucial: when only a part of the system has been delivered and is in operation, its performance is usually good, but if it has been designed and coded in isolation from the remainder of the system, its performance is likely to deteriorate as more of the system is provided and the operational load is increased. A 'system view' from the start is important.

It is also essential in planning deliveries to know what is possible. It would be silly for the developers to promise to include a given (say) five functions in a delivery if those five functions could not be developed and tested by the resources available in the time before the delivery. Thus, in planning a delivery there need to be estimates of how much effort each function will take for its development. The design should be drawn up to whatever level of detail is necessary for this.

If an entire sub-system is to be delivered, any sub-system with which it communicates needs to be designed to the point where the interface between the two can be clearly defined. Later changes to communications software can be difficult to implement, complex to test, and error-prone.

When one of a number of functions within a sub-system is to be delivered, the sub-system as a whole needs to be designed to the level at which the interactions between the functions is fully defined and any dependencies between them are obvious. It is not only futile to deliver a function if another on which it depends for its service has not yet been delivered, but it also diminishes the confidence of the users, for they do not have the use of a function which they had been promised. Further, if a dependency is only recognized when a function is already under development, there may be a rush to design and develop the function on which it depends in time for the delivery, and this can lead to the delivery being late, other promised functions not being delivered, and difficulties in testing the delivery.

The lesson is that the design of all sub-systems should be sufficiently detailed prior to the first delivery for the identification and definition of dependencies and interfaces. The need for this will be seen to be crucial in the context of scheduling deliveries and prioritizing functions for delivery.

### 9.5.4 Which Functions?

The early use of the system which ED offers cannot be optimized, and may not even be possible, unless there is a careful choice of which system functions should be provided at each delivery. The choice for the first delivery is particularly important, for it is an opportunity for the confidence of the users to be won. If the opportunity is not taken, and the users perceive the developers as failing to deliver on their promises, it is likely to take not one but a number of successful deliveries to reverse the impression.

Before any functionality can be provided, the skeletal system, consisting of the hardware and system software, must first be designed, purchased, installed and tested, so achieving this must be taken into consideration when the first delivery is being planned. It is worth explaining to the customer and users how each of these basic components contributes to the system as a whole, and how each is essential to the provision of the application functions which the users require. Remember that the users are unlikely to understand the basic system concepts and that their perception is simply of the developers programming their requirements. The fact that this programming is dependent on many other 'back-room' tasks, and on the preparation of the right system 'platform', will be lost on them unless you explain the point. Holding a workshop at which this is done is a good idea; and the prioritization of functions can be discussed at the same forum. I cannot emphasize sufficiently the importance of good and open communication with the users.

In planning the first delivery, the first thing to be established is the essential work to be done in setting up the system. This places constraints on the delivery: clearly, if it will take six months to carry out, the delivery cannot be made in less than that time. Further, if there is then a need to make the delivery as soon after that as possible, and the decision was taken to make it after (say) seven months, simple calculation shows that there is only one month available for the development (including testing) of applications functions. This may mean that a number of the most highly prioritized functions are excluded from the first delivery. Many project managers, in their desire to please the users, would ignore the obvious conclusion of impossibility and make a rash promise. But recognize the point that has already been made above — that to prove yourself unreliable at the start gives you an up-hill journey for a long way into the project. So recall Chapter 3's lesson of saying 'NO' and avoid folly. If you are going to get into trouble, do so through an unforeseeable circumstance, not for the want of being honest.

Starting with a list of all the functions to be provided by the system, the customer should derive a prioritized list. Given this, the developers should estimate the time, resources and cost of providing each function — or each of a chosen set, which should not merely be those with the highest priorities. Armed with this information, the relevant parties should attend the planning meeting. (The prioritization and planning processes are described in more detail in Chapter 12.)

Essentially, the planning of the first delivery should include the following activities:

1.     Identifying the essential system development to be carried out (as discussed above) and estimating the time and effort that it will require.

2.     Determining the date of the delivery. A number of factors may come into force in this regard. First, there is the political element: the customer may desire an early delivery, or a delivery on a particular date, in order to satisfy some business objective. This may be affected by the time to carry out the essential system development work. Then there is the time needed to develop one or more useful functions. Finally, there is a general desire not to keep the users waiting too long. Given that an ED project is likely to be long, it is reasonable to expect the first delivery after about six or nine months.

3.     Allocating functions to the first delivery is seldom a matter of simply choosing those of highest priority. As will be seen in more detail in Chapter 12, a number of factors intervene, such as:

       (a)     Some of the top-priority functions depend on other functions which have not yet been developed;

       (b)     The effort available does not allow more than one or two of the first five functions to be developed in the time, but, given that, there is then surplus effort which could be spent on developing one or more other small functions.

Thus, a balance must be struck so as to use the available effort efficiently while optimizing the effectiveness of the functions which are provided. Sometimes it is worth developing a function of relatively low priority because it would require only a small amount of effort and it could be put to use immediately. Similarly, it might be possible to identify a number of 'fast-track' functions which would offer immediate (even if not high-priority) value and which are quick to build.

At a planning meeting, the customer and users are likely to see things from one perspective and the developers from another. The project manager needs to maintain the balance by perceiving the advantages to the users of the developers' necessities, and vice versa. The good relationships which should be fostered throughout the project play a strong role in the planning meetings.

### 9.5.5 Use of Hardware

In many waterfall model projects, the developers are able to use the target system hardware as their development machine. The disadvantage of this is that when the system has been delivered, maintenance must be performed on the live system — or the system must be taken out of service for maintenance. As an alternative, development (and later maintenance) may be carried out on a machine which is not the target hardware, with the software transferred to the target hardware on delivery.

In ED the development machine cannot be forfeited when the first delivery is made. At that point, perhaps less than 10% of the applications software has been developed. So the provision of a development machine must be planned and budgeted for at the start of the project.

It is preferable for the development and target hardware and system software to be the same. Then, it may reasonably be expected that there will be no problems in 'porting' the software to its operational environment. In a big-bang project, resolving difficulties in porting the software to the target hardware often takes longer than expected and delays bringing the system into service, but at least they are dealt with before operation commences. This is so in ED at the first delivery. But after that, having to cope with such problems on an operational system, particularly if it needs to run for 24 hours per day, is a major inconvenience to the customer and users and can be the cause of bad feeling for a long time.

The case where the target system of an ED project is based on distributed or replicated hardware is also one for caution. Economy may be made by providing the users with a reduced system pending full functionality, with the developers having the use of one part of the target hardware (say one computer) on which to develop the applications software. The danger is that until the software is delivered, it has never been tested in an environment equivalent to its operational one. This suggests that its performance cannot have been fully validated. It would not be sensible to suggest that such an economy should never be made; the needs of and constraints on every project must be addressed in context. However, project and development managers should recognize the difficulties which ED imposes on the use of hardware in some cases. They should identify and assess the risks in their particular situations and advise the project board accordingly at an early stage.

## 9.6    PLANNING LATER DELIVERIES

### 9.6.1 The Second and Third Deliveries

If the time to the first delivery has had to be longer than the customer would have liked, and some highly-prioritized functions could not be delivered, it may be prudent to plan the second delivery for only a short time after the first (say, one month) and perhaps the third after a similar interval so as to provide an effective system. But then deliveries should settle into a regular pattern. While there is often a desire on the part of users to receive new functions and to have their proposed changes implemented quickly, there is also the need to deploy the development staff effectively and for them to work efficiently. The structure of the development organization needs to be designed for the long term, and this implies creating a flow of work through the team (as suggested in the previous chapter) rather than, say, having everyone writing code so as to maximize a certain delivery.

Planning of the second and third deliveries cannot wait for the completion of the first. It will be seen in the next chapter that the plan of a delivery must have been completed long before the previous delivery was made. The development of functions should be planned to minimize duplication of effort, so there needs to be a one-year rolling plan. This should include the bulk of the deliveries involved, with allowance for the addition of new requirements and rearranged priorities. Further, unforeseen changes crop up, and some changes proposed by the users also need to be implemented at short notice.

At the time of planning the first three deliveries, the number of requests for change following the first two cannot be predicted. It may be reasonable for the plans for the second delivery to be based almost entirely on the original specification, because changes based on the first delivery will take some time to be approved. But although the plans for the third delivery are drawn up even before the first is made, they should include a significant allowance for new requirements and changes. The temptation is to maximize the number of original functions included in it, and then, when important changes are approved, to try to include them as well. This leads to failed plans, broken promises, and a loss of the customer's and users' confidence. As development manager, be fair to yourself and leave some slack in early plans. It is of course a good idea to identify a number of functions which could be included in the delivery if only few changes are called for. Then you can astonish the customer and users by providing more than was promised. But do not overreach yourself and your staff.

### 9.6.2  The Effect of Validation on the Delivery Period

One factor which particularly affects the periodicity of deliveries is the time and effort required to test each new version of the system. As will be seen in Chapter 13, this can be considerable, and too short a periodicity increases the proportion of development time spent on validation, which cannot be carried out even partially in parallel with other development activities. If validation requires three weeks, it is clearly impossible to have a delivery period of less than three weeks. As the system grows, the validation time increases. It may in some projects be deemed acceptable to take short cuts, for example by revalidating only new or changed units of code, but even then the validation time can be substantial. In choosing a delivery periodicity, this factor should not be ignored.

A period of about three months between deliveries in a relatively large project is about as short a periodicity as should be aimed at. Less time than that is unlikely to be effective and puts too high a pressure on the developers. Indeed, as the project progresses, the pressure is likely to build up anyway. The users can be persuaded that a three-month interval is reasonable if the developers communicate effectively with them and if relationships are good. The onus is on the project and development managers to ensure that they are.

Then, the great test is to meet the delivery dates and be seen to be successful developers and reliable people. The most effective means of fostering good relationships are reliability, openness, and honesty.

### 9.6.3 The Planning Process

Once the first delivery has been made, development work may include:

- Functions as per the original specification;
- Change to what has already been delivered;
- New requirements due to a better understanding of what the system can offer and what is needed;
- Corrective maintenance.

As the second, third and fourth of these categories of work only arise once the system is in service, and as their content is increased with each delivery, there must be a re-planning process after every delivery. This includes a reassessment and re-prioritization of the development work and a review of the plans for the forthcoming deliveries. This process is described in Chapter 12.

Having determined what is to be included in a given delivery, it needs to be announced to the users. The customer representative is involved in the planing process and will already know, but the users need to be informed. There should be a set means of providing this information, as this not only increases the chance of most of the users receiving it but also is likely to generate interest.

We learned, and confirmed time after time, that communicating with users and keeping them informed of plans and progress is not only sensible but also essential. It is so easy for developers to become slaves to their deadlines and neglect to communicate with users. It is also easy to announce plans which do not materialize, and this antagonizes users and loses their confidence. The way to avoid neglecting the users is to impose discipline and formally arrange regular meetings. The way to obviate failure to fulfil plans is not to cease to announce plans, but to have a method of planning and managing development which maximizes the probability of fulfilling the plans. Having a configuration management system allowed us to plan and manage development effectively, and this is described in the next chapter.

### 9.6.4 Practical Issues at Delivery

Each project offers its own difficulties to the developers in making deliveries, and project and development managers need to identify the relevant issues and determine their solutions. Only then can they plan the installation of the new versions of the system with confidence. A few brief examples are offered here to indicate the sort of problem which might arise.

The first is the simple issue of downtime. If the users have come to rely on the system, even if it is not defined as needing to be 'non-stop', they are reluctant to lose it while the new version is being installed. Although they may have to lose it, it is not acceptable for the developers to demand the right to the easiest possible option. Negotiation is necessary.

This leads to the issue of the time of day when the delivery is made. If there is a genuine need for continuous system operation, it may have to be made between midnight and dawn. This then leads to the questions of whether the customer is represented on site during installation and whether users carry out acceptance testing. Arrangements must depend on the particular circumstances, including the nature of the system, the way in which previous deliveries have been conducted, and the relationship between the customer and users and the developers. I should mention, however, that good relationships during development can be destroyed by arrogant or unthoughtful behaviour by developers during delivery.

### 9.7    SUMMARY AND EXTRACTS

This chapter has given guidance on the planning which should be carried out in the early stages of an ED project. In particular, it has addressed the issues of specification, project planning, modelling the project, and delivery planning. The following extracts offer a sample of the points made in the chapter.

*   The accuracy of plans increases if they are reviewed at each stage of a project, when more information becomes available.

*   A specification of requirements is essential to the design of the system architecture, and the system architecture is essential to accurate planning, lower-level design and, thus, programming the software.

*   A broad specification (one with all or most of the requirements identified) is necessary for determining scope. A deep specification (one in which

the requirements are defined in detail) is necessary for determining the size and nature of the system.

- One of the most recurrent lessons which we have learned in software development is the importance of a good specification prior to the commencement of design or programming, but it is perhaps the lesson which we most consistently ignore.

- Even a well managed project which produces a well-engineered product may be perceived as a failure because it exceeds arbitrarily imposed time and budgetary limits ... Randomly imposed restrictions cause demoralization of development staff from the start, because the staff are persistently under stress to achieve what they know to be impossible.

- A rigorous adherence to plans can be as dangerous as having no plans, and an ED project manager needs to apply judgement in their use.

- A model may be a guide to what to do, but it should be quite clear what it is a model of, and it should not be employed outside its intended use.

- If a project's objectives change, it in effect becomes a new project ... New requirements, assumptions, constraints and risks may accompany the new objectives, and these should not be accepted by default, but rather assessed for their implications.

- Be reminded of the need not only to carry out the tasks necessary to setting the project on a sound course, but also to plan the time to do so.

- A thorough high-level design of the system needs to be prepared, verified against the system specification, and validated against the strategic objectives for the system.

- The short cut of a single designer rapidly drawing up a system architecture 'so that the more important business of detailed design and coding can be done' is likely to be a dangerous illusion.

- The design of all sub-systems should be sufficiently detailed prior to the first delivery for the identification and definition of dependencies and interfaces.

- We learned, and confirmed time after time, that communicating with users and keeping them informed of plans and progress is not only sensible but also essential.

- The way to obviate failure to fulfil plans is not to cease to announce plans, but to have a method of planning and managing development which maximizes the probability of fulfilling the plans.

# 10

# Software Configuration Management

## 10.1 THE ISSUES

Software configuration management concerns the control of software at all stages of its life cycle, from the coding of individual modules, through the integration of successively larger sub-sets of the system, to an operational system. Its purpose is to minimize errors, facilitate access to the software and the correction of errors, and ensure, among other things, that:

- Testing is methodical and thorough;
- Every unit of software, at whatever level of integration, is always traceable;
- Every version of every unit is identifiable;
- Storage of every unit is controlled;
- Access to every unit of software, at whatever level of integration, is facilitated;

- Changes are controlled;
- Systems are built only of the units and sub-systems which have been tested together;
- Documentation of all levels of development exists, is controlled, and is accurate and current.

In any development project, software configuration management is important. In an ED project it is doubly so, and it is more complex. With the first delivery, the system becomes operational. At the same time, development must continue, so the second delivery should already have been planned and its development commenced. It would not be feasible for the entire development team to work simultaneously on one delivery. As each delivery must go through the stages of planning, specification, design, module coding and testing, integration and testing, and system testing, the scheduling of deliveries could not be controlled unless a system of parallel working was in place. Having only one version of the system under development at any given time would lead to the following disadvantages:

- Staff skills could not be used optimally, and often not even efficiently;
- There would be a danger of too much new software being included in a delivery, and this would increase the difficulty and duration of debugging and the uncertainty of meeting delivery dates;
- If delivery N is not commenced until delivery N-1 has been delivered, adhering to the agreed delivery schedule becomes more difficult, and giving the customers and users early information on the content of a delivery becomes precarious.

So even from before the first delivery, there will always be more than one version of the system in existence at any given time, one live and one or more under development. As the composition of each delivery needs to be defined and its software identified from that of all others, it is important to design a method of configuration management and a staff organization which allow the concurrent development of more than one delivery, optimize the use of staff, and allow accurate planning of the content and dates of deliveries. Not only does keeping track of what is being done depend on it, but so does testing and the efficiency of development. According to the International Standards Organization, in its guidelines on quality in software [ISO 91], a configuration management system should:

- Identify uniquely the versions of each software item;

- Identify the versions of each software item which together constitute a specific version of a complete product;
- Identify the build status of software products which are in development or which have been delivered and installed;
- Control simultaneous updating of a given software item by more than one person;
- Provide coordination of the updating of multiple products in one or more locations as required;
- Identify and track all actions and changes resulting from a change request, from initiation through to release.

Our problem was not in finding a configuration management system, or in using it to control the first delivery (as in a waterfall model project), but rather in tailoring it and in designing the necessary procedures for controlling ED. The following descriptions are therefore concerned with these aspects rather than with the fundamentals of configuration management.

## 10.2  THE NEED FOR A DEVELOPMENT PROCEDURE

There are many configuration management tools to aid developers in controlling their software. However, like all software tools, they are hardware dependent—or, at least, system-software dependent. Thus, if you standardize on a tool before selecting your development system, it is likely that you will have to use your tool off-line. This has the disadvantage that it requires great discipline on the part of the developers to record every change to the software at the time it takes place, and it loses one of the great advantages of a configuration management tool—that it is an integral part of the development environment and thus provides both documentation and control of the development process.

It is therefore important for a configuration management system (CM system) to form the basis of the development environment and to provide a software library within which software at all stages of development is stored. It should provide configuration management facilities automatically, thus relieving the developers of the responsibility and the overhead of separate configuration management activities and avoiding the errors which are so likely to result from this. In other words, it should impose constraints on the developers and thereby guarantee control of the software.

For this, it is necessary to define the development process, step by step, and then to tailor the CM system to facilitate the process. A tool must support a method, and if you have not defined the method, a tool is more likely to be a hindrance than a help. It is rather like taking the time to define the problem to be solved and to prepare the requirements specification before commencing development: if this is not done, the project is likely to be ineffective. In the case of configuration management, the ideal would be to take the following steps, in order:

- Define the development procedure, including documentation standards;
- Document it;
- Ensure that all staff know and understand the procedure;
- Tailor the proprietary CM system to support the procedure;
- Define a procedure for the management and use of the CM system to ensure that it cannot be circumvented;
- Write standards in which the rules for the use of the CM system are embodied and train staff to understand them and adhere to them;
- Develop any software tools necessary for implementing the CM system and embody the rules in them.

At the top of the list is the working procedure for the development process. Everything else is built around this. However, while it would be nice for the development manager to devise an ideal method of working and then purchase a configuration management tool to support it, it is unlikely that the right tool would be found. It is more likely that the working procedure will depend, to some extent, on the capabilities of the support tool. Thus, the first step is to consider the hardware and system software which have been chosen for the development system, and to select a configuration management support tool which is compatible with them. Then the development procedure should be defined in the light of the capabilities of the chosen CM system, and the steps in the above list followed. It is an iterative process.

If the development procedure is ignored by the developers, software control becomes difficult, if not impossible, and considerable inefficiency is incurred. The project manager and development manager therefore need to ensure that the procedure is publicized, understood, universally accepted, and adhered to. They must provide training if necessary (particularly in large project teams). The CM system, procedures and rules which we evolved and which experience showed to work well are described in the next section.

## 10.3   THE CONFIGURATION MANAGEMENT SYSTEM

### 10.3.1   Fundamentals

A CM system which was compatible with the development system's hardware and system software was purchased to form the development environment and controlled library for the software. While the CM system would have been adequate for controlling a waterfall model development, it had clearly not been designed with ED in mind. It catered for any number of versions of any number of units of software, but it did not adequately cater for their integration into a number of different versions of the system, nor for many of the other aspects of ED control which are essential and which will be described below. We needed to tailor the CM system, design a procedure for its operation, and define rules for its management.

Essentially a CM system is a software library with mechanisms for uniquely identifying and documenting the software in it, constraints on the way in which the software is accessed and changed, and a means of facilitating the integration of the software units in building the system. We recognized that the goal of tailoring the CM system was to make it support our development process, so the first step was to design this. The following description reports on the way in which we tailored and used the CM system, but it also implicitly describes our development process.

We decided to allow for five concurrent versions of the system at various stages of development and we partitioned the software library so as to define five levels (see Figure 10.1) as follows:

- Level 1, the Test (T) level, at which module development and testing were carried out;
- Level 2, the Integration (I) level, at which the modules were integrated to form sub-systems and these, in turn, were integrated to form the system, with thorough testing taking place at each stage of integration;
- Level 3, the System (S) level, at which the system was validated;
- Level 4, the User (U) level, at which the system was made available for the customer to test prior to bringing it into service;
- Level 5, the Live (L) level, at which an exact replica of the in-service system was stored for examining problems and carrying out maintenance.

A working area was also provided at each level, partitioned from the system storage area so that changes made in the working area would only be integrated into the system intentionally and after thorough testing.

A CM system which caters for a number of versions of the system can easily be used to provide the levels defined above, simply by creating an appropriate means of numbering the units of software. That might be referred to as an 'implicit' system of control, with notional boundaries between the levels. We decided, however, to implement an 'explicit' control system by creating what appeared to the developers as physical boundaries between the levels. The transfer of a version from one level to the next required not only the usual configuration management controls but also a contract between the developer who wished to make the transfer and the manager who controlled the level to which the software was to be transferred. This apparently physical library structure turned out to be invaluable. It was easily understandable to developers who did not perceive their software as being identifiable only by a number, but who came to know exactly where their software was, why it was there, and what was required for it to gain transfer to the next level. The developers also understood clearly the need for the constraints which were

| Level | Working areas | CM system library | |
|-------|---------------|-------------------|--|
| 5 | | L level: copy of the live system for corrective maintenance | Maintenance |
| 4 | | U level: next delivery for customer's pre-release testing | Customer testing |
| 3 | | S level: integrated system being validated | Validation |
| 2 | | I level: integration and integration testing of software units | Development and verification |
| 1 | | T level: software units tested by their programmers | |

Figure 10.1 The software configuration management system structure

imposed on the control of their software, so they were almost invariably observant of the rules. This was a huge advantage; fewer breaches of the rules meant fewer instances of re-work and therefore greater efficiency.

Our design of the library thus made the CM system the basis of our development environment and integrated it with our development management. In this, it became both the primary development tool and a means of imposing discipline on the development process. Further software tools were then developed to move software units and systems upwards from one level to the next. Two rules were made, and the tools were designed to support them:

1.    No downward movement was allowed. This ensured that configuration records were not corrupted by indiscriminate changes and forced all changes to come from below. It should be noted, however, that changes made in the course of corrective maintenance needed to be reflected in the lower levels, and the mechanism for achieving this is described in Chapter 14.

2.    No skipping of levels was allowed. This ensured that no item of software advanced until it had passed all the appropriate tests.

## 10.3.2    Software Progress

Each level of the library possessed its own database which was tailored to the needs of storing and testing the software at that level. However, initial software development was carried out outside the library. Figure 10.2 shows that an individual programmer constructed a module of software to a specification, and tested it, using test specifications and test data previously prepared by the module's designer, until he was convinced of its quality. He then transferred it to the T level (the lowest level) of the library, where it was subject to spot checks by a member of the integration and test team (see Chapter 13). Test reports were prepared and copied to both the development manager and the programmer, and time spent by the latter on the re-work of faulty software units was recorded as a quality-related cost, as was the time taken for re-testing.

A unit of software did not have a standard, or even a maximum, length. Some years before, when using third generation languages (3GLs, e.g., COBOL, PASCAL), we attempted to limit the length of a module of software to 50 lines of code. Although this seemed good practice, and it minimized the number of logical errors within modules, it increased the number of interfaces and thus the complexity of integrated units. When we defined our CM system for ED, we were using 4GLs as well as 3GLs, and such a standard became impractical, as a program required far more lines of 4GL than 3GL code. With experience, we found it most practical to commission a programmer to build a function of the system (rather than merely the lowest level of module), while encouraging him to decompose this into as many modules as possible. Thus a programmer coded, compiled and tested small modules, and then integrated them into a function which he tested before introducing it into the T level of the library. On one particular project, the average length of transaction process functions written in a 4GL was about 2000 lines of code. 3GL functions averaged 300-400 lines of code, many being interface communication functions.

When the unit had been proven to conform to its specification at the T level, it was passed to the I level where it was integrated with other units of

| Level | Working areas | CM system library |
|-------|---------------|-------------------|
| 5 | | L level: copy of the live system for corrective maintenance |
| 4 | | U level: next delivery for customer's pre-release testing |
| 3 | | S level: integrated system being validated |
| 2 | | I level: integration and integration testing of software units |
| 1 | | T level: software units tested by their programmers |

Programmer's own test data    Software unit under development

**Figure 10.2** Initial development and testing done outside the main CM system library

software, written by the same programmer and others. The integration was carried out according to design plans, and each integrated sub-system was tested by the verification and validation team, using test specifications and test data prepared earlier by the designers. Again, test reports were compiled, filed under the reference of the delivery in preparation, and copied to the development manager and programmers. Again, re-work and re-testing at the T and I levels, due to programmer error, were recorded as quality-related costs.

At these two levels, where it was intended that most program errors should be detected and corrected, the modules and sub-systems were compiled with a debugger. This created an overhead of greater compilation time, but it provided the facility to step through the code, instruction by instruction, in search of an elusive bug. The debugger was seldom needed at the next three (system) levels, and was not used in the first instance. It was called into play, however, at the expense of considerable processor time, when a serious intermittent bug was present.

Successive levels of integration testing were carried out at the I level until, finally, the whole system for the delivery in preparation had been tested. This was then passed to the S level. Until now, tests had been designed to find bugs in the system and to verify that the software units conformed to their designs. Now, at the S level, validation tests were carried out to prove the functionality of the system as a whole and, thus, that the right system had been built. In other words, the product was not being tested for accuracy in the translation from a preceding stage of development, but for conformity with its original specification of requirements (see the V diagram of Figure 2.3 in Chapter 2).

When effectiveness had been proved, the system was moved to the U level where it was made available to the customer for pre-delivery testing, though the customer's staff did not always choose to avail themselves of the opportunity to carry it out (see Chapter 13 for a further discussion of this).

When it was time to prepare the system for delivery, it was passed from the U to the L level. Preparation time varied depending on the size of the system. On one project, where the system grew to almost a million lines of code, the time required was between one and two weeks. During this time, the code for the units of the system was generated, and the system was built and compiled (the method of storage of units was by original version plus successive changes — see Section 10.3.3). Then, each module used was recorded, with its version number and details of its links to other units, so that a complete configuration profile was created for the delivery. This was then documented and stored.

Next, a number of confidence tests were carried out to confirm functionality, check the new features of the system, and ensure that the system was that which had been validated at the S level. Finally, at the appointed date and time, the system was delivered to site. This was done via a direct link to each system in the field over which we not only delivered software but also applied controls to the system when this became necessary for maintenance.

### 10.3.3    Version Control and Storage

At each level of the library, there was a control program which recorded the arrival and presence of software units. For a new arrival, it recorded its name and gave it a version number; for a unit of the same name as one already encountered, it compared the new code with the old. If there were changes, it recorded them and allocated an updated number to the new version; if there were none, it did not change the version number. Having thus attended to identification, the control program organized the storage of the unit. What it actually stored were the original version and the successive changes made to it, each with its version number. This had the advantages that storage space was saved and previous versions were always readily obtainable, which was helpful when a new version caused serious problems. However, there was also a serious disadvantage which was that at each level the software needed to be both rebuilt and recompiled before it could be tested.

At the T and I levels, this was not too much of an overhead, but it certainly was at the S, U, and L levels, where the new version of the complete system was under consideration. A resulting further disadvantage was that, following system testing at the S level, the system was rebuilt twice more (at the U and L levels) before being delivered to site. A great deal of care therefore needed to be taken to ensure that the system built and compiled at the L level was exactly that which was tested at the S level. We thus developed a tool (a program) to check this. It made a record of the modules included in the S-level system, with their version numbers. It was then passed up with the system. At the L level, it was activated to test the newly built system against its own stored record, and it listed and printed out discrepancies. Of course, this program was stored in the same way as other modules and was not delivered to site as part of the system.

This method of storage was designed to save space. With a system as large as ours, it would not have been possible to store successive applications in their entirety. As shown above, the penalty was a time overhead. As the number of historic versions, and thus the number to be stored, increased, so did the time overhead, as each version could only be constructed from Version 1. We therefore decided to rationalize this by eliminating the earliest versions. Study of the pattern of our access to earlier versions led us to conclude that we were safe in retaining only four previous versions — which represented a year in time. Recreating the current system therefore involved applying a maximum of four sets of changes to the stored version, instead of a number which increased with time.

## 10.4 MAKING CHANGES

A bug may be detected in the software in any of the five levels of the library. While the policy should be for the defective module to be corrected at the lowest level of its existence (see Chapter 14 for expansion on this), there may be a need to access a module at any level, and sometimes to make an immediate correction. For example, if an application at the S level is faulty, but each of its component modules successfully passed their I- and T-level tests, it is necessary to find and correct the fault at the S level before re-introducing the changed modules at the T level, testing them, and passing them back up through the levels. Thus, it should be possible to access modules at all levels, via the working areas already mentioned and shown in Figure 10.1.

At the same time, however, there is the need to guard against two programmers making concurrent changes to a module (when the first new version to be replaced in the library would be overwritten by the second). The facility to avoid this is provided in most CM systems and takes the form of controlling access to the software. One means of doing so is by the use of two control commands, which we might call 'FETCH' and 'HOLD'.

The FETCH command might be defined to allow a copy of a software unit to be taken from the library but not replaced. A programmer could thus take a copy into a working area of storage, for example to test its integration with another unit or to experiment with a modification to it, but any changes made could not be introduced into the library.

The HOLD command might be defined to allow a copy of a unit to be taken from the library for the purpose of change and to hold the unit in the library frozen until it is returned (or until a time-out). When the unit is taken from the library, the system requires the programmer's name and password to be inserted. The system validates the programmer's right to make changes to the software and holds that unit, at that level, for that programmer. No one else is then able to HOLD the unit until the programmer has either replaced it, with the same or a changed version, or cancelled its HOLD status. A time-out may also be included to guard against an infinite delay in the event of the programmer going sick or failing to reset the unit's status for some other reason. In the event of a time-out, the return of the unit (changed or unchanged) must be precluded — to make a change, the programmer would need to apply another HOLD.

Changes to the system are thus possible under any circumstances, including emergencies, but they are always controlled. However, in controlling changes, attention must also be paid to the maintenance of historical documentation and the ease of access to earlier versions. Because a change may be made at any level, a simple version number which accompanies a software unit as it is passed up the levels would not guarantee uniqueness of change identification. For this reason, a unit does not take a version number with it as it goes from one level to another. Instead, it acquires a 'generation number' at each level. When it enters a level for the first time, it is allocated generation number 1, and each time it is changed at that level, either because of a change made at that level or because it is passed up from a lower level with a change, the generation number is incremented.

Thus, a software unit has a unique identity at each level. If its history is required, the generation numbers at each level, along with the dates and times of their creation, are printed out and assembled in chronological order.

## 10.5  OVERHEADS IN DELIVERIES

Although we always planned deliveries carefully, we did not at first make them at a regular frequency. We soon learned, however, that it is important to be regular, and experience led us to a three-month period. If we left it longer than this, the users thought that nothing was being done for them; if we tried to be more frequent, we forfeited efficiency because the overheads became too great.

The overheads took two forms. The first consisted of activities in the development environment, the second of activities on site. In development, there is a continuing need for modules and sub-systems to be built and tested (at the T and I levels), so these tasks should not be considered as overheads. However, this is not so at the system (S, U and L) levels.

If there is only ever going to be one delivery (as in the waterfall model — see Chapter 2), validation tests at the S level could be expected to be carried out only once. In ED they must be carried out for each delivery; moreover, they must be tailored to each delivery. Thus, for the first delivery, it must be clearly understood which aspects of the requirements specification are being met so that the test specifications can be designed to be thorough, but no more than appropriate. For subsequent deliveries, not only are there new tests, but many of the tests for the previous delivery will no longer be appropriate (because of changes to the functions being tested) and must be abandoned or replaced. As development proceeds, it is usually the case that the system grows with each delivery. Thus, if testing is to be thorough, its duration must increase, and after a few deliveries it may take several weeks, or even months. The nature, the thoroughness, and thus the duration of validation testing is therefore a prime consideration in the planning of the frequency of deliveries. It is not recommended that weekly, or even monthly, deliveries be attempted for a large system.

The overhead in S-level testing is high, and this is increased by the effort in any pre-delivery testing which the customer may chose to carry out at the U level. At the L level, there is the overhead of building and compiling the system for delivery to site, of creating the configuration profile, and carrying out confidence tests.

Then, on site, there is the overhead at the time of installing the new software. Even if this is only at one site, it may be non-trivial; if it is at several sites, even travelling time can be extensive. Although deliveries were made over links, we went to site to guide the users through the changes from the previous version, and on some occasions to train them in the use of new facilities.

In all cases, at any given site, normal operation must be ceased before the new version of the software can be loaded, so the timing and cost of system down-time must be considered. This may be in direct financial terms (if, for example, the system controls a production process), in terms of goodwill and market share (e.g., if the system provides a direct service to customers), in terms of a backlog of work (e.g., if the system provides a service to staff within the company), or in terms of risk (e.g., if the system carries out performance monitoring). In our case, the system was an essential tool to operational staff and was required 24 hours per day. Thus, not only did we have to minimize down-time, but we also had to carry out installation at times of least activity — such as in the foreday — and this added to the inconvenience and cost of deliveries.

When normal operation has been suspended, any databases on the system must be dumped to disk for security. This allows their reconstruction in the case of corruption during the testing or operation of the new version of the system. When the copies have been taken, the new software is loaded, and appropriate tests are carried out to ensure that the system is functioning correctly. These are not system tests, but confidence tests for the developers and comfort tests for the users. It is most important for the users to be comfortable with the new system, and although they should already know what to expect of it, the developers should spend time with them at each delivery — perhaps a considerable time — taking them through the changes, training them in the use of new screens, menus, and applications, and, generally, making sure that they understand and approve of the new system. With this type of attention, which helps them to understand the system, they are almost certain to approve of it, particularly if their questions of why certain hoped-for improvements weren't implemented are answered sympathetically.

Without such attention, even if understanding is easy to achieve, approval may be withheld. Never forget that while the customer representative is involved in system-level decisions, the users are not, and they should not be taken for granted; nor that a developer may have more contact with some users than the customer does; nor that public relations is part of everyone's job, including a developer's.

## 10.6  MANAGING THE CONFIGURATION MANAGEMENT SYSTEM

Each level of the CM system library should be the responsibility of a named manager. In our case, we allocated the responsibilities for the levels to the team leaders whose roles we considered to be most appropriate to them (the structure of the development team is discussed in Chapter 8 and shown in Figure 8.3). Thus, the L level was under the jurisdiction of the support team leader, the U and S levels were under the system test team leader, and the I and T levels under the design and coding team leader.

The main responsibilities at each level were maintaining the integrity of the software within the level and ensuring that it was not advanced to the next level until it had passed all appropriate tests and the manager of the next level was ready to receive it. Leaving the manager of a lower level to pass software up when it was ready rather than when the manager of the higher level was ready to receive it was found to be risky. In most cases, all went well, but when a problem occurred there was likely to be a disagreement over what had in fact been transferred. Our solution was to lay down a procedure which decreed the following:

1.      A transfer should only take place when the manager of the higher level is ready to receive the software;

2.      The manager of the lower level should document a list of all the units to be  transferred, with their version numbers, along with a statement (a guarantee) that they had been thoroughly and successfully tested according to the pre-designed test specification and test cases;

3.      The manager at the higher level should check the list, ensure that all, and only those, units which were expected (i.e., necessary for the delivery in question) were included, and then agree to accept the transfer and sign it off.

Under this procedure, any discrepancies between what was expected and what was offered could be resolved before the transfer was made. Reference to the plan for the delivery was almost invariably sufficient to reveal which units were missing or surplus. The content of units did not need to be checked at this stage. If a unit was present and of the correct version number, it was fair to assume that the changes made to it had been those specified. If they were not, responsibility was in any case clearly identified. We found that this procedure and the clearly defined management responsibility for the integrity of the levels, and the peer pressure which it implied, were sufficient to ensure harmonious, accurate, and timely transfer of the software up the levels.

## 10.7  CONCURRENT DEVELOPMENT

It was mentioned in Chapter 9 that a rolling one-year delivery plan was maintained. At four deliveries per year, this amounts to plans (of varying degrees of detail) for the next four deliveries. Given that some system functions are large and will require considerable development effort and time, it is certain that software modules of the next two, and perhaps the next three deliveries, will be under concurrent development.

At the T level, this does not pose a problem, for the modules are developed in isolation and are not obviously a part of any given version of the system. But it is preferable not to attempt to move the modules for a given delivery to the I level until its predecessor has been moved up to the S level. It would be possible to fool the system into accepting them by appropriate numbering, but this then places an onus on the I-level manager to make the necessary adjustments prior to each system being passed to the S level. 'Keep it simple' is an appropriate maxim in this case. To minimize confusion, the I-level manager should not accept any modules which are not defined as part of the next delivery.

## 10.8  OVERHEADS IN EFFORT

If a CM system is to be effective, development not based on it should not be tolerated. If all staff are to use the CM system, they need not only to be aware of it but also to understand it and the advantages which it offers them. They need to know how to use it and to have access to guidelines on it and to the procedures and rules to be observed in its use. They also need to know the management structure based around it.

In order to achieve these aims, a great deal of effort may need to be expended in writing the guidelines (or standards) on the use of the CM system, in documenting the procedures to be observed and the forms to be used in achieving signed-off transfers of software, and in training the staff in all aspects of the CM system. Frequently the effort involved in such activities is ignored or forgotten when project plans are prepared, with the result that when such tasks are carried out (not far into the project) it becomes clear that the plans will not (cannot) be met. This is failure on the part of the project manager to put a suitable project infrastructure in place (see Chapter 9), and it is hugely demoralizing to staff, who from the start are faced with a project which, as they see it, cannot be successful.

A remedy applied by many project managers is to deny the staff the necessary training on the grounds that there is not sufficient time and that, anyway, 'they don't need training for such simple procedures'. But in the absence of training, who instructs them in the simple procedures? They are only simple when you understand them. This remedy leads to staff resenting the fact that their training is denied and becoming indifferent to the procedures in question, and this leads to a decline in moral, efficiency and effectiveness. Saving on necessary training is false economy.

The need for developing project-specific standards and procedures, not only for a CM system but also for many other aspects of the project (such as programming), should be recognized from the outset. Further, such standards and procedures are not a luxury but a necessity. They should be considered as part of the project infrastructure, and if their development and implementation are left too late, problems are certain to ensue. The project manager must identify them and see that they are designed, developed and brought into effect at the earliest possible time.

## 10.1  SUMMARY AND EXTRACTS

This chapter has explained the importance of a configuration management (CM) system to evolutionary delivery projects. It described a CM system which resulted from experience and was tailored until it provided a sound environment for software development and the control of five concurrent versions of the system.

Not only are CM system rules required for achieving adequate control, but also management procedures for governing the system. These were explained.

If ED is to be successful, a project manager needs to introduce a CM system and the associated rules and procedures at the initiation stage of the project. The system described in this chapter provides a guide to what is necessary and a model on which he can build.

The following extracts from the text make some of the points of the chapter.

- A tool must support a method, and if you have not defined the method, a tool is more likely to be a hindrance than a help.

- A CM system is a software library with mechanisms for uniquely identifying and documenting the software in it, constraints on the way in which the software is accessed and changed, and a means of facilitating the integration of the software units in building the system.

- The transfer of a version from one level [of the CM system] to the next required not only the usual configuration management controls but also a contract between the developer who wished to make the transfer and the manager who controlled the level to which the software was to be transferred.

- Our design of the library made the CM system the basis of our development environment and integrated it with our development management. It became both the primary development tool and a means of imposing discipline on the development process.

- Time spent on the re-work of faulty software units was recorded as a quality-related cost, as was the time taken for re-testing.

- In ED they [validation tests] must be carried out for each delivery; moreover, they must be tailored to each delivery.

- The nature, the thoroughness, and thus the duration of validation testing is a prime consideration in the planning of the frequency of deliveries. It is not recommended that weekly, or even monthly, deliveries be attempted for a large system.

- While the customer representative is involved in system-level decisions, the users are not, and they should not be taken for granted.

- If a CM system is to be effective, development not based on it should not be tolerated. If all staff are to use it, they need to understand it and the advantages which it offers them.

- The need for developing project-specific standards and procedures, not only for a CM system but also for many other aspects of the project (such as programming), should be recognized from the outset.

# 11

# Change Control

## 11.1   THE ISSUES

The most significant advantage of ED is its offer of an early opportunity to recognize the need for change to a system and its requirements. If the offer is acted on, the perennial problem of building a system which does not meet its users' requirements can be minimized. Necessary for this, however, is a persistent and critical assessment of the efficiency and effectiveness of the functions already delivered and a careful control of the requests for changes to be made. Feedback from users can be expected to provide evidence of efficiency, but the managers who sponsor the project should assess the effectiveness of the delivered functions in meeting business objectives.

ED thus allows the potential for a system to keep pace with changes to its requirements. Early modification can be made to software already delivered, and, importantly, original requirements now obsolete can be cancelled, thus saving the effort and cost of their ineffective development.

The price for this advantage is the plethora of requests for change (RFCs) which may arise and have to be handled during the development of the system. They may have a variety of causes, among them:

- Operational changes;
- New or altered business objectives;
- Changed environmental conditions or working practices;
- Organizational changes;
- A desire by users for more efficient working;
- New or amended legislation or international agreements or standards relating to the system's functions or data;
- Errors in the original requirements;
- A newly defined strategic scope for the project;
- New ideas which seem good at the time.

If all RFCs were accepted for development, they would form a body of work unlikely to be completed, and if given high priority would preclude further work on the original specification. They therefore need to be controlled and vetted, taking into consideration their value to the users, their value to the business, their conformity to strategy, their priority, and the estimated effort, cost and elapsed time of their implementation.

While the great advantage of ED is that it allows and encourages early change, if this change is not controlled, it can have a disastrous effect on a project. Indeed, control of change is a significant component of the control of the project. In this chapter, the procedures which we developed for controlling RFCs are described. An adjunct to these procedures is the prioritization of work, and this is described in the next chapter.

## 11.2  REQUESTS FOR CHANGE

In discussions of the specification of requirements in Chapters 3 and 5, the inevitability of change was emphasized, and the previous section proposed that uncontrolled requests for change can lead to an uncontrolled project. To impose control on change, it is first necessary for the project and development managers to define what an RFC is and how it should be handled, and to publicize this to all participants in the project. We found that a satisfactory definition could not be limited to what an RFC is, but needed also to state clearly what it is not; and that defining how it should be handled meant documenting a formal procedure. Before stating a definition of an RFC, however, it is worth examining its possible sources, and also the sources of work which should not be defined as an RFC.

Once the first delivery has been made and brought into operation, there are four categories of work to be carried out on the software.

1.  Continuing development as per the original specification of requirements. When the specification is signed off early in a project, it is deemed to be the basis of design and validation of the system. Thus, in the absence of requests by the customer to make changes to it or to the software already delivered, all development is according to the original specification. This category of work, therefore, does not contribute to RFCs.

2.  Developing functions which are newly specified, having not been included in the original specification, or which were included but are now re-specified. Such work is the result of an RFC to the specification. This category of development work may arise in many ways, for example, as the result of users' feedback on deliveries already made, of changes in the customer's organization or operational practice or business objectives, or simply through making corrections to the specification.

3.  Making modifications to software already provided which conformed to its specification. Although the RFC results from experience with the software, it is in fact a change to the requirements on the system.

    End users are often not familiar with the original specification, and being frustrated by what they perceive to be a failure of the system to support them as they would now like, regard the discrepancy as a system fault. Overcoming this demands close liaison between the developers and the users.

    Modifications in this category may be large or small, but they frequently take the form of changes to screen lay-outs, data fields, or menus. An example of a change whose origin was beyond anyone's control was one which resulted from a new international standard. Having to adhere to the standard required a change to the size and format of a certain data field which was a part of numerous records on the system — and the changes had to be made by the internationally agreed date of implementation.

4.  Correcting delivered software which was shown not to conform to its

specification. This constitutes software maintenance, the process for which is described in Chapter 14, but it does not involve a change to the specification of requirements and so is not considered an RFC (this is important for accounting purposes).

Categories 2 and 3 result from changes either to the specification or the system as delivered so far. Category 1 does not involve change, and category 4 consists only of corrective amendment. A definition of a request for change is therefore based on categories 2 and 3 and states that 'A request for change (RFC) is a formal, documented request, authorized by the customer representative and the strategic representative, for a change to the specification of requirements on the system. The change may be to requirements not yet satisfied or to requirements already met on the system so far delivered; it may be to cancel stated requirements, or to add entirely new requirements. Maintenance changes to correct the system so as to meet its specification are not RFCs.'

## 11.3 A PROCEDURE FOR HANDLING REQUESTS FOR CHANGE

### 11.3.1 Preamble

It is not suggested that the procedure described here is the only one possible. However, the procedure is not merely a theoretical proposal but a method which was developed as the result of need and experience and which was used and found to be effective. It was developed evolutionarily over a period of time, until finally it seemed to cover all the aspects of change control we found to be important.

At the beginning of the project, there were in place a set of change control principles which had been devised for traditional big-bang delivery projects. While these formed a good basis to build on, they did not ensure the degree of change control essential to ED. Three deficiencies come to mind. The first is that they contained no mechanism for strategic control over proposed changes. The second is that if the effort or cost of the change was judged to be less than 10% of the estimated cost of the stage of the project, the change did not require the approval of the project board, and this led to the developers being swamped by requests for small changes which may not all have been essential and which together may have cost more than 10% of the stage budget. The third deficiency was that the only procedure for vetting RFCs before they were presented to the project board was the automatic approval of those thought to be insignificant in cost (less than 10% of the cost of the stage, as mentioned above). The project board, therefore, was forced to spend a great deal of time in discussion of the merits of RFCs. It was decided that the customer representative needed to carry out a greater degree of preparatory assessment. This initial change led to the evolution of new procedures which were formally documented. Their operation was monitored by the project board and improvements were incorporated iteratively.

It is recommended that in each project the project board should make a minuted decision to adopt and abide by clearly defined procedures which should then become a formal and integrated part of the project's documentation. Their use should be subject to quality assurance, for procedures alone do not make a good project; it is a culture in which their value is recognized and which drives their use which is the telling factor. But procedures are indispensable to consistency in achieving both efficiency and high standards. For managing change, there needs to be a formal procedure which includes vetting, documentation, quality assurance, and authorization. The procedure described below was proved by experience and could be tailored to meet differing needs.

### 11.3.2    Initial Documentation

It can be expected that in ED the most prolific source of RFCs will be the users of the delivered functions. With experience of the system, they discover that the specified requirements are not quite what were needed, for example: the information now required to execute a certain function is distributed over two screens and it would be better if it was all on one, that once you become familiar with the system the use of menus is inefficient, and so on. Most users' RFCs are perfectly reasonable, but in many projects there would be no remaining development effort to implement new functions if they were all to be implemented. It is therefore necessary to vet them and only implement those which are proven to be essential.

Early in our projects we were inclined to accept RFCs direct from users. As we found ourselves submerged in them, we began to be discerning over what we accepted. But that had two detrimental effects: our relationship with the users began to deteriorate because they saw us as denying them the changes which were important to them, and our overload did not subside as we were now spending a great deal of time in vetting the RFCs. We came to realize that the users' managers and the customer representative should be the ones to decide which changes should be implemented. We therefore insisted on their involvement.

As will be seen below, changes which are to be implemented by the developers need to be formally specified. But given that many if not most users' RFCs are unlikely to be accepted for implementation, it would be a waste of effort to prepare detailed specifications of all of them. Yet, if they are to be understood and vetted, they need to be documented. So the first stage of the RFC procedure (see Figure 11.1) is 'initial documentation'. This should identify:

- The system to which change is requested;
- The proposed change (and the specific requirements in the original specification, or previous RFCs, to be affected by it, if these are known);
- The reason for the change;
- The benefits of the change;
- Any requirements in the original specification, or any previous RFCs, not yet implemented, which would be obviated by the change (if these are known);
- The date by which the change is required (or preferred).

Initial RFC documentation is often made by users not accustomed to writing and, in some cases, not good at it. Yet, if the documentation is to be correctly interpreted and not cause added work through being ambiguous, too brief, or too casually written, it must conform to a minimum standard which should be defined within the project. Such a standard should include the document's source details, such as author, date, and version number.

The above refers to users' RFCs. Certain RFCs, such as those demanded by the business because of changes in business objectives, new product lines, international agreements, and legislation, will already carry strategic authority to proceed to development and would not require initial documentation and vetting. They would normally advance directly to the 'formal specification' stage of the procedure (see below and Figure 11.1).

### 11.3.3    Initial Vetting

Very often users' managers remain remote from projects. Neither are they the end users nor are they sufficiently senior to be the system's customer or even to be involved in the planning or authorization of the project. Unless the senior managers are careful to include them, they are in danger not only of being out of touch but also of feeling alienated. They are then reluctant to contribute to

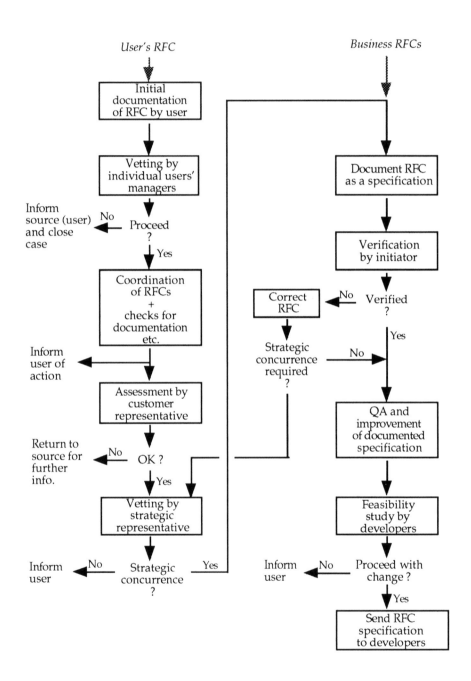

**Figure 11.1** A procedure for handling requests for change

the project: they are already busy and, as they see it, they have already been excluded, so why should they take gratuitous steps to be of assistance when they may not even be appreciated? This of course is a worst-case situation, but it is surprising how frequently it comes about.

Yet, it is the users' managers who are best placed to determine the users' needs, to support the users in fulfilling them, to vet the users' proposed changes to the system, and in doing so to coordinate them and eliminate redundancy; also to step back from the detail in which the users themselves are immersed and help the users to distinguish value-adding changes from those which are merely convenience-adding.

The next stage of the change control procedure should be the vetting of the users' RFCs, preferably by the users' managers. If users' managers are to carry out initial vetting the customer representative must involve them in the project, help them to understand what is required, and work with them to achieve it. Ideally, the manager of each user should vet that user's RFCs in the first instance and then pass them to the customer representative who has overall responsibility for the vetting and for coordinating the RFCs. Responsibilities at this stage should be to:

- Ensure that all RFCs passed on to the customer representative are value-adding;
- Ensure that no RFC is contrary to working practice or would undermine management's control or monitoring procedures;
- Eliminate RFCs which are trivial or unnecessary;
- Remove redundant RFCs;
- Combine RFCs which are complementary;
- Ensure that all RFCs passed on to the customer representative are documented according to the standard for initial documentation;
- Keep the users informed of what action is being taken and explain why RFCs have not been approved.

If this is to take place satisfactorily, the users' managers must understand the project, recognize its benefits to them, and feel a part of it. It should be the customer's organization which brings this about, but, as observed above, this does not always (or even often) occur. Thus, although the users' managers are not normally within the jurisdiction of the project, the project manager and development manager should be conscious of the need to attract their interest and acquire their participation from the start. The project manager should encourage the customer representative to include them in project planning and not to by-pass them in carrying out requirements capture with the end users. The development manager should not by-pass them in forming relationships with the users, holding meetings with them, or disseminating information to them.

### 11.3.4    Coordination

From users' managers, RFCs are submitted to the customer representative who has the task of:

- Recording and numbering them;
- Ensuring that all necessary information is present;
- Detecting and eliminating duplication;
- Ensuring coordination so that common themes or requirements are identified;
- Determining any repercussions of the RFCs, for example whether they would obviate the need for a previously specified requirement.

Some or all of these tasks may already have been carried out by the users' managers. Indeed, the customer representative may define the initial vetting so that it includes them. But the issue here is not so much who performs the task but who formally has responsibility for it. So the customer representative performs at least a quality assurance role. It would be normal for the customer representative to delegate the coordination and checking of the RFCs to the user coordinator, but the procedure should be such that the customer representative cannot shed the responsibility and is held liable for problems caused by flaws in the execution of the task.

When the user coordinator (or the customer representative) is unable to understand an RFC, or when there are recurrent problems, RFCs may be returned to their source for more complete information, or the user coordinator might visit users or their managers for discussion of the proposals or of the shortcomings.

### 11.3.5    Strategic Concurrence

When coordination is complete, the remaining RFCs are submitted to the strategic representative for approval.

The purpose of this is not to examine whether the proposed change is a good one, for the strategic representative may not have the detailed knowledge of the system or its application to make such a judgement. Rather, it is to ensure that it is within the business objectives for the system. The requirements in the original specification required strategic concurrence to show that they lay within the strategically determined scope of the project and that they contributed to the business' objectives, rather than merely meeting end users' requirements. If RFCs are not subjected to the same scrutiny, it would be possible for a project which commenced on a strategically approved path to be diverted into becoming an expensive irrelevancy.

Given that there are numerous changes during an ED project, the customer needs to recognize the need for strategic participation throughout the project, rather than merely at the beginning.

### 11.3.6    Formal Specification

RFCs should under no circumstances be communicated to the developers other than in documented form and with the appropriate authority. Further, they should be written with all the care associated with the original specification: experience suggests that more rework is carried out as the result of doing the wrong thing in the first place than of doing the right thing wrongly — in other words, as a result of ineffectiveness rather than inefficiency. If effectiveness is to be achieved, there must be a clear specification of what needs to be done, which is always the first principle of quality.

Time and effort are saved by not preparing specifications for RFCs until they have been approved and given strategic concurrence, but then it is important for them to be documented formally. Some believe that ED implies a 'let's-get-on-with-it' attitude and that formal documentation is a hindrance to 'getting things done quickly', but experience shows that a certain formality improves the chance of having to do something only once. Continuous 'doing' without pausing to plan what should be done incurs unrecognized inefficiency.

So the RFCs which have achieved strategic concurrence, including those which have their origins at business level, need formally to be specified (this implies formality in adhering to standards and does not imply the use of mathematical language).

Normally the responsibility for the authorship of RFC specifications rests with the user coordinator, but procedures could call for some or all of the work to be done by the users' managers or the users themselves. The author needs to take care with those attributes which are important to a specification —

correctness, completeness, consistency, traceability and non-ambiguity. Moreover, the specification should not be treated as an independent document but should be written as an adjunct to the original specification, with clear statements of how it relates to it, of which original requirements are to be changed, of which should be replaced, and of which otherwise affected.

### 11.3.7    Verification

On completion of an RFC specification, the user coordinator should seek its verification by its initiator — or initiators, if the RFC is a composite of a number of others. If the RFC has been changed intentionally since its initial proposal, perhaps by its initiator's manager, this will need to be explained to and discussed with the user who initiated it. But there are also occasions when the intention of the original proposal has been corrupted during the several stages since it was first drafted. Then the RFC should be redrafted and a decision taken on whether the alterations are such that the newly drafted RFC must be resubmitted for strategic concurrence.

### 11.3.8    Quality Assurance

Document quality is something that not many mangers seem to give time to. On the one hand they think it is not very important, and on the other that it is easy to achieve. Yet, whenever we inspect a document, even one previously inspected, we find numerous errors, at least some of which would have resulted in inefficiency or ineffectiveness later on in the project. In the case of a specification, a defect could have considerable effect if not detected until the software is in service. By the ten-to-one rule, if it would cost one unit of currency to repair a specification defect found at the specification stage, ten times more to fix if the defect is found at the design stage, a hundred times more if it is found at the software build stage, and a thousand times more at the operations stage. Given that the corrective action must always commence at the specification and work through to where the defect was found, this rule is not far from the truth.

It should therefore be a part of the change control procedure that all specifications are subjected to quality assurance, and I recommend the use of Fagan's Inspection [Fagan 76, Redmill 88]. As in all inspections, one of the inspectors should be an intended user of the document, which in this case implies a system designer. This provides an added viewpoint to the inspection, it gives the development team early warning of the proposed change, and it ensures that they can understand it.

Responsibility for achieving quality assurance should rest with the customer representative, though it is usual for the inspection to be arranged by the user coordinator. The inspection report should show that the document is acceptable before the customer representative submits the specification to the next stage of the process.

### 11.3.9   Feasibility Study

The RFC should now be sent by the customer representative to the development manager with a formal request to estimate the effort and cost necessary for implementing the change. Whereas this formal approach is essential for maintaining the integrity of the project and for budgeting and accounting, it should not be the first that the development team hears of the proposed change. As suggested in the previous section, one of the design team would almost invariably have inspected the document. Moreover, it would be exceptional for the development team not to have been consulted, in the early stages of the proposal, for their advice on the difficulty, cost, planning and wisdom of the change.

It might also be suggested that the feasibility study should be carried out before formal documentation, so that time is not wasted on documenting those RFCs which are not to be proceeded with. However, two things mitigate against this. The first is that the developers should have been consulted informally at an earlier stage, with the result that the vast majority of RFCs to get to this stage will in fact be implemented. The second is that it is not until the RFC is documented formally that it is fully specified in all its detail. Accurate estimates of the time, cost, difficulty and effects on the rest of the system of implementing it can only be made in the light of this.

So the developers carry out a feasibility study, whose manpower and cost are recorded for later accounting (for payment by the customer). Many proposed changes are trivial, and their studies are brief. Others require studies of considerable depth in order to estimate the effort needed for the change and to deduce any effects on other parts of the system and thus any resulting secondary work. In all cases, the feasibility study report to the customer representative should contain:

- The manpower required to make the change;
- The cost of this manpower;
- Any capital costs involved, for example, the upgrade or purchase of new hardware;
- An assessment of any changes in staff allocation or skills necessary to implement the change;
- The predicted impact of the change on other parts of the system, for example, on the response times of other functions;
- The impact of the change on external matters, such as the timing or content of outputs, or on work practices.

### 11.3.10  Decision on Whether to Proceed

With the above information, the customer representative is responsible for deciding whether to commission the change. The fact that an RFC has gone through the procedure described in this section means that the change is desirable. However, even now it may be turned down because of its cost, its impact on the system, the manpower or elapsed time necessary for implementing it, or because of any of these combined with the fact that it is of such low priority that it would never be likely to be implemented (although the latter reason should have been detected earlier).

In coming to a decision, the customer representative is briefed by the user coordinator who should have discussed the matter within the coordination team (see Chapter 8). Further, if there is doubt as to whether to approve the RFC, he would normally consult the manager of the user who submitted the request in the first instance. In the end, however, the customer representative must make the decision.

If the customer representative decides to cancel an RFC which originated for business rather than end-user reasons, it is usual to take the decision in consultation with the strategic representative, for there may be reasons for the proposed change of which the customer representative is not aware. In a few cases, when a change originates from, or would affect a senior customer, the customer council (see Chapter 8) may need to be involved in the decision.

When the decision to proceed has been taken, the customer representative should send the specification of an approved RFC, with a request to implement it, to the development manager, with a copy to the project manager. As the development team will be aware of all RFCs (having carried out feasibility studies on them) and may have made provision for some of them in appropriate delivery plans, they should also be advised of which RFCs have been cancelled. The RFC is also added to the customer representative's prioritization list (see the next chapter) so that its scheduling can be determined.

### 11.3.11  Remarks on Formality

The above procedure has laid some emphasis on formality. Observing formality can save time rather than waste it. But formality does not need to be staid. It is possible and desirable to maintain friendly and cooperative formality. In many parts of this book the importance of good human relationships is stressed. With the users and developers communicating regularly and harmoniously, it is usual for all RFCs to be discussed between them before the formal procedure is invoked, and for all parties to be aware of their progress. Formality does not imply, and should not be taken to imply, either inefficiency or a draconian regime. But it is often assumed to be based on inflexibility and, alas, it often turns out that way unless it is well managed, and unless it is applied within an appropriate culture. Management, therefore, needs to be aware of the type of culture which exists, to be alert to the type which is required, and to attend to the business of developing and nurturing it.

### 11.4  DOCUMENTATION OF REQUESTS FOR CHANGE

All RFCs submitted are recorded and their documentation retained in the project files. For those which are implemented, the ideal might seem to be for the regular production of a new version of the whole requirements specification to incorporate all RFCs to date. But this requires dedicated staff effort, which is in short supply in most projects. Our solution was to mark-up the original specification of requirements so that it contained references to the RFC specifications. Our procedure for doing this was for one member of the design and coding team to carry out the marking-up and another to check and sign it off. On the one hand, this was an expedient, but on the other, it carried a significant advantage which was that, in keeping the RFC specifications separate, we not only saved effort but also achieved an audit trail of changes which was much clearer than would have been possible had they been built into new versions of the original specification of requirements.

However, the system design documentation needs to be updated when each modification is made. Except for emergency maintenance modifications, no changes should be made to the software until its specification has been dealt with as described above and its redesign is complete. In our case, this was not only facilitated but also ensured by our staff organization. As described in Chapter 8, the development team was organized so that the flow of work was in accordance with good practice. As a single person was never charged with specifying or designing the software units which he was to build, he could never carry out these tasks out of sequence. Processes and procedures should always be identified and defined independently of staff organization, never to fit in with it. The organization may then be adjusted, if necessary, to facilitate the procedures. Too often, quality is forfeited by forcing working practices to conform to an obsolete and inappropriate organization.

## 11.5  THE USERS' VIEW

Those most directly affected by the efficiency and availability of a system are usually its on-line users. It is they who are inconvenienced by poorly formatted screens, slow response times, and long-winded menus, so it is they who submit the majority of the RFCs. Yet, from a business point of view, it is often their RFCs which are seen as being of lowest priority. Thus, many of the changes which users think of as being essential to their work are cancelled or delayed.

The problem is often not that the business view prevails, but that the users don't know of it. They are usually of lower rank and not involved in strategic decisions, so if they do not receive feedback on the RFCs which they have submitted, they may be forgiven for thinking that nothing is being done to help them. Further, if they are not advised of the procedures described in this chapter, they blame the developers for any delays.

Given this, we took a number of initiatives (also mentioned in other parts of this book) to create a good relationship with our users and to share information with them. When we explained such issues as how many RFCs we had to deal with, the concept of value to the business as well as to the end user, the need for and the methods of vetting RFCs, the prioritization process, and how we planned and developed deliveries, the users were immediately more supportive of us and keen to be patient over their own demands. Human beings are naturally reasonable; if approached sympathetically, with openness and honesty, they tend to respond likewise. But if their past experience is of a contrary approach, their previously conditioned response may prevail for a time. Change occurs when trust is developed.

In most companies that I have dealt with, users' managers do not adequately play the role of intermediaries between their staff and the project, nor between their staff and their business as a whole. If there was better communication between managers and staff, including interpretation and discussion of the business' objectives and the strategic decision-making process, and particularly including feedback on how, and how well, the staff's output contributes to the business' objectives, I am convinced that morale, efficiency and effectiveness would all improve. When staff are neglected, or not well informed, they feel demoralized and their work suffers. Sympathetic human contact is the first step in the remedy of this. Honest and open feedback is the next. Feedback is a fundamental engineering principle and the basis of control, and receiving early feedback on the operational system is the great advantage of ED. We can gain advantages by providing feedback to our staff. We need to be more concerned to do so, placing their work not only in the local context, but in the business context as well.

## 11.6  SUMMARY AND EXTRACTS

This chapter first defined 'requests for change' in terms of what they are and what they are not, and then presented a step-by-step procedure for handling them. Responsibilities for the various steps are clearly placed on the project participants defined in Chapter 8.

The described procedure was developed in evolutionary projects, improved in the light of experience, and found to work well. It could be tailored to form the basis for the control of change in other projects.

The following extracts do not describe the procedure, but they make some of the chapter's points.

- Feedback from users can provide evidence of efficiency, but the managers who sponsor the project should assess the effectiveness of the delivered functions in meeting business objectives.

- If change is not controlled, it can have a disastrous effect on a project.

- The project board should make a minuted decision to adopt and abide by clearly defined procedures which should then become a formal and integrated part of the project's documentation.

- If RFCs are not subjected to [strategic] scrutiny, it would be possible for a project which commenced on a strategically approved path to be diverted into becoming an expensive irrelevancy.

- The customer needs to recognize the need for strategic participation throughout the project.

- More rework is carried out as the result of doing the wrong thing in the first place than of doing the right thing wrongly.

- A certain formality improves the chance of having to do something only once. Continuous 'doing' without pausing to plan what should be done incurs unrecognized inefficiency.

- Whenever we inspect a document, even one previously inspected, we find numerous errors, at least some of which would have resulted in inefficiency or ineffectiveness later on in the project.

- It is usual for all RFCs to be discussed between them [users and developers] before the formal procedure is invoked, and for all parties to be aware of their progress.

- .Formality does not imply, and should not be taken to imply, either inefficiency or a draconian regime ... Management needs to be aware of the type of culture which exists, to be alert to the type which is required, and to attend to the business of developing and nurturing it.

- In keeping the RFC specifications separate [from the original specification], we not only saved effort but also achieved an audit trail of changes.

- Processes and procedures should always be defined independently of staff organization, never to fit in with it ... Too often, quality is forfeited by forcing working practices to conform to an obsolete and inappropriate organization.

- If there was better communication between managers and staff, including interpretation and discussion of the business' objectives ... and particularly including feedback on how, and how well, the staff's output contributes to the business' objectives, I am convinced that morale, efficiency and effectiveness would all improve.

# 12

# Prioritization of Work and Delivery Planning

## 12.1 THE ISSUES

The first delivery in an ED project is a turning print, the point at which the project meets a fork and sets out in two directions — further development on the one hand and operation and maintenance on the other. It is also the point at which the rate of change within the project increases significantly.

In providing customers with service earlier than otherwise, one of the purposes of ED is to invite review, with change if necessary, so that the specification of requirements, and thus the system, may continue to reflect the real needs of the customers, the users, and the business as a whole, rather than merely the requirements which were expressed in the specification. It is well known that users only begin to understand their needs when their system is delivered to them, and that they are then stimulated to seek changes to it, so change is almost certain to ensue. But not only the users but also 'the business' may seek change, and there may be many strategically inspired changes to the system. Actually, many of the business-originated requests for change (RFCs) would have arisen anyway; but with the system already being partially in service, communication of them is stimulated early rather than at the end of the project.

The first delivery is planned early in the project and must include the hardware and system software, the applications features essential to a basic system (for example, a man-machine interface, help modules, and certain menus), and some other functions (as discussed in Chapter 9) which are deemed to be of high priority. Similarly, the planning of the second delivery (and perhaps the third) is also at least partially based on the prioritization of the requirements in the original specification.

When the first delivery has been made, the prioritization process needs to become dynamic. The system becomes an entity which must change with each delivery, and each delivery invites change to the requirements on the system as a whole, both to those parts already in service and those to be developed. As RFCs arrive, re-prioritization is essential if the most needed functions or changes are to be implemented earliest, if non-value-adding requirements are to be identified and cancelled, if deliveries are to be planned effectively, and if development effort is to be optimized.

Moreover, it is important for the developers not to have the responsibility for prioritization. While they can contribute to the process, it should be those who desire the system's functionality who determine the relative importance of the functions.

Prioritization does not need to be a complex matter, and it is not difficult to devise a satisfactory procedure. However, too often it is not carried out, and when it is, it causes problems because the procedure is not formal and the wrong persons are involved. Experience leads to two recommendations: first, that re-prioritization should be carried out at the planning stage of each and every delivery, and second, that there should be a formal procedure for it. The subsequent sections in this chapter describe a procedure (see also Figure 12.1) which is designed to identify and involve the appropriate participants and define their roles and interactions.

Whereas prioritization is a principal part of the planning of a delivery, it will be seen that the delivery plan depends not only on the prioritized list of functions but also on the logistics of carrying out the intended development work.

## 12.2    PREPARING THE PRIORITIZATION LIST

### 12.2.1    Preamble

From the time of planning the first delivery (see Chapter 9), there exists a prioritized list of all functions which have been specified for development. What is discussed here is therefore the process of adding to and subtracting from this list and re-prioritizing its contents. The list as it exists must be the starting point of the process.

As the customers have commissioned the system and will use the functions provided by it, they have the prerogative, and indeed the responsibility, to prioritize their requirements. Within the project, this responsibility lies with the customer representative. At the same time, some requirements on the system are defined by the business for strategic reasons, so the strategic representative will also have the right to negotiate, or even to impose, priorities. There may also be work which the development manager needs to carry out, for example, to implement testing tools or quality assurance tools on the system, and there may be development work which the project manager wishes to be done, for example to introduce a measurement function as the basis for monitoring progress. Thus, these four parties are all necessarily involved in the prioritization process. It may be noticed that they comprise the project board (see Chapter 8), so their meeting to prioritize functions and to plan deliveries is in fact a project board meeting with a special purpose.

One possible means of prioritization would be to hold a single meeting of the four parties for the purpose. But the responsibilities for the process are not equally divided among them, and this is unlikely to be an effective use of time. A great deal of preparatory work should be done prior to such a meeting, particularly by the customer and strategic representatives. If the preparatory work has not been completed satisfactorily, debate at the meeting may far exceed decision, and decisions may be conditional on the agreement of others not present. A formal procedure is therefore necessary to ensure that the meeting, when held, is effective. The paragraphs below reflect a procedure which evolved over time and which experience showed to work well. As will be seen, effectiveness depends on the final meeting of the four participants covering both the prioritization and the delivery planning processes.

## 12.2.2    The First Draft of the New Prioritization List

As prioritization is intended to be for the benefit of the customer, it is the customer representative who should carry the responsibility for initiating the process. The end of the process is the prioritization and delivery planning meeting which should produce a new prioritized list which is agreed by all four parties. The beginning of the process is the preparation by the customer representative of the first draft of the new list.

The main source of amendments to the existing prioritization list usually consists of the users' RFCs which have been through the approval process and have been passed to the development manager for implementation. These are already in the possession of the customer representative. There is another source of changes on the customer's side of the project, and this consists of any RFCs initiated by the customer at a senior level. Such RFCs are the responsibility of the strategic representative and will be discussed in Section 12.2.3, but in some cases they may be included in the customer representative's preparations.

As described in the previous chapter, it is the user coordinator's responsibility to understand clearly each RFC so as to facilitate the vetting process. If there was any uncertainty about any of them, it should have been discussed with the RFC's initiator. Included with a description of an RFC is the required (or preferred) date of its implementation, but defining a date does not necessarily clarify the importance or urgency of the RFC, so a part of the user coordinator's discussion with the initiator should be to establish these issues. The information and understanding gained by the user coordinator is used not only in the vetting process but also in determining reasonable completion dates for the RFCs and establishing their relative priorities.

The user coordinator, on behalf of the customer representative, also needs to understand the implications of each RFC. In requesting a certain change, a user is not likely to be aware that it might obviate the need for some other requirement previously specified (either in the original specification or as an earlier RFC). But recognizing such implications is important, for it saves costs — whereas other changes may increase them. When it comes to the prioritization list, it is important not only to rearrange priorities but also to remove obsolete requirements from it.

So the user coordinator may carry out most of the re-prioritization work, but the customer representative should retain the responsibility for it. Based therefore on his own knowledge, on the briefing of the user coordinator, on the urgency of the functions to be developed, and on the manpower, cost, and

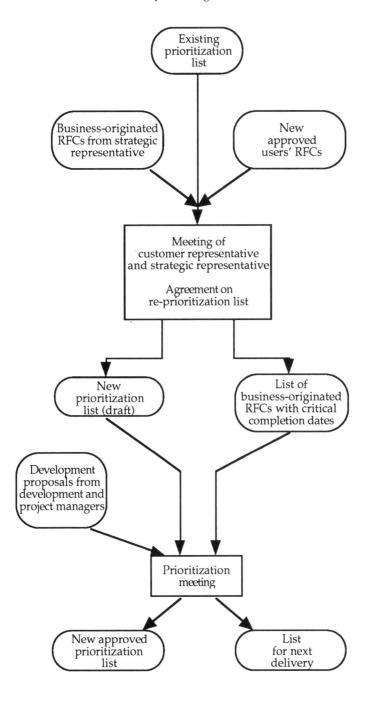

**Figure 12.1**  A prioritization procedure

elapsed time estimated for their implementation, the customer representative produces a new priority list, inserting new requirements, allocating new priorities to old functions, and removing superseded requirements.

On occasions, when there are RFCs from a number of customer domains, the customer representative may need to seek advice from one or more other senior managers, or even to convene a customer council meeting in order to determine relative priorities.

The result of the customer representative's efforts is a new draft prioritization list (see Figure 12.1). Given that the whole reprioritization process must be carried out after each delivery, the project manager should formalize the process and set deadlines for completion of each of its stages.

### 12.2.3   The Strategic Representative's Responsibility

The strategic representative on the project has two main tasks. The first is to ensure, during the RFC vetting process (see Chapter 11), that only strategically justifiable development is approved. The second is to see that all strategically important requirements are completed on time.

The strategic representative's responsibilities in the prioritization procedure are therefore to bring to the process any new RFCs introduced for strategic reasons and to ensure that they are scheduled for timely delivery. This role may be seen to consist of two parts. The first is to prioritize the strategically-based RFCs relative to other functions on the prioritization list; the second is to ensure the appropriate delivery scheduling of those RFCs with definitive completion dates.

Thus, the two functions of creating a prioritization list and scheduling the provision of the functions are linked, so it is important that at the end of the procedure the meeting of the four board members covers both prioritization and delivery planning (see Section 12.4 below).

Strategically-based RFCs would normally have been passed by the strategic representative to the customer representative for inclusion in his preparations. The customer representative and the strategic representative both represent the customer organization, so it is appropriate that they should agree their requirements and resolve any differences which they may have over priorities before coming to the prioritization and delivery planning meeting. Once the customer representative has proposed a new prioritization list, they should meet to discover and resolve any conflicts between them. It is not always possible to resolve all disagreements in advance of planning the deliveries because, as will be seen in Section 12.3, there are a number of reasons why a delivery cannot be composed simply of the functions of the highest priority. Given this uncertainty, there is sometimes a need for the strategic representative to maintain a separate list of changes (or new requirements) whose completion dates are critical and must not be compromised. Thus, the customer representative's list is of relative priorities and the strategic representative's requirement may be for absolute delivery dates. Both requirements need to be presented at the prioritization and delivery planning meeting.

It could reasonably be argued that what goes on between the customer and strategic representatives is in the customer's domain and should not be the concern of the project manager. But experience shows that their involvement in the reprioritization process may not occur unless the project manager has some say in it and unless there are clear definitions of what should happen, who should be involved, and when it should occur. In creating the project infrastructure (see Chapter 8), the project manager should be careful not only to define the procedures for the way in which prioritization (and other processes) are to be carried out, but also to obtain the agreement of all essential participants in them that they understand the procedures and agree to adhere to them. So the prioritization procedure needs to be defined and should include at least:

- The re-prioritization to be carried out by the customer representative;
- The prioritization list to be produced by the customer representative;
- The input to be made by the strategic representative;
- The meeting to be held between the customer and strategic representatives to agree the customer representative's prioritization list and to discuss the absolute requirements for RFCs on the strategic representative's list.

The strategic representative also needs to attend the prioritization and delivery planning meeting.

### 12.2.4    The Development Manager's Responsibility

The development manager provides a service to his customers. So under normal circumstances he should attempt to meet their demands rather than determine them. However, he has a  responsibility to make deliveries as effective as possible and to make development as efficient as possible. In discharging the latter responsibility, he may find it necessary to develop software support modules or tools — for example, to facilitate configuration management, or to monitor the performance of the system and test conformity with certain requirements such as the times of response.

Such additions to the development programme are not always welcomed by the customer. Although logic suggests their necessity, they are perceived to be outside the contract and as not properly occupying development effort or time. However their development cannot occupy zero time; nor can they in most cases be developed outside the project by others, for they usually need to be integrated with the system under development. Moreover, even if their development is not paid for by the customer, it distracts some effort from one or more other system functions and thus delay them. The development manager therefore needs carefully to prepare the case for their inclusion in the development schedule before putting it to the other project participants, particularly the customer representative. He should identify his needs, their importance, the reasons why they need to be developed within the project, the reasons why they have not been developed earlier, and, importantly, their value to the customer.

Such proposals for change should be agreed between the project manager and development manager prior to the prioritization and delivery planning meeting and included in the documentation sent to participants by the project manager in advance of the meeting.

It is also possible for the developers (particularly the designers) to detect the need for system features which have not been specified. For example, many customers omit security functions from their specifications and it may be the designers who detect the need for routines to restrict access to the system and monitor security. Such proposals from the developers should be submitted at any appropriate time by the development manager to the customer representative but should not be proposed at the prioritization and delivery planning meeting. If the proposal is accepted by the customer representative, it would need to be submitted back to the developers for an assessment of the effort and cost involved, according to the procedure described in the previous chapter. When this has been done and the RFC approved, the customer representative would determine the new function's priority and bring it to the prioritization and delivery planning meeting as part of his prioritization list.

### 12.2.5    The Project Manager's Responsibility

The project manager cannot assume that everything will go according to plan or procedure. One of his functions is to put monitoring and quality control procedures in place so as to ensure that nothing goes unchecked. Thus, three weeks before the prioritization and delivery planning meeting he should receive the new prioritized list from the customer representative, ensure that it has been approved by the strategic representative, and receive any proposals for software to support the development process from the development manager. In addition, the project manager may himself wish to specify software development in support of the project, for example, of a software module to collect or analyse project management data. In such a case, his support team would document the requirement and include it with the other documentation mentioned above.

When he (or his support team on his behalf) has ensured that there are no omissions or superfluous entries in the customer representative's list, the project manager dispatches all the above information to the other participants (the members of the project board), along with an invitation to the prioritization and delivery planning meeting, which should have been scheduled well in advance. Due to the difficulty of bringing more than two managers together at short notice, we had a policy of scheduling all regular meetings a year in advance, with confirmation of the next meeting and extension of the schedule occurring at each meeting.

### 12.2.6    The Meeting

As at other project meetings, it is normal for the project manager to chair the meeting, the objectives of which are to develop a new, agreed, prioritized list of functions to be developed and to plan the contents of subsequent deliveries. As shown in Figure 12.1, the inputs to the process are the customer representative's newly prioritized list, any proposals for development which the development and project managers might have, and the strategic representative's list of business-originated RFCs. The two purposes are integrated, and as it is seldom possible to separate them and treat them in series, they should be carried out in parallel. The outputs of the meeting are a new prioritization list and the plans for future deliveries.

### 12.2.7    Timing

The prioritization and delivery planning procedure needs to be carried out with the same periodicity as deliveries. With deliveries at three-monthly intervals, we re-prioritized four times per year, and we carried out the process soon after each delivery. By the time delivery N was made, the development of delivery N+1 was already well advanced, so with the exception of the most urgent business requirements, no changes could be made to it. Thus, after delivery N, we made a final plan for delivery N+2 (almost six months into the future), reviewed the plan for delivery N+3, and made an initial plan for delivery N+4. We thus maintained a rolling one-year plan.

## 12.3   PRIORITIZATION

The first issue is to confirm that the strategic representative concurs with the prioritization list submitted by the customer representative. Agreement should have been achieved between the two representatives prior to the meeting, but the chairman should still establish the situation. Often, if the prioritization list does not contain business-originated RFCs, the strategic representative does not have an interest in the relative priorities of users' RFCs, and concurrence is irrelevant. On the other hand, some users' changes may have buisness-level implications, in which case the strategic representative may wish to exert influence or even to impose authority.

The next issue is to accord priorities to the items introduced by the project manager and the development manager. As the customers consider the development to be for their benefit, it is not always easy to convince them that this 'extra' work and the resulting diversion of development staff would be to the benefit of the project. The attitude sometimes seems to be that if the development manager wants software routines to improve development efficiency, he can make them in his own time. The development manager may need to point out that with all his time being dedicated to the project, he has no time of his own. However, it is proper that he should demonstrate the benefits of the work before being allowed to expend effort other than on the specified requirements.

A lesson here is that development tools for testing, monitoring, or achieving efficiency should be a part of the project infrastructure and should be considered at the start of the project. They cannot always be purchased off-the-shelf, nor their need predicted in time to develop them at the start of the project, so the possibility of the need to develop or tailor them should be explained to the customer from the outset, and time and effort allowed for this in the development plans. When unforecast requirements arose, our experience was that with the project manager appointed to be the arbiter of disputes, there was always a fair resolution, even when the customer representative and the development manager were both adamant that their needs should be pre-eminent and immediate.

The result of the first part of the meeting is, therefore, a new, up-to-date, prioritized list of requirements for development, including any put forward by the project and development managers. This is then used during the second part of the meeting, and remains valid until prioritization is repeated.

## 12.4   DELIVERY PLANNING

Typically, the customer representative would like the functions to be delivered in precise order of priority, and as many as possible at each delivery. So would everyone else. But because this is almost never possible to arrange, the voice of the development manager carries a great deal of weight in this part of the meeting. It is therefore important that the development manager is sufficiently experienced and authoritative to present his view and to emphasise the error and disadvantages of promising too much.

Again the project manager is the final arbiter, but here decisions depend more on logistics, common sense and discretion. More compromise is necessary, for there are many reasons why the priority list is only the starting point and the guide to the delivery plan. In the main, these reasons centre around the use of development effort, typical examples, illustrated by three figures, being given in the sections below. Figure 12.2 shows the previous delivery plan, with A—M being the requirements scheduled to be developed. Figure 12.3 shows the customer representative's new proposed prioritization list, with suggestions for deliveries defined by dotted lines. Figure 12.4 shows how delivery N+2 changes from the proposal as the result of practical constraints.

### 12.4.1   Delivery Already in Development

As seen in Chapter 10, at least two, and usually three, deliveries are under development at any given time. Thus, it may be that a requirement of

Requirement

```
A
B
C                    Delivery N (just made)
─────────────────────────────────────────
D
E
F                    Delivery N+1 (next delivery)
─────────────────────────────────────────
G
H
I
J                    Delivery N+2 (planned)
─────────────────────────────────────────
K
L
M                    Delivery N+3 (planned)
─────────────────────────────────────────
```

**Figure 12.2** The previous delivery plan

previously high, but now diminished, priority is already near to completion. For example, this is the case with Requirement I (but not Requirement H). In the previous delivery plan (see Figure 12.2) Requirements I and H are both scheduled for delivery N+2. The customer representative's re-prioritization

Requirement

```
D
E
F                    Delivery N+1
- - - - - - - - - - - - - - - - - - - - - -
G
R
S
J
X                    Delivery N+2
─────────────────────────────────────────
K
I
Y
P                    Delivery N+3
─────────────────────────────────────────
T
H
M
O
```

**Figure 12.3** The new priority list

Requirement

```
         D
         E
         F                    Delivery N+1
      ─────────────────────────────────────
         G
         Z
         T
         M
         J
         I                    Delivery N+2
      ─────────────────────────────────────
         S
         X
         K
         R                    Delivery N+3
      ─────────────────────────────────────
```

**Figure 12.4**  The final decision on delivery N+2

reduces their urgency (see Figure 12.3), so it might be expected that they would be forced out of this delivery. However, as Requirement I is already integrated into the delivery, and its removal would incur extra effort, it is retained in the final plan for delivery N+2 — at the expense of Requirement X (see Figure 12.4). But the development of Requirement H is not yet far advanced, so it is relegated to a later delivery, commensurate with the customer representative's new prioritization list.

### 12.4.2    Changes To The Same Software Unit

If all foreseen changes to a given software unit can be made at the same time, a great deal of time and manpower can be saved, particularly in testing at all levels. The development manager therefore needs to be accurately briefed on which units would have to be modified, and which would be otherwise affected, during the implementation of RFCs or original requirements. For example, Figure 12.3 shows Requirement S as having a high enough priority to be included in delivery N+2. However, the development manager knows that while Requirement G is being implemented it would be sensible to implement Requirements T and M. They are of lower priority, but the effort to deal with them would be halved if they were combined with Requirement G. The meeting must then decide whether to implement Requirements G and S now and not save the effort and time (an improbable decision), to implement

Requirements G, T and M now and defer S, or to implement Requirement S now and defer G, T and M. As Requirement G is of higher priority than S, the second choice is likely (see Figure 12.4), given that the inclusion of Requirements T and M does not delay the delivery. It is important for the periodicity of deliveries to be maintained and for the actual dates to be met once they have been set. We aimed to schedule each delivery to within two weeks either side of three calender months from the previous one.

The above paragraph shows the complexity of planning deliveries. If thorough analyses of requirements and RFCs have not been carried out, the information necessary for delivery planning cannot be available. The project manager needs to ensure that all necessary preparation has been carried out, otherwise the prioritization meeting becomes a detailed analysis session rather than a decision-making process.

### 12.4.3   Large Jobs

There are times when the high manpower necessary for implementing a given requirement would preclude parallel work if it were needed within a short time. Except in the most urgent cases, this is to be avoided, as a balanced effort across a number of tasks is usually desirable, from both developers' and users' points of view. Thus, while Requirement R (see Figure 12.3) would seem a candidate for delivery N+2 because of its priority, if its demand on resources is such that it would be the only requirement provided in that delivery, it would be deferred (see Figure 12.4).

### 12.4.4   Dependencies

On occasions, the development, testing, or successful operation of one software unit depends on the existence and correct operation of another. The second unit may, for example, be a communications module, a man-machine interface facility, or a performance monitoring routine. If the second unit does not exist, its development has to be advanced, in spite of an apparently lower priority, if its dependent unit is to be implemented.

The documentation of RFCs should include references to any related requirements in the original specification as well as information on the impact of the proposed change on any other requirements or functions. The maintenance of such cross-references ensures that the extent, scope and impact of the work to be done are clearly defined. The project manager should verify that this information is available at the delivery planning meeting so that there is no uncertainty about the amount of work being accepted for a delivery.

### 12.4.5    Strategic Requirements

The strategic representative may need to insist on certain requirements being accorded high priorities. For example, Requirement Z is introduced at short notice into delivery N+2 for this reason (see Figure 12.4).

Experience shows that when changes are necessary for the business to meet essential target dates, for example for compliance with international standards or agreements, or to benefit the organization, everyone on the project is willing to cooperate entirely, provided that the requirements and the reasons are communicated. However, if there is reason to believe that the strategically-determined priority is artificially high, or the completion date unnecessarily stringent, compliance is not assured. For example, if a new function is to support a new product, and it is known that the product will be late, it may be felt that the original completion date for the function could be relaxed, to avoid a stressful rush or to make way for a function which would be more immediately useful. Similarly, it is not unknown for senior managers to impose unreasonable (and, from a buisness point of view, unnecessary) deadlines on developers because the completion of a certain function by a certain time would bring them (the senior manager) a bonus. In my experience, developers resent this not because of the reason (why shouldn't the manager look out for himself?) but for the deceipt which often veils the reasons given for the deadline.

So the strategic representative is likely to get his way if he is seen to be honest and reasonable but to encounter opposition if not. If disagreement is expected, the project manager should seek a resolution with the customer's senior management before the meeting. Otherwise, on rare occasions, he might take an action point at the meeting to resolve the matter subsequently.

### 12.4.6    Form of the Delivery Plan

All requirements to be developed within a delivery will already have been specified in detail, either in the original specification or as an RFC. It would therefore be ineffective for the delivery plan to include their full specifications. It is therefore sufficient for the delivery plan document to identify each by its title and number, with reference to the document in which it is fully specified. Quality assurance of the delivery plan should include checks to ensure that each requirement is uniquely and unambiguously identified, that its scope and boundary are clearly defined, and that its cross-references are correct.

## 12.5  SUMMARY AND EXTRACTS

To gain the greatest benefits from evolutionary delivery, the most highly prioritized functions should be delivered earliest. So, with requirements changing throughout the project, re-prioritization at the same frequency as deliveries is a necessity. In addition, however, there are several practical issues which place constraints on the contents of deliveries and force compromises on their planning. The issues of re-prioritization and delivery planning are therefore continuous and mutually-influencing processes.

This chapter has presented a procedure for regular re-prioritization and delivery planning — one which was arrived at iteratively in practice and which worked well. It identifies those who should be involved and defines their responsibilities. From it, project managers could design detailed procedures to suit the particular circumstances of their own projects.

The following extracts make some of the chapter's points, though they do not describe the procedure.

- Prioritization does not need to be a complex matter ... However, too often it is not carried out, and when it is, it causes problems because the procedure is not formal and the wrong persons are involved.
- Experience leads to two recommendations: first, that re-prioritization should be carried out at the planning stage of each and every delivery, and second, that there should be a formal procedure for it.
- It is important not only to rearrange priorities but also to remove obsolete requirements.
- Due to the difficulty of bringing more than two managers together at short notice, we had a policy of scheduling all regular meetings a year in advance, with confirmation of the next meeting and extension of the schedule occurring at each meeting.
- The prioritization and delivery planning procedure needs to be carried

out with the same periodicity as deliveries. With deliveries at three-monthly intervals, we re-prioritized four times per year, and ... maintained a rolling one-year plan.

- Development tools for testing, monitoring, or achieving efficiency should be a part of the project infrastructure and should be considered at the start of the project.

# 13

# Testing

## 13.1 THE ISSUES

Testing is a touchy subject. Most developers are not trained in it and do not care to spend their time on it. Many find it boring, do not appreciate its importance, and prefer to think their job complete when a program has been written, at which time testing is merely to provide confirmation of good work.

Managers do not often attempt to shift the developers' attitude in favour of testing. Have you ever come across a conversation like the following?

Manager: 'All this testing takes a lot of time. What do you want to do it for?'

Developer: 'To find the bugs.'

Manager: 'How do you know there are any bugs?'

Developer: 'I don't.'

Manager: 'Then what do you want to do all this testing for?'

The manager has the last word. He saves money by not sending the developer for training in testing and he saves time on the earlier stages of the project by minimizing testing. But then he incurs huge cost and time penalties on account of the greater difficulty in finding and fixing bugs later in the life cycle: during validation, or acceptance testing, or when the system is already in service. The ten-to-one rule applies: it states that a fault introduced into the system in stage N of the life cycle costs ten times more to eradicate at stage N+1 than it would have done at stage N, 100 times more at stage N+2, etc. Of course, the figure of ten is not definitive; it might be eight in some cases, twelve in others, or even five in some; but the principle stands: it is more difficult and more costly to repair a fault the longer you leave it (or the longer it remains undetected).

Testing is an integral part of software development. It needs to be an integral part of programming. Then, completing a program becomes an iterative process of programming, testing, correcting, testing, and signing off the program as having met predetermined test criteria. To achieve this mode of working, and, indeed, the attitude necessary for it, programming needs to be defined, in education, as an integrated coding and testing process, and taught as such. Software engineering and programming courses should include instruction in testing theory and techniques, and success in team and individual student projects should require evidence of their use. Only then will there be a change from the culture of perceiving testing as an 'extra' to perceiving it as an integral and essential part not only of development but also of programming.

Because of having to change not one but several versions of the system, late corrections in ED are even more time-consuming and expensive than in waterfall model development. It is therefore cost-effective to achieve correctness at the earliest possible stage. This implies good development practice and thorough testing at the T level (see Figure 10.1 in Chapter 10).

The methods we adopted for testing are discussed in Section 13.3 and 13.4, but first, an enquiry is made into what we should seek to achieve from testing.

## 13.2 TESTING AND CONFIDENCE

Testing can prove imperfection by finding a single fault, but it cannot prove perfection. So what is it for? It is intended to give confidence. It is a risk-management activity. If this statement seems odd, consider this: if there were no risk attached to getting something wrong, there would be no point in testing it. One could simply bring it into service, correct errors as they are revealed, and lose nothing by doing so. But the greater the risk attached to getting it wrong, the more important it is to get it right and the more carefully one would test it.

An example of recognising testing as a risk-management activity is the practice of 'beta releases'. In this, the customer perceives an advantage in gaining early experience of a product and accepts that it may not yet have been thoroughly tested. The supplier believes that he will lose nothing if bugs in the software cause some problems to the customer and that he will gain a great deal if the customer puts the software to the test and reports any bugs to him. A difficulty may arise if the customer experiences more than a reasonable amount of trouble, so the supplier must carry out sufficient testing in advance of the beta delivery to avoid losing customers. How much testing is sufficient? This is a matter for the supplier to decide in each case. In effect, what he is doing in making the decision is carrying out risk management.

As the value of having and using a product increases, so does the cost of not having and using it, perhaps because of a fault. Moreover, the greater the cost of making changes to the software, the greater the value of getting it right in the first place. Thus, for a large system, of value to its users and provided by ED, there is likely to be significant advantage in carrying out thorough testing of each delivery and attempting to ensure that it is 'right'.

So we want to carry out thorough testing. But testing is expensive. Given that we can never prove perfection, we want to avoid testing beyond the point of significantly diminished returns — that is, we want testing to be cost-effective. So we need to understand the cost of there being a bug in a delivered system — the cost to the customer and the cost to the maintainers. In other words, what are the risks?

But in most projects, ED and otherwise, the problem is not that the risks are difficult to identify, but that no one has endeavoured to identify and assess them. As a consequence, there is usually no risk-based determinant of what should be tested or how much testing should be carried out. The result is that many organizations over-test — that is, they attempt to test exhaustively. In other words, they try to acquire 100% confidence of there being no errors in the system, rather than a level of confidence commensurate with the risk of loss of the system. Naturally they fail, for it is impossible to test any but a very simple software system fully in a finite time.

Testing is intended to give confidence. It should not be mistaken for a means of proving that there are no remaining faults, for it cannot do this. If testing reveals no faults, it is wiser to conclude that the tests were inadequate than that the system is fault-free. Of course, the tests may have been adequate to provide the desired level of confidence, given that this is known.

On the other hand, the derived level of confidence could be spurious. Suppose that the tests were poorly designed? They may, for example, be trivial but repetitive. Then, a large array of tests, perhaps executed over a long period, could only provide confidence in the sub-set of the software which had in fact been tested — actually, over-tested. But, in ignorance, the confidence might be extended to the whole system. This would be costly, both in the testing itself and in the later consequences of maintenance. So we ask, what is the minimum level of testing required in order to secure the desired level of confidence? And we come full circle, for this question cannot be answered unless we understand two things. First, we need to understand the consequences of errors being in the system — and this has traditionally not been done in software development. Second, we need to understand how to test (otherwise we run into the problems mentioned above, for example, of over-testing in ignorance) — and typically software testers have neither expert knowledge nor broad experience of testing.

## 13.3   TESTING IN EVOLUTIONARY DELIVERY

Testing takes a great deal of the developers' time in ED. It is carried out at every level (it is the customer's responsibility at the U level) of the process (see Figure 10.1 in Chapter 10), and when something is found to be erroneous and has to be corrected, it is returned to the lowest (T) level, corrected there, and re-tested. It is therefore crucial for testing to be carried out both efficiently and effectively. Every test must count.

If the temptation to economize on testing is unwise in other forms of development, it is positively dangerous in ED. Yet the attitude of, 'why spend much on it now if we are likely to change it anyway,' is not unlikely. But beware: if you are contemplating minimizing testing, be sure that you understand the risks which you think you are reducing and, equally importantly, those which you are taking.

### 13.3.1   The T Level

It is said that modules of code should be tested by an independent verification and validation team — independent, that is, of the programmers. The argument is that if a programmer errs in interpreting the design and thus builds a bug into the code, he will test for the bug as though it were a correct feature. In spite of this exhortation, very few organizations practise independent testing.

In our projects, we did not provide independence in the testing of the lowest level of software modules (though we did at the integration levels). Yet, we achieved high-quality software. We attributed this principally to five factors:

- Training the programmers in testing;
- Giving the programmers clearly defined responsibility for the quality of their code;
- A system of 'mini contracts' between staff at the different levels of the CM system (so that T-level programmers were 'contracted' suppliers to the I-level team) and checks on the delivery times and the quality of products through peer pressure;
- The facility for independent random checking (or auditing) of software at the T level;
- The recording of re-work and re-testing as quality-related costs.

The first of the above points is self-explanatory. The second is only what most of us would agree is altogether proper: that each person should be responsible for (and should take a pride in) his work. Yet, it is not uncommon to find programmers not being expected to accept responsibility for either the quality of their work or the timing of its delivery. My experience is that while a lax environment (which reduces quality) seems to be easily accepted by programmers (and other staff), higher expectations are appreciated even more — and what is more, they are responded to.

The third point was simply that we created customer-supplier relationships between each other. The awareness that others are dependent on you and the peer pressure which this generates tend to provide an incentive both to do the work and to take a pride in it. You know that your product will be used and that you will receive feedback about it.

The fourth point refers to the random checking of code. Our system was this. Programmers wrote their code in the T level working area, which was in fact outside the control of the CM system (see Figure 10.2 in Chapter 10). They were responsible for implementing the designs of the module designers and verifying a faithful translation from design to code. When they had satisfied themselves that this had been achieved, they transferred their code into the T level (proper) of the CM system and were responsible for carrying out pre-designed verification tests on it. As a form of independent quality assurance, spot checks could be carried out, usually by someone from the integration and test team, using the test cases for the module in question created by its designers.

The final point in the bullet list above refers to an *understanding* by the developers of the principles of quality. Too often management talks *about* quality but fails to take the trouble to train staff and follow the training with support. More importantly, they even more often fail to provide leadership in quality by demonstrating a concern for it in their behaviour. Training, support and leadership enable the staff not only to recognize the words but also, and more importantly, to understand the principles and how they relate to *them* in *this* situation. Our staff understood the principles of quality. A great deal of emphasis was placed on 'getting it right' at the T level. The programmers understood why this had to be so, and they had no doubt about the seriousness of their responsibility. Testing is expensive, and re-testing as a result of getting it wrong in the first place was recognized by the programmers as a quality-related cost.

When it was time to pass a module of completed code to the I level, the programmer concerned notified the appropriate person that it was ready for delivery. It was only passed up when the recipient agreed to accept it, and at that time the programmer signed it off as a quality product. Signing off a product has a marvellous effect of focusing the mind on the guarantee which is implied in the signature and the responsibilities which lie behind it. Their signatures implied that they had good reason to believe their modules to be of the required quality, that they accepted responsibility for this belief, and that they recognised that any rework would be recorded as quality-related costs against them.

## 13.3.2 The I Level

When software arrives at the I level, it does so as disparate modules coded at the T level by different programmers. At the I level, these are integrated, and the interfaces between them and the larger (integrated) units tested. If all modules were integrated at the same time, the likelihood of the product not working satisfactorily and the difficulty of diagnosing the problem would both be increased. The system therefore needs to be integrated in stages, with the modules being brought together in an order defined (ideally) by a logical incremental increase in the functionality of the system.

It takes time to integrate the modules of a system and to test thoroughly the functionality of the larger and larger units created in the process. If the delivery is to be on schedule, the modules must be delivered from the T level on time and their development schedules must be based on the integration plan. Planning at the I level is the basis of the development of each delivery.

It would be convenient to draw up the integration plan for a delivery from a knowledge only of the functionality of the modules. But this would be impractical. A module which the integration team would like to introduce into the process at an early stage may be the one which will take longest to develop. So the plan needs to be drawn up with reference not only to the ideal order of integration but also to the estimated development effort required for each module in the delivery. In planning, there should be discussion between the two teams involved, and there may need to be compromises on both sides, with the integration and test team accepting a non-optimum order of delivery and the programming team juggling its staff so as to put extra effort onto some modules to accelerate their development. In our case, the decision-making process was eased by the fact that the design and coding team leader was responsible for both the T and I levels.

The integration plan should not be drawn up in isolation, but in the knowledge of the requirements of the higher levels of the CM system: the anticipated time for validation of the system at the S level (based on the experience of previous deliveries), the arrangements with the customer for pre-delivery testing at the U level, and the known time to build the system and carry out confidence tests at the L level. Only with such integrated planning, and then with the programmers' commitment to the integration plan, can the developers be confident of making their deliveries on time — and, as has already been observed, it is crucial to confidence and morale for them to do so.

As mentioned in Chapter 10, a debugger was used in testing at both the T and I levels. This incurred an overhead in compilation time, but it provided the facility for stepping through the software instruction by instruction in the event of an elusive bug. Given that these two levels (and particularly the T level) were the only ones at which detailed 'destructive' testing (i.e., attempting to break the system) could be carried out, it was worth doing it well.

### 13.3.3   The S Level

At this level, validation is carried out to prove functionality rather than primarily to find bugs. Naturally, however, no bug found should be ignored.

The point worth remarking is the effect that the time taken for system validation has on ED. At the first delivery, it is likely that only a small percentage of the total software is delivered, so validation may take a relatively short time. But as the system grows, the time taken increases rapidly. There is the time taken, not only to carry out the testing, but also to design the tests. Nor can tests designed for previous deliveries be relied on to be reusable. As pointed out in Chapter 11, the work on deliveries after the first is of four types, of which changes to previously delivered sub-systems or modules often predominates. So the previously designed tests must also be changed.

Our systems grew rapidly, and they soon required six weeks for validation. At this stage, many organizations may consider whether it is acceptable to reduce validation by leaving unchanged parts of the system untested, on the assumption that the changes will not have affected them. In very critical systems this is a dangerous assumption. But again we return to an assessment of the risks. If a residual bug could cause serious loss of life, or the collapse of a business, full validation may be unavoidable. If on the other hand the risk is not so high, it may be feasible to trade off the chance of failure against a saving in validation time. A rule cannot be laid down for the solving of the problem; the important thing is to be aware of the need for decision.

One thing is certain, however, and that is that talk of a delivery per week, or even per month, needs to be taken with a pinch of salt. If validation takes six weeks, it is not possible to have a delivery period of less than that time. Moreover, if the period is made to be exactly equal to the validation time, the implied commitment is that a number of developers must work permanently on validation, and this will almost certainly not be the most effective way to employ them. A balance must be struck between satisfying the customer and users with frequent deliveries and using the development staff effectively.

### 13.3.4   The U Level

This level provided the customer (and the users) with the opportunity of carrying out pre-delivery tests on the system. What we found was that after the first delivery, on which they carried out acceptance testing, the users considered their involvement in testing to have ended and they did not like the idea of having to make further time for it. The attitude derives from waterfall model projects, in which the system is delivered in one big bang and acceptance is a one-off process.

The advantage of not having the customer carry out tests, whether they are called 'acceptance tests' or 'pre-delivery tests', is that it saves the developers' time. The disadvantage is that the developers do not obtain the benefit of the customer's or users' viewpoints in designing the tests. This is a significant drawback, for the developers often cannot envisage how the users will employ the system or what they will expect of it, so they fail to test it in many modes of operation, some of them remarkably obvious (once they have been pointed out).

Once we discovered the value of the users' involvement in designing tests, we strove to ensure that they were always a part of the team which did this. Good relationships with the customer representative and the user coordinator enabled this participation, often in spite of opposition from users' local managers who argued that their staff were too busy with essential work to be diverted to 'doing the developers' work for them'.

The U level was therefore used less than the other levels, but we always maintained it to provide what we considered a necessary customer facility. Of course, the customer has the choice of whether to trust the developers and not test the system, or to apply full and rigorous tests to every delivery, or to take some intermediate course. But beware of seeing the customer or the users as a threat, or of hoping for them to stay out of the way. Their testing is of value to the development team and they should be encouraged to participate.

### 13.3.5    The L Level

The purpose of the L level was described in Chapter 10. The tests carried out there took the form of 'confidence checks' that the system to be delivered to site and brought into service was that which had been configured and validated at the S level. Other tests carried out at the L level were for the purpose of maintenance, which is described in the next chapter.

### 13.4    ACHIEVING CONFIDENCE THROUGH TESTING

The way in which we used the configuration management system for carrying out the testing process was described in Section 13.3. The remaining question is how did we achieve confidence in our software while making testing cost-effective.

Inadequate testing leaves errors which will result in the costs of later loss of service, aggravation to the customer and users, and correction. On the other hand, too much testing costs a great deal, while still not guaranteeing freedom from errors. Can the right balance be struck? Can we minimize the risk of future costs while not spending excessively now? A fact which warns us never to be cocksure is that the dependability (reliability, safety, etc.) of a system is less a function of the number of faults found or the number remaining in the system than on the consequences of the residual faults. A single fault can lead to a critical failure, or to complex and expensive correction of the system. Our confidence in testing should always be tempered by this fact. Thus, in critical systems, reliance is not placed entirely on fault avoidance (good development practice) and fault removal (testing and correction), but also on the inclusion of fault tolerance (redundancy in design and recovery procedures) which can add considerably to the cost of the system.

Yet, there are a number of points which, if observed, can justify increased confidence in the testing of the system. The following list of eleven testing principles does not purport to be exhaustive, but it consists of those points which we found to be most important, both in achieving effective testing and in giving us confidence in the quality of the tested software.

First, design software with testing in mind. For example:

- Keep modules simple and short;
- Minimize the number of inputs to the module and allow only a single output;
- Design only one function into a module (strong cohesion);
- Make each module as independent of all others as possible (weak coupling);
- Build checks for the validation of input data into the code;
- Produce explicit, structured, complete design documentation.

This affected the programmers at the T level, and the integration and test team members were encouraged to check for these features at the I level.

Second, keep the programming simple and structured. 'Clever' programming often leads to complexity, an increase in the likelihood of bugs, and a decrease in test coverage. Again this principle was appropriate to the programmers, and it was looked for during code inspections.

Third, designers (not programmers) with the aid of trained testers should design the test plans and test cases for the software, in accordance with the principles of the V development model (see Figure 2. 3 in Chapter 2).

Fourth, the test plans and test cases should be subjected to thorough quality assurance. For this we used Fagan's Inspection.

Fifth, all developers should be trained in testing principles and practice. We did not find programming courses which integrated testing with programming, so we ourselves conducted short courses in testing in the context of programming.

Sixth, the development manager should create and nurture the culture of testing, not merely as an integral part of development, but as a natural part of the programming process.

Seventh, use a static analysis tool to check that code conforms to the defined rules of structure and the standards laid down. This assumes that in the project there are defined rules; if there are not, there is every reason to doubt the quality of the code being produced.

Eighth, use one or more complexity measures to get a feel for the complexity of each program or unit of code. If a program's complexity is above average, or above some defined figure, it may be deemed necessary to carry out extra tests on it, or to take extra precautions to ensure that thorough test coverage is achieved. However, these are not the only options. It is often preferable to rewrite the program in a simpler way, perhaps redesigning it and breaking it down into two or more smaller modules. Although many people baulk at the thought of this, arguing that it is a waste of time, it is usually not as time-consuming as carrying out extra tests now and still having to do more than average debugging later. The programmer already understands the problem to be solved and the algorithm for solving it, so the second attempt gains from the experience of the first and can be surprisingly quick and effective.

Ninth, choose test cases carefully, so as to achieve full coverage while avoiding duplication. Let us consider a trivial example (similar to one which I observed in practice). A module consists of a function whose inputs are intended to be integers between 1 and 75. Now, it is known that many problems occur at boundary values, so it is suggested that test values of 0, 1, 2, 74, 75 and 76 would be useful. Similarly, extreme out-range values present problems, so appropriate test values are necessary — say, 917 and -254. Finally, a mid-range value is essential for validating the function — say, 39. Thus in this simple example (ignoring non-integer values), a minimum of nine tests are necessary. However, to prove the module, the tester (the programmer) used values of 1, 5, and all values at intervals of 5 up to 75 — a total of 16 tests. He neglected thorough testing at boundary values, ignored extreme out-range values altogether, and over-tested with mid-range values. Thus, of the necessary nine tests he carried out three, achieving 3/9 (one third) of the minimum necessary coverage, at 16/9 (1.77) times the necessary cost. Beware of deriving false confidence from apparently extensive testing, when in fact extremely limited coverage has been achieved.

Tenth, test what the module should not do as well as what it should. The large number of tests carried out in the example of the previous paragraph gave the tester high confidence that his software was sound. Yet, he had merely tested the program's function over and over again. This is in fact the part of a program which is most often correct. But he had not tested those parts of the program which were most likely to contain errors. In practice, he should also have used non-integer test data to check the validation of input data.

Eleventh, test thoroughly at the earliest stage (the T level in our ED structure). This is in fact the only stage at which exhaustive testing can be carried out, for at later stages the assumption is made that individual software units are of good quality, and tests are focused on functionality and interfaces. Do not forget the ten-to-one rule: if the later assumption of quality is false, a great deal of re-work will need to be carried out, first at the basic level and then at higher levels.

Many of these principles concern the consideration which programmers must have for testing, rather than the activities which the testers must carry out. This reinforces the affirmation that programmers should not be encouraged to think of coding as an independent discipline but should be taught to perceive it as having testing integrated with it. It was our programmers' awareness of testing, combined with our integration and test team's awareness of the principles of 'test-oriented programming', which gave us the necessary level of confidence in the quality of our products as we delivered them. Too much emphasis cannot be placed on this. In ED each delivery is a working system, not a prototype, and, as we shall see in the next chapter, maintenance can be complex and expensive, so assuring the quality of deliveries is of high importance. Effective testing is crucial to ED.

## 13.5  SUMMARY AND EXTRACTS

This chapter has explained the processes used for testing at the various stages of an ED project. In doing so, it identified the responsibilities of and between the relevant project participants. It also addressed the point that it is confidence and not perfection which can be derived from testing, and it described the means by which confidence in the quality of software can be arrived at.

The following extracts are examples of the points made in the chapter.

- It is more difficult and more costly to repair a fault the longer you leave it (or the longer it remains undetected).

- Completing a program becomes an iterative process of programming, testing, correcting, testing, and signing off.

- Programming needs to be defined, in education, as an integrated coding and testing process, and taught as such.

- Testing ... is intended to give confidence. It is a risk-management activity. If there were no risk attached to getting something wrong, there would be no point in testing it.

- There is usually no risk-based determinant of what should be tested or how much testing should be carried out. The result is that many organizations over-test.

- If testing reveals no faults, it is wiser to conclude that the tests were inadequate than that the system is fault-free.

- If you are contemplating minimizing testing, be sure that you understand the risks which you think you are reducing and, equally importantly, those which you are taking.

- While a lax environment (which reduces quality) seems to be easily accepted by programmers (and other staff), higher expectations are appreciated even more — and what is more, they are responded to.

- If the delivery is to be on schedule, the modules must be delivered from the T level on time and their development schedules must be based on the integration plan. Planning at the I level is the basis of the development of each delivery.

- Beware of seeing the customer or the users as a threat, or of hoping for them to stay out of the way. Their testing is of value to the development team and they should be encouraged to participate.

- The development manager should create and nurture the culture of testing, not merely as an integral part of development, but as a natural part of the programming process.

- Beware of deriving false confidence from apparently extensive testing, when in fact extremely limited coverage has been achieved.

- Test what the module should not do as well as what it should.

- Test thoroughly at the earliest stage (the T level). This is in fact the only stage at which exhaustive testing can be carried out, for at later stages the assumption is made that individual software units are of good quality, and tests are focused on functionality and interfaces.

- It was our programmers' awareness of testing, combined with our integration and test team's awareness of the principles of 'test-oriented programming', which gave us the necessary level of confidence in the quality of our products as we delivered them.

# 14

# Software Maintenance
# — Definition and
# Procedures

## 14.1 THE ISSUES

Software maintenance is traditionally understood to consist of any work
carried out on the software after a system has been brought into service. For
example, James Martin referred to it as '... changes that have to be made to
computer programs after they have been delivered to the customer or user'
[Martin 1983]; and Glass and Noiseux said that 'Maintenance is the process of
being responsive to user needs — fixing errors, making user-specification
modifications, honing the programs to be more useful' [Glass 1981]. These
defining statements are affirmed by the acceptance of three 'dimensions' of
software maintenance, namely 'perfective', 'adaptive' and 'corrective'
maintenance [Swanson 76], where perfective and adaptive maintenance involve
making changes to the software to keep up with changing needs, and only
corrective maintenance is the fixing of incorrect software.

Such broad definitions of maintenance are unique to software. Changes to the functionality of hardware would traditionally be recognized as redesign and redevelopment, as distinct from maintenance which would only refer to the correction of defects. However, with hardware the maintenance work (such as the replacement of failed items) is discernibly different in kind from redesign and from the addition of new functions, while for software there is no replacement of worn out parts, and programming for redesign is not different in kind from programming to fix a defect. So, particularly with reference to the waterfall development model, it easily became accepted for the stage of a system's life cycle following acceptance into service to be called 'maintenance', with no distinction being made between the reasons for the work being done.

Even though the large maintenance teams retained by most companies typically spend most of their time implementing new requirements rather than making corrections, the companies have not concerned themselves with identifying improvements to their systems. A disadvantage of this is that the systems are valued at their original development cost, and added value is not accrued in the company's assets register.

A further result of lumping all work together as maintenance is that, in order to give the impression of a project being completed on time and within budget, project managers may compromise on meeting the specification and deliberately leave development work undone, to be carried out under the disguise of maintenance after the system has been accepted into service. The tragedy is that this is often done with the connivance (overt or covert) of senior managers who are less concerned with quality than with publicizing the 'successful' completion of a project. But who suffers from this? The developers, for while the project manager is praised for having completed the project on time, they are left with having to spend considerable further time on 'maintenance' of a system which is in fact of good quality.

So, defining software maintenance as embracing all types of work has had its disadvantages, but the easy path for most companies has been to accept it. Senior managers have stayed clear of the foreign world of computers, 'maintenance' teams have grown by doing whatever has been asked of them, and finance departments have avoided revaluing computer systems when new functionality has been added to them. But the traditional definition of software maintenance has only been justifiable if the system has been delivered in one 'big bang' — and even then it should have entered its operation and maintenance stage in its completed state rather than with some of its original specification still to be met.

But when ED is employed, maintenance and development cannot be separated by a point of time. As soon as the first delivery is made, maintenance activities are likely to become necessary, while at the same time development must continue. To abide by the old definition would be to decide that development ends at the first delivery and that all subsequent work is maintenance. As less than 10% of the requirements specification may then have been met, this is clearly absurd. Moreover, given that maintenance should always be accorded immediate attention, it is important for it to be distinguishable from continuing development. If all work is maintenance, the development team must forever be 'fire fighting'. We all need the stimulation of 'pressure' from time to time, and most of us react to it by increasing and improving our effort and output, but it should not be the norm. If it persists for too long, its effect becomes counter-productive: the response changes from stimulation to resentment, and morale deteriorates. One is poisoned by an excess of one's own adrenaline.

Given the limitations of the traditional definition of software maintenance, it is important to redefine it, at least in the context of ED, and this is done below.

Having a more appropriate definition of software maintenance is the first step towards controlling the after-delivery service to the customer. It relieves the pressure on the developers, for it provides a basis for distinguishing between maintenance work, which is afforded immediate attention, and requests for change (RFCs), which should be directed through the change-control procedures described in Chapter 11.

The next step is to have procedures for carrying out the maintenance. These should describe methods of working which ensure efficiency in the effort of maintenance staff, effectiveness in the work they do, and satisfaction to the customer. Beware of thinking that achieving effectiveness is the same as affording satisfaction. It is not so. Effectiveness is one consideration, and a necessary one, but customer satisfaction is not the result of an objective recognition of correctness; it stems from a subjective perception of all contributing factors, including speed of service, attitude, politeness, and feedback. As well as defining maintenance in a manner appropriate to ED, this chapter describes maintenance procedures and their management which evolved with experience and which were found to be effective.

## 14.2 REDEFINING SOFTWARE MAINTENANCE

It was shown in Chapter 11 that once a delivery has been made there are four categories of work to be done on the software.

1. Continuing development as per the original specification of requirements;
2. Developing newly specified functions;
3. Making modifications to software already provided which, although conforming to its specification, was shown by use not to meet the users' actual requirements in one way or another;
4. Correcting software which was shown not to conform to its specification.

The first three categories of work are development, and only the fourth is maintenance. An appropriate definition of software maintenance would therefore be, 'Modifications made to software found after delivery not to conform to its specification, in order to make it conform to its specification.' This is a return to the older concept of maintenance used in hardware systems.

From time to time, it may be found that although a unit of software does not conform to its specification the users discover that the original specification was wrong or no longer applicable. The modifications to be made will therefore need to be re-specified. In such cases, the non-conformity should be recorded, but the effort required for the modifications should be costed against development and not maintenance.

## 14.3 A PROBLEM TO BE RESOLVED

As developers, the above definition of software maintenance suited us well, our greatest problem being in agreeing with our customers and users on which work fell within it — though I should add that this was mainly in the early days before we invested special effort in maintaining good relations with them. When people are wary of each other, their eagerness to find differences in their views seems to be stronger than their will to agree; when their relationships are harmonious, it is the other way around.

We experienced little problem in agreeing on which work fell into categories 1, 2 and 4 (see Section 14.2.1 above). The trouble was with 3. If users found that a function did not perform as required at the time of use, the natural tendency was to record the fact as a defect of the system. They did not at first find it easy to recognize that the problem was (or even, might be) in their specification.

But whose fault was it? Had we, the developers, not written a large part of the specification, albeit with information derived from the customer and users? One of the most difficult and demanding stages of the project life cycle is requirements capture, the success of which relies on considerable skill, experience and patience on the part of the analysts, committed and continuous participation on the part of the customers and users, and extensive verification and validation by both. Could we honestly declare that we had played our part faultlessly? We realized that we had to share the blame. Whereas we demanded professionalism of ourselves in all stages of development, we could not expect the same of our users. It was not their job or their domain of expertise. We would have liked it to be different, and I am convinced that customers could and should participate a great deal more in their projects and, by doing so, improve the chance of their success. Indeed until they do, they will not receive optimal systems. Nevertheless, it was not enough to stand back and cast blame. A system which did not meet the users' requirements, even if it conformed to its specification, did none of us any good; and it certainly didn't serve the users' business.

We therefore set out to do two things. The first was to improve requirements capture and requirements expression (in the specification). The second was to create a relationship with our customers and users such that disputes were in the first place unlikely to arise and in the second place easy to resolve. A number of actions were taken on the first count, one being to increase emphasis on prototyping prior to specification. This has the twin effects of attracting the users' participation and obtaining from them statements of requirements which could be verified.

Among the actions taken on the second count (that of improving relationships) were the introduction of more formal meetings, more informal visits, more openness about our problems, and the provision to the users of a help line for the rapid resolution of their problems. The effects were increased contact, communication, honesty and understanding. Customers and users have rights to certain expectations, and our being defensive or arguing that their expectations are excessive will not change them. However, we found that if we explained our problems, their inclination was to be sympathetic. Similarly, it is to our advantage to express sympathy for their problems, even when we are unable to solve them as they would like. Being open evokes human warmth and reasonableness.

The results of our initiatives included greater professionalism all round, a better understanding of each others' problems, fewer issues to resolve, a sounder basis for the resolution of issues which did arise, and a stronger willingness to find the best solutions rather than to apportion blame. Having been involved in numerous software projects, and having observed and read about countless others, I believe this was a considerable achievement.

As to the issue of categorizing maintenance work, greater involvement in the project and greater discernment of the necessary attributes of a specification led our customers and users to recognize the inadequacies of their specification as well as of our work. At the same time, the formal procedures introduced for handling requests for change (see Chapter 11) ensured that requirements expression improved considerably and was subject to extensive quality control.

## 14.4  ADVANTAGES

By defining software maintenance as only those activities resulting from non-conformity to specification, a number of advantages accrue, both to the customer's organization and to the developers.

### 14.4.1  Need for a Definition

The first advantage is simply having a clear definition. With the old 'understood' definition being altogether inappropriate to ED (and misleading and inexact in other circumstances), a new and more appropriate definition was not merely desirable but essential.

### 14.4.2  Quality Measurement

A second advantage is that there is now the basis of a measure of the quality of development work. Measuring and publishing maintenance costs (the cost of poor quality) has the effect of eliciting pride when the figures are low, both in absolute terms and as a proportion of the original development costs. It also has the effect of stimulating the will to reduce them in the future, and it provides the basis of measurable targets for quality improvement initiatives. If maintenance is not distinguished from development, there is no such incentive.

It should be pointed out, however, that the 'basis' for quality measurement does no good of itself. It is taking measurements, publishing the results, deriving comparisons with past figures and setting new targets for the future, and defining improvement initiatives in collaboration with the staff which are the stimulating factors. Good management is the determinant. The insensitive use of measurements can demotivate development staff.

### 14.4.3    Budgeting and Accounting

A third advantage is to the business, in budgeting and accounting for the project. Now the finance department can obtain the actual undistorted cost of the materials and labour required to bring the system into service with all its functionality, and increased functionality is recognized as added value to the system and can easily be quantified and included as such in the company's assets register. Moreover, by recording the costs of carrying out the four categories of work (see Section 14.2), the costs of both poor development and poor specification can be quantified. Reference has already been made to the efforts which we made to improve both. Other managers might choose to base improvement projects on the derived quality-related costs.

### 14.4.4    Planning Deliveries

A fourth advantage is in prioritizing work for subsequent deliveries. Maintenance was accepted by us as having to be done independently of other development work. We had to find time for it, urgently if necessary, so it always received a high priority. All other work was subject to prioritization. This had the effect of drawing attention to the category 3 modifications, many of which were considered urgent by the users, but it alleviated the pressure which would have been placed on the developers if all 'urgent' modifications were classified as maintenance and had to be made immediately. By putting clearly defined procedures in place, and managing them, all parties are enabled to have a clearer and more realistic view of what it takes to implement a development project.

## 14.5  NECESSARY FEATURES OF A MAINTENANCE PROCEDURE

Software maintenance must take place within the development environment's control system — the CM system described in Chapter 10 — where a copy of the operational system is stored in the L level exclusively for the use of maintenance staff. The design of a maintenance procedure must therefore be integrated into the software control mechanisms, and the staff organization and management should match the procedure.

In ED there are at any time a number of deliveries in preparation. Without care, maintenance changes made at the L level could easily be cancelled, perhaps very quickly, by the next delivery or the one after that. Any procedure must ensure that this does not occur.

Maintenance, however, is not only procedural but managerial as well: by its nature, it must be based on decisions taken in the light of current evidence. For certain routine functions it is an advantage to have rigid procedures which provide both guidance and discipline. In maintenance, however, where corrective action must be balanced by the need to sustain operational service, flexibility is essential. Procedures should be a framework for management responsibility, decision and action.

A minimum set of maintenance goals, to be considered when developing maintenance procedures is:

- The response to users should be rapid and efficient;
- A decision-making process should exist for determining exactly what action is necessary;
- Urgent action should be identified and taken immediately;
- Non-urgent corrections may be deferred, perhaps to a later delivery, but always with the agreement of the customer representative;
- All maintenance changes are formally documented, both in maintenance records and in the system's design documentation;
- No changes should be inadvertently reversed or overwritten by a subsequent delivery;
- Notification of action taken is formally provided to the original reporter of the problem;
- Principles should be defined for the management of maintenance procedures, and for the interaction of managers in the development organization in conducting and monitoring maintenance work.

These are not necessarily the only goals of a maintenance procedure, and a reader wanting to set up procedures may have other criteria related to particular circumstances. However, note that of eight stated goals, three (the first, fourth and seventh) are concerned with the customer or the users. Maintenance has a direct bearing on them. They have already received the product — reasonably expecting it to conform to its specification — and have (or believe that they have) found it to be defective. The developers are at fault for getting it wrong, and they should recognize this. Maintenance consists not only of product care, but of customer care as well.

## 14.6  THE WHEREWITHAL FOR CARRYING OUT MAINTENANCE

As a minimum requirement, there need to be clear definitions of:

- Responsibility for carrying out maintenance;
- Call-out procedures, for example, how users should contact maintenance staff, whether staff can be called outside of normal working hours and, if so, how it is decided who is to be on duty at any time;
- Procedures for the way in which maintenance staff deal with users at the time that problems are being reported and at all subsequent stages of the maintenance process;
- Allocation of staff to maintenance, whether their time is shared between maintenance and some other function and, if so, what priorities apply;
- What facilities the maintenance staff have, for example, for interrogating the live system, shutting down the live system, and testing fixes before installing them on the live system.

Referring to Figure 8.3, responsibility for maintenance is assumed to be invested in the support team leader. He would of course normally delegate tasks to his staff, and he may need to arrange with other team leaders to carry out certain work, but he cannot shed the responsibility for the execution and integrity of maintenance work.

Experience suggests that most reports of problems arrive by telephone. In our case, a list of the support team's telephone numbers (at work) was held by the operations staff, so rapid contact could be initiated even by novice operators. However, familiarity and friendship, resulting from regular site visits, led most calls to be made to best-known individuals.

As our support cover was 24 hours per day, some of the team had modem-connected terminals at home, but the choice of whom to contact outside of normal working hours was limited by an agreed and published emergency rota. The team also had direct links to all operational systems. As mentioned in Chapter 10, they loaded new deliveries over their links, and could exert full control over the live systems. With terminals, they were able to carry out all user functions, monitor system activity, and also initiate and control diagnostic tests.

If initial tests on the live system did not solve a problem, the team had the exclusive use of the L level of the CM system library. They used this for carrying out diagnostics. Having developed and tested a correction in the programmers' area of the library, they again used the L level system for carrying out tests prior to delivery of the repaired version of the software.

The first thing a maintainer should do is to obtain as much (verbal) information about the problem as possible. Then, as the fault could be the user's rather than the system's, he should talk the user through whatever operations seem likely to overcome the problem or resurrect the system.

In our case, if this wasn't successful, the maintainer logged in and assumed control of the live system in an effort to discover the problem — taking care not to interrupt service if the system was still operational. If the problem could not easily be found, the maintainer resorted to exploring the system or carrying out diagnostics on the L level of the CM system.

When the fault was found, an assessment was made of its impact on the system and its users, and of what it would take to fix it.


## 14.7  CARRYING OUT THE WORK

### 14.7.1  Decisions to be Made

The main question to be answered is, when should the fix be implemented? There is a balance to be achieved here: in many cases the users want a fault to be corrected as soon as possible, but this increases the complexity of handling the fix, for implementing it at the L level introduces the possibility of its being overwritten by a subsequent delivery. It is therefore most convenient if the correction is deferred and included in a later delivery. The lower the level of the library at which the fix is introduced, the less complex it is to control it. If the impact of the fault is great, the fix may need to be implemented as soon as possible, but introducing it at the L level imposes the greatest problem.

Suppose that the next delivery is already at the U level and scheduled for delivery in three weeks time; could delivery of the fix wait for that? Or, if the fault is intermittent, its impact is low, and the change is extensive (though, perhaps, conceptually simple), it may be preferable to design the fix into the delivery which is now at the T level. This would delay its implementation by perhaps six months, but it would be the most convenient solution from the developers' point of view, and it would ensure thorough design and testing. It would also eliminate any possibility of the fix being reversed by the next delivery and it would almost certainly be the cheapest solution (Figure 14.1 shows an example of this situation).

### 14.7.2    The Rule to be Applied

If the fix is to be introduced above the T level, precautions, partly procedural and partly managerial, must be taken against the possibility of it being overwritten by a later version of the software. One of the rules governing software within the CM system library is that there should be no movement downwards (see Chapter 10). Software should only move upwards through the levels of the library. The question then is, how is this rule applied to controlling maintenance changes? The principle is that, with the exception of corrections made at the L level for immediate delivery, all changes are made at the lowest level of the library at which the software module to be changed is the same as in the version which needs to be changed. Clarification of this

| Level | Working areas | CM system library |
|-------|---------------|-------------------|
| 5 | | L level<br>Live system (Version N) |
| 4 | | U level<br>Version N+1 (waiting for customer's<br>pre-delivery tests) |
| 3 | | S level<br>Version N+1 (system tests completed) |
| 2 | | I level<br>Version N+2 (partial integration<br>testing in progress) |
| 1 | Fix<br>carried out<br>here | T level<br>Version N+2 (units being tested) |

**Figure 14.1** Maintenance fix carried out on Version N+2 of the system at the T level of the CM system library

rule is given in the examples in Sections 14.7.4 and 14.7.5. Further, if any precautions are to be successful, responsibility must be defined.

### 14.7.3    Responsibility

In all cases, the support team leader is responsible for ensuring the correct implementation of the fix and its integrity in versions of the software already under development. In most cases, his staff decide what the fix should consist of, and design and document it. If appropriate, they implement it in the L level version of the system, test it there, and then implement it in the operational systems. Then they must in all cases pass the fix to the team leaders who have to implement it in the other versions of the system that are already in preparation. Later, as each of those versions reaches the L level, the support team's documentation for the appropriate delivery prompts them to ensure that the fix has been included and to test that it has been correctly implemented. For example, in the case suggested in Section 14.7.1, where the fix was implemented in Version N+2 (see Figure 14.1), the support team would test for it in that version, but not in Version N+1.

If it has been decided to defer implementation of the fix, there needs to be a discussion between the support team leader and the team leader currently responsible for the delivery in which it will be included as to who will design and develop it. On some occasions the support team may design and develop it, on others they may design it and leave development and initial testing to the other team, and on yet others it may be sufficient for them to provide a specification of the problem to be overcome rather than a design of the fix. In no case, however, can the support team leader relinquish responsibility for the fix, so he must ensure that it is implemented in the agreed delivery and test for its presence and correctness when the delivery reaches the L level.

### 14.7.4    Implementing a Fix at the L Level

Let us suppose that the fix is to be implemented immediately at the L level and thus in the live system. When this has been done, the question is, what is the lowest level at which the software modules affected are unchanged from those at the L level? We will assume, in this example, that in the next delivery (Version N+1) there has been no change, but that Version N+2 includes a change to those modules (see Figure 14.2).

| Level | Working areas | CM system library |
|-------|---------------|-------------------|
| 5 | Immediate fix made here | L level<br>Live system (Version N) |
| 4 | | U level<br>Version N |
| 3 | Fix made at L level introduced here | S level<br>Version N+1 (undergoing system testing) |
| 2 | | I level<br>Parts of Version N+2 being integrated |
| 1 | Problem to be re-solved here when other changes are made | T level<br>Version N+2 (units being tested) |

**Figure 14.2** Maintenance fix made at the L level — library status and activities

Once the support team leader is confident of the fix and has delivered it to site, he arranges for its inclusion as it stands in Version N+1, at the S level. The system test team leader incorporates the new versions of the modules into the system and decides what tests are necessary for proving the fix to his satisfaction.

As Version N+2 of the system includes changes to the modules involved in the fix, the fix as introduced at the L level cannot be incorporated at the T level. The fix must be redesigned, along with the other changes to the module, into Version N+2. Thus, a specification of the problem to be cured is passed from the support team leader to the low-level design and coding team leader for inclusion in Version N+2 at the T level. This creates a change to the definition of the delivery. The fix is therefore redesigned into Version N+2 of the system, and tests at the all levels of the library are designed to exercise it.

The support team leader retains responsibility for the fix and must test for it at the L level when both Versions N+1 and N+2 of the system arrive there.

### 14.7.5   Implementation of the Fix is Deferred

If the support team leader considers that the best course is to defer implementation, he puts the case to the development manager. If the latter agrees, concurrence is sought from the customer representative. As the support team knows the system intimately, as they are on call in case of a recurrence of the problem, and as the decision can be reversed at any time, the customer representative would usually accept the support team leader's recommendation.

How a fix might be implemented when deferred is shown in the following example.

Let us suppose that it is decided to introduce the fix in the delivery of Version N+1 which is, as shown in Figure 14.3, now undergoing system tests at the S level.

Version N+1 must remain at the S level until the fix has been included in it. However, the fix must be made at the lowest level that the software modules are consistent with those at the S level, so, if the modules to be changed are the

| Level | Working areas | CM system library |
|---|---|---|
| 5 | | L level<br>Live system (Version N) |
| 4 | | U level<br>Version N |
| 3 | | S level<br>Version N+1 (undergoing system testing) |
| 2 | | I level<br>Parts of Version N+2 being integrated |
| 1 | Fix carried out here | T level<br>Version N+2 (units being tested) |

Figure 14.3  Maintenance fix deferred to T level — library status and activities

same in Version N+2 as in Version N+1, the change must be made at the T level. In this example, let us assume that Version N+2 includes no change to those particular modules.

The fix is therefore made and tested at the T level and the changed modules passed to the I level. There they may be integrated and subjected to new integration tests before being passed to the S level. If by now the schedule for Version N+1 to be passed up from the S level is behind schedule, it may be decided to pass the changed ('fixed') modules straight on to the S level to replace their previous versions which have until then been a part of the Version N+1 system. The justifications for this are that, first, there will be tests at the S level which could detect any faults in the fix, second, the L level team will be available to deal with any problems in operation if a fault did slip through into the delivered system, and third, that the tests at the S level, though carried out in parallel with the further progress of the fixed system, should uncover any faults, perhaps in time to correct them before Version N+1 is delivered to site from the L level. This is not a recommendation not to test at the I level, merely a reminder that in practice compromises sometimes need to be made. When they are, they should be justified and a fall-back position determined. Again, it is pointed out that testing is most effective when the risks involved are identified and understood.

Alternative to passing the changed modules straight to the S level is to carry out integration testing at the I level. This is always preferred if there is time, and always essential if the risks attached to a bug existing in the operational system are too great.

Once the fixed modules arrive at the S level, the system test team leader must decide what tests are necessary for gaining confidence, at that level, in the integrity of the fix. Remember that testing is a risk management activity, and that what the designer of tests is doing is assessing the risks involved in failure, and planning a means of acquiring confidence that they have been reduced to an acceptable level. As the fix was not a part of Version N+1 from the beginning, the previously designed system tests will not cater for it. However, there is now the certainty that the tests on Version N+2, at all levels, will be redesigned to exercise the fix formally and thoroughly, so bugs which slip through in Version N+1 should be detected in the testing of Version N+2. So the system test team leader must use judgement. There is also the back-up of the continuing responsibility for the fix of the support team leader who must check for its presence and effectiveness in both Version N+1 and N+2 when they arrive at the L level.

When Version N+1 has passed its system tests, it is passed up to the U level and, eventually, via the L level, to the systems in the field. Occasionally, the work involved in this type of deferred maintenance causes a delay to a delivery, but extra pre-delivery effort (which comes to be a planned part of the support team's schedule) usually avoids this.

## 14.8  MODULE HISTORY

If a module or unit of software had a version number which it retained as it moved up the levels of the CM system library, changes made anywhere above the T level would put the version numbers out of sequence. To avoid such a complication, version numbers are not used by the CM system for individual software units (only for complete versions of the system). Instead, use is made of the 'generation number' (see Chapter 10) which is updated each time a module is updated or replaced at a level.

Briefly, what happens is this. When a module enters a library level for the first time, it acquires generation number 1. Then, it can only be updated at that level by use of the HOLD command. When this happens, its generation number is incremented, and this carries on for as long as the module exists at that level. When it is moved up to the next level for the first time, it acquires generation number 1 there. It thus obtains an identity at each level, and this is updated to reflect the number of times it is altered at that level.

There is one case where caution may need to be applied, and that is when a changed module is passed up the levels to replace an earlier incorrect version of the same module, as in the example of Section 14.7.5 above. Then the change to the existing module at the given level does not result from the use of the HOLD command. Three points are worth making.

The first is that because the fix is made at the lowest level at which the module is unchanged from its versions at higher levels, when it reaches a given level it should functionally be the same as its earlier version when that reached the level in question. This means that the manager with responsibility for the level is 'starting with a clean slate'. However, the other two points to be made are in consideration of possible complications.

The second point is that if the title of the module is the same as that of its predecessor, it should automatically receive a generation number equivalent to its predecessor's incremented by 1. In other words, the system should be such that a module cannot exist at any level in two versions with the same generation number.

The final point is that a check must be made of whether changes had been made to that module at that level prior to the arrival of the new version. Let us consider an example. Module X arrives at the S level and is accorded generation number 1. During system testing a change is made to it by use of the HOLD command, and its new version now carries generation number 2. A fix is made to the same module at a lower level and a new version with the same name arrives at the S level and is given generation number 3. We must now ensure that the necessary change which was earlier made at the S level is included in the module. If it was not included in the fix at the lower level, it must now be made, using the HOLD command, and this would create a new version of the module with generation number 4.

## 14.9  DOCUMENTATION

The two examples in Section 14.7.4 and 14.7.5 demonstrated the procedures for incorporating maintenance within the CM system. Maintenance changes also need to be documented.

Because of the definition of maintenance (see Section 14.2), it is given that the specification of requirements needs no change. The question then is, did the error first occur in the design, or in the software itself? The design documentation is, therefore, checked as part of the support team's maintenance procedure. If the design is found to be incorrect, the correction to it is documented and verified, and thus included in the next formal issue of the design documentation.

In all cases, the issue of up-to-date documentation for the software is automatic, as this is an integral function of the CM system and a part of the software production process. With each module and unit of software, the programmer must produce descriptive documentation in conformity with project standards, and this is enforced by the CM system. Quality assurance should always include checks for conformity to standards.

In all cases, too, the problem is recorded in the maintenance log, and all time taken in repairing the fault, at all levels, is recorded and accrued against quality-related costs.

## 14.10 ONE FURTHER POSSIBILITY

It was shown in Chapter 10 that the processes of building and testing a system and documenting its configuration profile at the L level require that the system is moved from the U to the L level up to two weeks before it is due to be delivered to site. During this period, the L level does not contain an exact replica of the live system, and efficient maintenance may be compromised.

The first thing to note is that, as a last resort, the live system can be regenerated at the L level. This, however, is avoided if possible, and the usual preference of the support team is to implement a fix in the new version of the system and to accelerate its delivery. This implies having to create, in the new version, the conditions under which the failure occurred. If the failure repeats itself, the fault can be diagnosed, and the fix produced, tested, delivered, and built into later deliveries, as already described. If the failure does not occur, it may be hypothesized that the particular fault which caused it is not being delivered in the new version. This is not always a wholly correct assumption, but one could waste a great deal of time testing for the fault.

As far as maintenance goes, the support team manager must use discretion in determining the risk involved in bringing the new version into service. In many cases the risk is not great, for once the new version is in operation, its replica will exist at the L level and maintenance can again be optimized, as described above. For safety-related systems, this would not be a satisfactory situation — but, then, ED of such systems may not be either. Given the particular circumstances, development and project managers must decide on what guidelines to provide to maintenance (support team) managers and what discretion to allow them within the guidelines.

## 14.11 SUMMARY AND EXTRACTS

This chapter has shown that a tight definition of software maintenance is required for evolutionary delivery, and it has provided an appropriate definition.

It has explained in detail a maintenance process for ED and given examples of how the configuration management system defined in Chapter 10 is used to facilitate and control the process. Project and development managers could base a procedure for maintenance appropriate to the circumstances of their own projects on this.

The following are extracts from the chapter.

- To give the impression of a project being completed on time and within budget, project managers may compromise on meeting the specification and deliberately leave development work undone, to be carried out under the disguise of maintenance after the system has been accepted into service.

- The traditional definition of software maintenance has only been justifiable if the system has been delivered in one 'big bang' — and even then it should have entered its operation and maintenance stage in its completed state rather than with some of its original specification still to be met.

- Customer satisfaction is not the result of an objective recognition of correctness; it stems from a subjective perception of all contributing factors, including speed of service, attitude, politeness, and feedback.

- When people are wary of each other, their eagerness to find differences in their views seems to be stronger than their will to agree.

- By putting clearly defined procedures in place, and managing them, all parties are enabled to have a clearer and more realistic view of what it takes to implement a development project.

- The design of a maintenance procedure must be integrated into the software control mechanisms, and the staff organization and management should match the procedure.

- Maintenance is not only procedural but managerial as well: by its nature, it must be based on decisions taken in the light of current evidence ... Procedures should be a framework for management responsibility, decision and action.

- Principles should be defined for the management of maintenance procedures, and for the interaction of managers in the development organization in conducting and monitoring maintenance work.

- Maintenance consists not only of product care, but of customer care as well.

# 15

# Evolutionary
# Delivery Culture

## 15.1 THE ISSUES

Traditionally, the objectives of a project manager have been stated as: to complete the project on time, within budget, and to specification. Almost invariably in software development projects at least one of these is not met, and too frequently none is met (typical causes of failed projects were discussed in Chapters 3 and 4).

The three objectives are simple to state and simple to understand. Management understand them and set them as their criteria of judgement of a project, and two of them at least — time and budget — are easy to measure. There are of course games which are played to contrive project success. For example, the completion (at last) of a late and over-budget project may be celebrated with a fanfare — because it meets the last agreed completion date and budget (perhaps agreed only a couple of months earlier). Or a project manager may compromise the specification so as to 'complete' the project within the defined time and budget, leaving the developers to continue the work of developing the system under the heading of maintenance. But such devices are contrived knowingly, and at least the objectives are easily definable.

What is the goal of an ED project? It cannot be to 'meet the specification', for it is recognized at the outset that there will be changes, perhaps numerous and far-reaching changes, to the original specification. Can our goal be to meet time or budget criteria? If we cannot be definitive in the specification, on what can we estimate the necessary time and budget? We need to reconsider.

Estimation is not merely obtaining an idea of the project's likely time and resource requirements. It also provides the basis for defining the project's terminating criteria and judging its success. A reassessment of these issues implies a re-evaluation of the culture necessary for the success of ED projects, in both senior management and the developers.


## 15.2  PROJECT GOALS

If the goal of a development project is not to meet a defined specification, what is it? If we step back from the specification and inquire into the more fundamental reasons for the project, we arrive at the business objectives. In many, if not most, waterfall model projects, the business objectives hardly play a role: they are not determined, or not communicated to the project manager, or communicated only vaguely, or not used as the basis of monitoring the project. The result is that they often are not met. But at least in such projects there is the specification to fall back on. Success can be claimed if the system meets the users' requirements. But are the users' requirements and the business objectives not the same? No. The users' requirements are means of meeting the business objectives — if they are specified in accordance with them (see Chapter 7). But if the users' requirements are not specified in accordance with the business objectives, adhering to them leads to a strategically ineffective project (and system). Moreover, even when they start out meeting the business' strategic needs, the users' requirements can alter drastically during the project — hence the need for the participation of a strategic representative. However, a strategic representative is not a common component of waterfall model projects.

In ED, it is possible for there to be so little change to the requirements during the project that the original specification retains its integrity throughout. Don't count on this, but if it happened, success could be claimed for meeting the specification. However, in general, experience shows that it is essential in ED to be clear about the business objectives for the project, and to monitor both project progress and requests for change against them. This requires a change in the culture of both senior management (in the customer's organization) and project management.

In an organization commissioning ED projects, the senior managers need to develop the culture of thinking strategically, planning strategically, expressing their strategic plans so that they are clear to their organization, and monitoring effort (including project effort) against the strategic plans. It may be argued that this should be the case in all organizations, and I would agree, but in most it is not so. In ED, the business objectives are essential as project goals.

## 15.3 ESTIMATION

Typically, senior management bases its approval of a project on time and budget estimates. If in ED we are aiming at a moving target, how can we with confidence make predictions? Again we must have recourse to the business objectives for the project. But how are these translated into estimates of budget and time?

The answer is that they cannot be translated directly, because the business objectives are stated at too high a level. They do not contain the detail (for instance, that contained in a requirements specification) which allows decomposition into system functions, the deduction of the tasks necessary for creating the functions, and thus the time and resources needed to carry out the tasks. So we cannot make confident estimates from the objectives; we need a specification for that. It was pointed out in Chapter 9 that in ED we need a good specification to start with. From this we can make estimates, and these may be used as a first approximation to what we expect of the project.

Prior to a specification being prepared, however, senior management needs to devote greater consideration to the *value* of meeting their objectives. When one or more business objectives are to be met by a computer system, there should be an estimate by senior management of what those business objectives are worth and whether there are time constraints on them (for example, if a new product is to be competitive, it may need to be developed within a certain time, and it may be uneconomical to take longer to produce it). The developers (via the project manager) should be asked if they can meet the objectives at a certain budget and within a given time — and in most cases a feasibility study would be carried out to determine the answer. As pointed out above, a statement of business objectives is usually at too high a level to allow reliable time and budget estimates to be deduced directly, so the feasibility study would involve the determination of the main functions necessary to meet the objectives and the capture of the principal requirements necessary to those functions. This would result in a quickly produced partial specification for the purpose of initial approximate estimates.

If the feasibility suggests that the developers could not meet the stated objectives within the defined constraints, the reasons should be examined. Often, compromises can be made. Perhaps the objectives can be pruned so that an adequate system can be developed within the defined constraints; sometimes some objectives can be met within a given time while others are deferred — and ED is particularly useful in allowing such a compromise.

Then, given clearly defined objectives, with value and time constraints which have been shown by a feasibility study to be reasonable, a specification may be drawn up and more accurate estimates based on it. If the estimates are much different from the previously defined constraints, now is the time to resolve the problem, not with the users but with senior management. This process follows that proposed in Section 9.3 of Chapter 9.

Thus, instead of a project being approved because it seems a good idea, it should be subjected to checks for its value and for the feasibility of completing it at a cost (in time and budget) equal to or less than its value. This brings senior management far more into the business of project definition and assessment than hitherto. It is a change which is long overdue, and would benefit not only ED projects but waterfall model projects as well.

## 15.4 REAPPRAISAL

Once the project has commenced, the project manager should review it regularly, with respect not merely to the requirements specification, but, more importantly, to the defined business objectives. With such a basis for monitoring, it would not be acceptable to run out of money or time unexpectedly. The project manager would need to detect well in advance that progress was such that the objectives would not be met within the budget or time, or both.

Immediately, senior management would be approached for a reappraisal of the project, and, given that there are good reasons for the impending failure, questions such as the following would need to be raised: Are the business objectives worth more than we previously determined? Would they still be valid if we spent more time meeting them? Should we terminate the project?

When the progress of a project is monitored against objectives rather than against the completion of tasks, project managers need to be prepared to change course when necessary and to use judgement to determine when it is necessary (see [Worsley 97]), that is to say, they should be prepared to vary their tactics appropriately so as to meet the strategy — and this cannot be done if there is a determination only to follow procedures. Procedures are rules for those who do not possess a deeper understanding, and for achieving the various advantages of a consistency of approach, but at some organizational level there need to be wise decisions on their use. They should be tools to be used to best advantage by thinking project managers.

Regular reappraisal suggests that in some cases it may be appropriate to cease the project. An advantage of ED is that if a project were abandoned, there would usually be an operational system, and if there had been an effective prioritization process, the functions in operation would be among those of greatest value to the users and the users' business.

In our projects, there was perpetual change, due not only to new functions being called for, but also to a continuous perception by the users of ways to improve those which had already been delivered. In advance it was impossible to forecast the project time or budget, for the changes could not have been predicted. How, in such circumstances, can criteria for the termination of the project be defined? Reappraisal offers repeated opportunities to abort the project if the gains are not commensurate with the investment in them. But there may be circumstances in which it is advantageous to a business to allow 'project drift' away from the objectives. This suggests a further criterion for continuing the project.

If more is being provided than was originally intended, those who want the added features would argue that they are essential. But are they worth what is being spent on them? A relevant question is whether or not they are within the original objectives for the project. If they are, then, as additional functions, they need to be assessed for strategic concurrence by the strategic representative on the project. If they are not within the original objectives, then it is the objectives rather than the functions which need to be reappraised.

The culture of regular reappraisal of ED projects implies not only

determining strategic objectives but also, and importantly, working to them —
and monitoring the work to make sure that it remains within them. It calls on
senior management not to leave system development projects to end users and
inexperienced project managers, but to define them and their criteria for
success and to appoint competent and experienced project managers. It calls
on them to understand projects, and to demand that their project managers
plan and monitor projects according to the objectives and assess the project
results against the defined criteria for success. Moreover, it calls on senior
management to be careful how they judge the success of a project.

## 15.5  JUDGING SUCCESS

In our early days on ED projects, we found that we worked harder than ever
to keep up with the changes which the users and customer representative
requested. We found too that our work was not recognized because our
achievements did not meet the traditional success criteria: we did not meet the
specification within the estimated time and to the defined budget.

At first, we responded to changes until we became submerged in them.
Gradually, we improved the situation by evolving change-control and
prioritization procedures and better relationships with the system's users. In
doing so we achieved a great deal — in retrospect that is clear — and after a
year we had a better relationship with our users than we had ever had before.
They were pleased with our mutual relationship and pleased with the deliveries
which they received. But senior management were not the users. They did not
see or touch the system. Their criteria for success were based on the early
estimates of budget and time to meet the initial specification (on which their
authorization of the project was based). When, after two years, we had not
approached completion, we were seen by senior management as having
failed. The demoralization of the staff was huge. They had worked long hours,
achieved greatly, and satisfied those who had previously been antagonists
(the users), only to find that according to inappropriate criteria they were
deemed to have failed. Moreover, the judgement of failure was passed by
those with the greatest influence — but the least understanding. It took some
time to rekindle morale.

Senior management need to have different criteria of success for ED
projects. Their criteria need to be based on strategic planning and business
objectives. If this will take a long time to come about, project managers should

not wait passively for it. They can change the way in which senior managers view projects by providing them with appropriate information — as suggested in Section 15.7.

## 15.6 CUSTOMER PARTICIPATION

Senior managers tend to be busy, and it is unusual for them to perceive project participation as having a high-priority call on their very full days. Yet, in many places in this book I have emphasised the importance of the involvement of customers in their projects. The 'customer representative' (see Chapter 8) is defined not only as sitting on the project board but also as having a number of responsibilities (such as approving requests for change) and being available to make decisions (such as regarding the priority of functions to be developed). These tasks are not trivial. Not only are they important to the smooth progress of the project (and so affect the efficiency of the developers), they are also important to the nature of the product (and so affect the effectiveness of the project). To discharge them conscientiously, and thus to provide value to their own businesses, customer representatives require time and an understanding of the required system. Until senior managers who are customers take their projects seriously, recognise their involvement in them as an essential part of their job rather than an inconvenient diversion from it, and accord them the time they need, their projects will continue to fail or to result in ineffective systems (which amounts to failure, though it may be concealed).

Many development projects cost millions of pounds or dollars. Yet, many customers treat them less seriously (both in defining their objectives and in their personal involvement) than the purchase of a car. But customer participation is crucial, not only at the requirements stage, but at all stages. Those projects in which continuous participation is seriously invested are the ones most likely to produce systems which satisfy real business needs.

## 15.7 CULTURE OF THE DEVELOPERS

It was observed in Chapters 11 and 14 that after the first delivery there are four categories of work to be done on the software:

1. Continuing development according to the original specification;
2. Developing newly specified functions;

3.  Modifying delivered software which, although in conformity to its specification, does not to meet the users' current requirements;

4.  Correcting software which does not meet its specification.

Given the need to distinguish between the work done on the four categories, we developed a culture of accounting. The development manager inculcated into the team leaders, and the team leaders into their teams, an understanding of the four categories of work and of the importance of accounting for their time spent on them. Each week we documented the manner in which our time was spent, and we began to include these records in the project manager's monthly reports to senior management. When we were questioned as to progress, we presented our records, which often showed more effort being invested in making changes than in progress against the original specification. We took opportunities to emphasise this point to senior management, and to explain the reasons for it, until they began to understand ED, the demands which were placed on the developers, and the way in which the projects were progressing. To avoid misunderstanding, we also emphasized the benefits of ED, and we encouraged the users to bring these to the attention of their own management. We demonstrated how the real requirements differed from the original specification, and why meeting them was an evolutionary process. Slowly, a culture change began to take place. Slowly, the criteria for project success evolved away from simply meeting original estimates.

(Note that I am not advocating *carte blanche* for the developers, but rather a recognition of the impossibility of estimating accurately in the face of unpredictable change. Estimates should certainly be made, and planning and monitoring should be based on them for the requirements on which they were made. But their continuing validity should be monitored. Changes should be *valued,* as proposed in Section 15.4, and new estimates made for them. The trouble comes when old estimates are used as criteria for success after they have ceased to be valid.)

I suppose that the most likely readers of this book will be developers and project managers. If you are involved in, or going to be involved in, an ED project, note the need for a new culture, not only in the developers but also in senior management. (If you are involved in waterfall model projects, you may also recognize the need for a new culture there.) If senior management are not already strategic thinkers and planners, they are unlikely to initiate the change, so it is you who must help them to understand the new needs of ED. If you do not, it is you and your staff who will suffer, for you will forever be striving to meet impossible targets. ('So, what's new?' you may ask. But that's another issue.)

As for the developers' culture, I would like to end with a couple of remarks, one on quality and the other on relationships with users.

With regard to quality, it is not often that I come across a development team with a real understanding of it. Almost all want to do a good job, few would intentionally do a bad one, and many adhere to certain quality procedures, such as carrying out document reviews. But adhering to a procedure or meeting a standard is not the end of it. Having five or six people review every document may achieve a high level of quality (and it may not), but is it in every case cost-effective? What would have been the penalty for missing one or two of the errors which were found? What might we have lost if in one case we only used three people on the review? Procedures tell us what to do, but not how to judge. Unless we develop an understanding of quality, we will not develop judgement of how to achieve it; and we are unlikely to achieve it cost-effectively.

I believe that one problem is that development managers and team leaders do not invest sufficient responsibility in team members for the quality of their work. If instead of decreeing that certain quality assurance procedures should always be carried out, managers called on each individual developer to achieve, assess and justify the quality of their work, it would create both a need and an incentive to understand quality better and to be more judgemental in achieving it. While the ideal is always to achieve and assure high quality, it is also true that there are times when we need to balance risks. Yet, few developers consider the cost (the risk) involved in poor quality when they are under pressure to meet an impossible (or merely difficult) deadline.

Unless we understand the cost of poor quality, quality remains in the procedures rather than in our culture. In Chapter 14 I mentioned that in our team we defined maintenance as a quality-related cost. This had a salutary effect on the developers. 'What does that mean?' they were prompted to inquire. It meant that faults in the software caused us to divert highly skilled people from development to maintenance, creating a debit of time and money on the project. The initial question had been answered, but the debate had only begun. It led to a deeper interest in quality and a deeper understanding of it. Such an understanding can lead to a quality culture rather than a quality regime (see [Levene 97]). With so many interactions in an ED project of any size, with so much testing and so many points at which it is necessary to assess the risks before committing resources to something, a genuine quality culture in the development team is important. What is more, such a culture rubs off on anyone who works closely with you, for they cannot help but perceive its 'rightness'. Users and developers on other teams begin to see things in a new light. Sounds magical, doesn't it? But such a culture does not develop on its own, nor overnight. It requires insightful leadership over a prolonged period. If you are a project manager or development manager, start planning next year's changes now.

The second matter which I wanted to remark on was the developers' relationship with the users. The better and more open it is, the better the chance of a successful project. In fact, we found that the greatest asset to the project was a close relationship with our users. Regular communication with them, through both formal meetings and informal encounters, is essential. You want them to appreciate your deliveries, to respond with feedback on how they can be improved, and also to understand why you cannot meet all their demands all of the time. So work closely with them, tell them your problems and listen to theirs. And tell them the truth. If that's not a new culture, good for you, but in most cases it will be.

## 15.8  SUMMARY AND EXTRACTS

This chapter has examined the culture required for successful evolutionary delivery projects. It has made recommendations, many of which are also applicable to waterfall model projects.

In particular, the following subjects were discussed: the use of business objectives as the foundation of projects, the need to reassess how the judgement of success or failure of a project is determined, the participation of senior management in the definition and management of projects, the basis of estimation of project time and budget, the relationships between developers and users, and the understanding and judgement of quality.

Following rules gets us some way towards success much of the time. But being highly successful most of the time depends on more than that; it depends on those attributes, such as attitude, which determine our culture. Procedures and standards are necessary but not sufficient; if we want quality software, we developers of software must develop our attitude, our understanding of quality, our psychology, and our professionalism. We must manage better and delegate more responsibility. Our expectations of our staff must increase.. We must become better managers, better engineers and more professional.

The following extracts make a few of the points of the chapter.

- Estimation is not merely obtaining an idea of the project's likely time and resource requirements. It also provides the basis for defining the project's terminating criteria and judging its success.

- If the users' requirements are not specified in accordance with the business objectives, adhering to them leads to a strategically ineffective project (and system).

- Senior management needs to devote greater consideration to the *value* of meeting their objectives.

- When the progress of a project is monitored against objectives rather than against the completion of tasks, project managers need to be prepared to change course when necessary and to use judgement to determine when it is necessary.

- The culture of regular reappraisal of ED projects implies not only determining strategic objectives but also, and importantly, working to them — and monitoring the work to make sure that it remains within them.

- Senior management need to have different criteria of success for ED projects. Their criteria need to be based on strategic planning and business objectives.

- Those projects in which continuous [customer] participation is seriously invested are the ones most likely to produce systems which satisfy real business needs.

- The trouble comes when old estimates are used as criteria for success after they have ceased to be valid.

- Procedures tell us what to do, but not how to judge. Unless we develop an understanding of quality, we will not develop judgement of how to achieve it; and we are unlikely to achieve it cost-effectively.

- Such a [quality] culture rubs off on anyone who works closely with you, for they cannot help but perceive its 'rightness'. Users and developers on other teams begin to see things in a new light.

- We found that the greatest asset to the project was a close relationship with our users.

# References

[Boehm 88]

Barry W Boehm: *A Spiral Model of Software Development and Enhancement.* Computer, May 1988

[Checkland 90]

*Checkland P B and Scholes J: Soft Systems Methodology in Action.* John Wiley & Sons, Chichester, UK, 1990

[Fagan 76]

Fagan M E: *Design and Code Inspections to Reduce Errors in Program Development.* IBM Systems Journal 15 (3) 1976

[Ferraby 91]

Ferraby L: *Change Control During Computer Systems Development.* Prentice Hall International (UK), 1991

[Glass 81]

Glass R L and Noiseux R A: *Software Maintenance Guidebook.* Prentice-Hall, New Jersey, 1981

[ISO 91]

International Organisation of Standardisation: *Quality Management and Quality Assurance Standards — Part 3: Guidelines for the Application of ISO 9001 to the Development, Supply and Maintenance of Software.* ISO, 1991

[Levene 97]

Levene T: *Getting the Culture Right.* In Redmill F and Dale C (eds): Life

Cycle Management for Dependability, Springer-Verlag, UK, 1997

[Martin 83]

Martin J and McClare C: *Software Maintenance — The Problem and its Solution*. Prentice-Hall, New Jersey, 1983

[Redmill 88]

Redmill F J, Johnson E A and Runge B: *Document Quality — Inspection.* British Telecommunications Engineering 6 (4) January 1988

[Redmill 89]

Redmill F J: *Computer System Development: Problems Experienced in the Use of Incremental Delivery.* Proceedings of SAFECOMP '89, Vienna, December 1989

[Redmill 97]

Redmill F: *Practical Risk Management.* In Redmill F and Dale C (eds): Life Cycle Management for Dependability, Springer-Verlag, UK, 1997

[Swanson 76]

Swanson E B: *The Dimensions of Software Maintenance.* IEEE Computer Society, Proceedings of 2nd International Conference on Software Engineering, October 1976

[Worsley 97]

Worsley C and Lee L: *Third Generation Project Management.* In Redmill F and Dale C (eds): Life Cycle Management for Dependability, Springer-Verlag, UK, 1997

# Further Reading

Andersen E S, Frude K V, Haug T and Turner J R: *Goal Directed Project Management*. Kogan Page in association with Coopers & Lybrand, 1988

Brooks F P Brooks Jr: *The Mythical Man-month*. Addison-Wesley 1982

DeMarco T and Lister T: *Peopleware — Productive Projects and Teams*. Dorset House Publishing Co. 1987

Gilb T: *Principles of Software Engineering Management*. Addison-Wesley, 1988.

Meredith J R and Mantel S J Jr: *Project Management — A Managerial Approach*. John Wiley & Sons (Second edition) 1989

Ould M: *Strategies for Software Engineering — The Management of Risk and Quality*. John Wiley & Sons, Chichester, UK, 1990

Sommerville I: *Software Engineering*. Addison-Wesley (fourth edition) 1992

# Index

# TITLES IN THIS SERIES